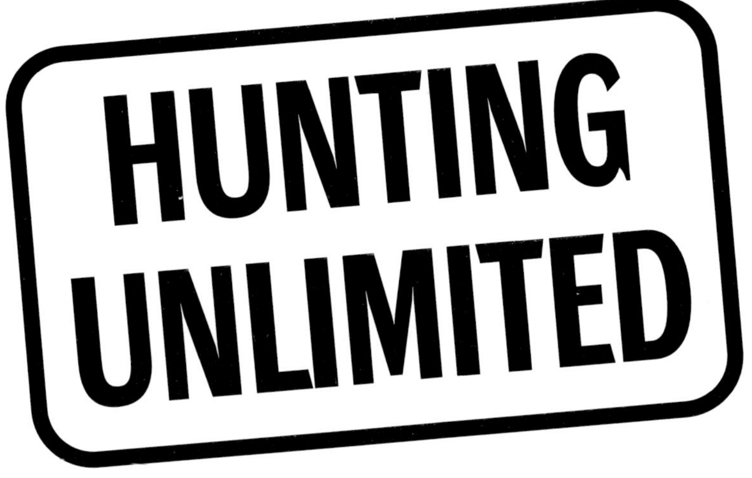

Shooting Birds With a Camera

TOM ANDERSON

If you like hunting but don't like strictures,
You ought to try shooting pictures.

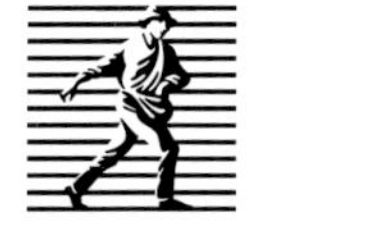

SIMON & SCHUSTER CUSTOM PUBLISHING

Cover photos: Osprey in Flight (front)
Cedar Waxwing (back)

All photographs by Tom Anderson

Printed in the United States of America

10 9 8 7 6 5 4 3 2 1

Please visit our website at www.sscp.com

ISBN 0–536–01832–4

BA 98595

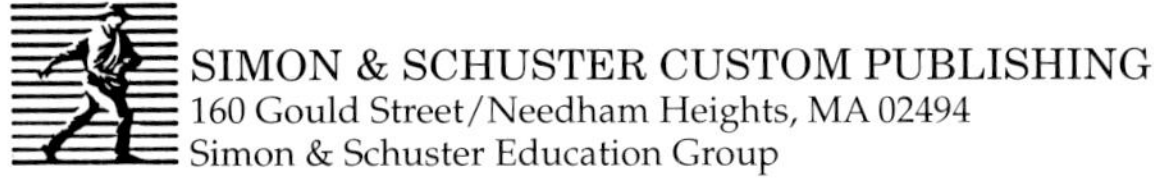

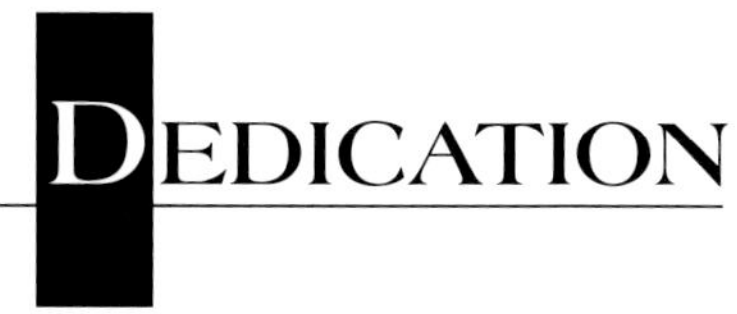

Dedication

To Mary Pat and Our Flock

Our world abounds in awe-inspiring natural beauty. It can be found all around us, sometimes in the most unlikely places. In our preoccupation with other priorities, it's easy to neglect the effort needed to truly see it. It's an effort, however, that will be abundantly rewarded.

My enduring fascination with nature,
particularly my interest in birds,
has greatly enriched my life.
I can think of few more precious gifts
than to inspire a similar passion in others.

ACKNOWLEDGEMENTS

My thanks are due to the many people who have urged and encouraged me to produce this book. It has truly been a labor of love. Thanks also to my son, Matt for his help in scouring the copy for errors and to my son Ted for opening the door to my publisher. I am especially in debt to Steve Pollick, Outdoors Editor of *The Toledo Blade,* for his foreword which is not only generous in its comments, but does a superb job of articulating the theme and essence of what I have tried to express.

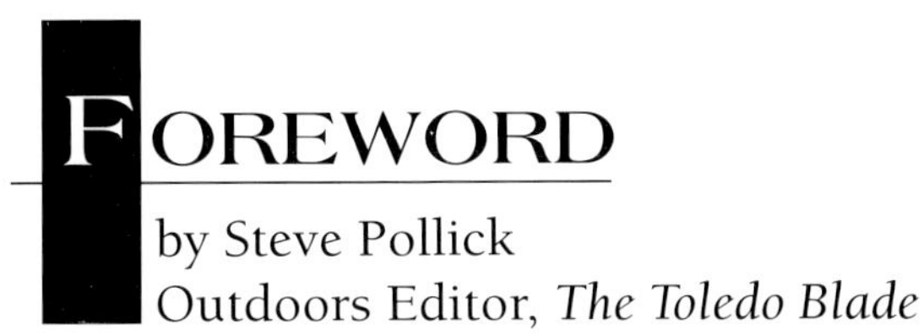

FOREWORD

by Steve Pollick
Outdoors Editor, *The Toledo Blade*

Hunting, one of man's earliest survival skills, is ages more ancient than agriculture. Man was a hunter and gatherer long before he was a farmer or herdsman. Thus hunting, the pursuit of wild animals for food, is deeply rooted in the human psyche. Its appeal or draw, even today, remains relatively close to the surface in many of us, much to the confusion or consternation of others among us for whom this particular call of the wild is dead.

Thus, even though hunting, per se, is unnecessary for obtaining food today, at least in well-fed western societies, it remains very important to many persons. These are the ones who feel the inexplicable pull and attraction, even the need, to don the skin of the predator and to use senses and skills nowadays mostly dormant, if not moribund, in modern humans who too often are isolated from the realities of nature and its endless cycle of life and death.

Moreover, hunting as an ancillary activity today is deeply steeped in tradition, style, custom and ceremony. In other words, there is a lot of room for interpretation. Enter Tom Anderson, bird hunter. Enter Tom Anderson, naturalist. Enter Tom Anderson, photographer.

Tom, with much urging from friends, relatives and acquaintances, here and now has committed to print his thoughts on hunting, particularly hunting in a unique and different way, namely with a camera. He demonstrates how he has been able to combine hunting, nature study, and photography into one consummate pursuit, and how he arrived there in more than 60 years afield.

As the following pages unfold, the reader will see as well that Tom does not hunt with just any camera. In more than 30 years afield, photo-hunting birds, he has developed and perfected equipment and techniques that on one hand closely mimic hunting with a shotgun, and on the other hand mimic hunting with bow and arrow, this latter in terms of stealth and patience required to close with the "game" at hand.

The marvelous results of his hunts, and his choices of equipment and methods, are confirmed in the many pages of wonderful character studies of birds, from songbirds and shorebirds to game birds and birds of prey. Nowhere does Tom urge those who hunt more conventionally and traditionally to lay down their arms. Nor does he urge non-hunters to so begin. But he makes an enthusiastic case to join him in what has become for him a passionate pastime.

Contents

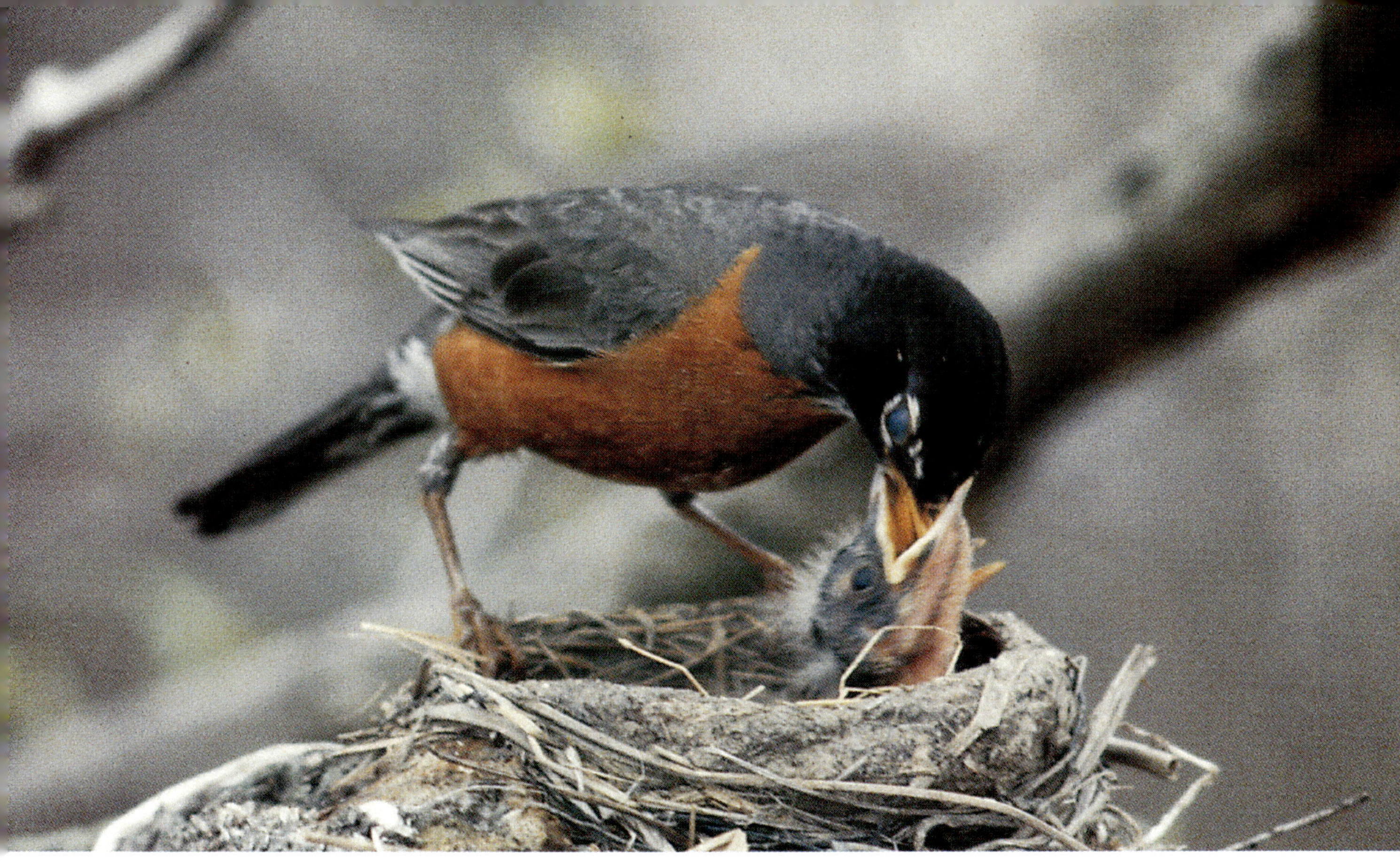

American Robin

I think that I have never heard

A poem as lovely as a bird.

A bird whose hungry mouth is prest

Up to its mother at the nest.

(With apologies to Joyce Kilmer)

A Blue Jay and a Rifle

I have been an avid hunter for more than sixty years. For the last thirty I've been shooting birds whenever and wherever I've had the opportunity. I've shot them at all times of the year, both during the day and at night, but particularly during their breeding season when they are at the peak of their beauty. I've even shot them on their nests. I've shot them in public parks and in crowded cities, from my car and from a baited blind. Most of them were shot with a Canon and then some were blown up in my darkroom. During all that time, not a feather has been ruffled nor have I run afoul of the law.

For as long as I can remember, I've been intrigued by the wonders of nature, but my greatest fascination has been with birds. I grew up on a farm in northwest Ohio near Toledo, and much of my childhood was spent exploring woods and fields or poking around the banks of the stream upon which our home was built. Before I reached my teens, I was intimately familiar with every square foot of the beautiful 110-acre piece of land I have called home for nearly all of my life. My wife, Mary Pat, and I have built our home and raised our family there. So have three of my brothers, and my sister.

Over the years, Toledo has expanded so that our property, once almost five miles west of the city, now lies within its limits. In late 1995 most of it was given to the Toledo Metropark system so its natural beauty will be preserved for the enjoyment of many generations to come.

Two key events occurred in my early years that shaped the direction of my life, piquing my interest in nature and the outdoors. The first was finding a dead Blue Jay. The second was the purchase, at age 12, of my first and only .22 rifle for the princely sum of five dollars.

I was ten years old when I found the Blue Jay. I brought it to my mother and asked her if we could have it mounted. Through a friend, she located a taxidermist and sent it to him. I'll never forget what a thrill it was when the mounted specimen was finally delivered. The jay seemed alive again, and I could study its beauty at my leisure. I determined then and there that I wanted to learn taxidermy. With a little research, my parents found that one of their friends was an accomplished amateur taxidermist. He agreed to give me lessons, and that marked the beginning of a hobby that lasted thirty-five years.

With my new rifle, I spent hours at target practice. Within a few months, I had graduated from shooting at tin cans on fence posts to tossing them up and hitting them in flight. Learning to shoot came naturally to me and I loved it. At the age of fourteen I was given a twelve gauge shot gun for Christmas. I will long remember the thrill of my first day of pheasant hunting on the opening day of the following season. I was hooked on hunting! For many years thereafter, the opening day of hunting season was the most eagerly anticipated day of the year for me.

Shortly after I began my taxidermy lessons, my father was able to secure a federal permit to possess migratory birds. This permit allowed us to own federally protected specimens but it did not permit killing them. Once our friends learned of my hobby, I was kept well supplied with birds found dead on the road or, more often, beneath plate glass windows. In the ensuing years, my taxidermy skills improved considerably and I developed a modest collection of mounted specimens.

Upon the death of my father, the permit was transferred to me, and I continued to add to my collection of mounted birds. In the early 1970's, the terms of the permit were modified to allow me to maintain my current collection, but prohibited the acquisition of any new protected species. Although disappointed with this change, I was in complete agreement with the reasons behind it. For an unscrupulous collector, a permit to possess could easily be interpreted as a permit to kill. With the increasing emphasis being placed on conservation and protection of endangered species there was really no valid reason to add to my collection. So my taxidermy ended, but my fascination with birds did not.

To fill the void left by the loss of my hobby, I decided to try my hand at bird photography. My early attempts were not overly rewarding. I found very quickly that it wasn't easy to get a good picture of a four inch long warbler that seldom sat still for more than a second or two. And if it did sit still, the minimum focusing distance of my telephoto lens wouldn't let me get close enough for a really good shot. Somehow, I thought, there must be a better way.

Then in a camera store an unusual looking piece of equipment caught my eye. It seemed to belong in a gun shop rather than a camera shop. It was called a Follow-Focus Outfit, made by Novoflex and had just arrived from Germany. A quick review of the features of this unique apparatus told me that this was the "better way" I'd been searching for. I bought it on the spot and since that day, I've shot thousands of birds with it, including 400 species in the United States. More than eighty percent of the pictures in my collection and in this book have been taken with it. Although technological advances in lenses and cameras have made it virtually obsolete, it will probably remain a part of my arsenal until either it wears out or I do.

As I was developing my extensive collection of slides, particularly of birds of northwestern Ohio, I began to get invitations to give programs throughout the region. It seemed that each time I gave a program to a group, I was invited by another to do the same. Since those early days, I have presented slide programs to thousands of people in a wide spectrum of organizations. I continue to be surprised at the level of interest shown and how many express amazement at what can be seen literally in their own backyards.

Often, after giving a program, someone would ask, "When are you going to publish some of your pictures?" Until now, my answer has always been that photographing birds was a hobby that I took up solely for my own enjoyment and that I really had never given any serious consideration to writing and publishing a book. I knew that technology in the publishing business was improving so rapidly that the task would probably be much easier as time passed. What finally convinced me to get going, however, was my realization that the same couldn't be said about myself.

Although most of its appeal might be in the photographs, my intention is not merely to produce another book about birds or about wildlife photography. This is a book about hunting—hunting birds with a camera. I hope the following pages will give you a sense of the fun and pleasure it has brought me.

GUN OR CAMERA?

As a hunter who always got a kick out of shooting a shotgun, let me list some of the reasons I get an even bigger kick out of shooting a camera.

1. I don't have to eat what I shoot.

Historically, of course, the main purpose of hunting was to put food on the table. In this country, at least, that has long since ceased to be an important factor. In fact, many hunters (myself included) consider appropriate disposal of game somewhat of a chore, particularly when you know you can get a better and much cheaper meal at the local supermarket. Since I began hunting with a camera, there has been no game to be cleaned or given away, nor have I felt compelled to invite my friends to a game dinner to empty my freezer.

2. There is no closed season and no license is required.

If you follow common rules of courtesy, there are very few limitations on where or when you can hunt with a camera. I take my camera with me any time I might see something worth shooting.

3. It is completely safe for all concerned.

From the game's perspective, I'm sure this one would be at the top of the list. Every year people are killed or injured in hunting accidents. I have never heard of any injury being inflicted by a camera.

4. It is more challenging.

I have found that getting a good picture of a bird is far more challenging than downing one with a gun. Even with the best of equipment, a good picture demands proper lighting conditions and the right surroundings. The bird must also be caught in an appealing attitude. In addition, good shots often call for quick reaction and a steady hand.

5. There is at least as much opportunity for excitement and suspense.

For me, at least, the primary appeal of hunting, whether with a gun or camera, has always been the excitement. I have found hunting with a camera to be every bit as thrilling as hunting with a gun. Not knowing for certain whether you've made a good shot until your film is developed provides an additional measure of suspense.

I am also convinced that hunting with a camera has sharpened my powers of observation and increased my appreciation of the beauties of nature that surround us. As you might suspect, when out in the field, I have not confined my shooting to birds alone. I am constantly looking for the opportunity to get a good picture of a deer, a squirrel, a beautiful butterfly, a wild flower or an interesting insect.

Perhaps now you can understand why I have put away my guns and do my hunting with a camera.

Hunting birds can be a lot more fun
If you bring your camera and leave your gun.

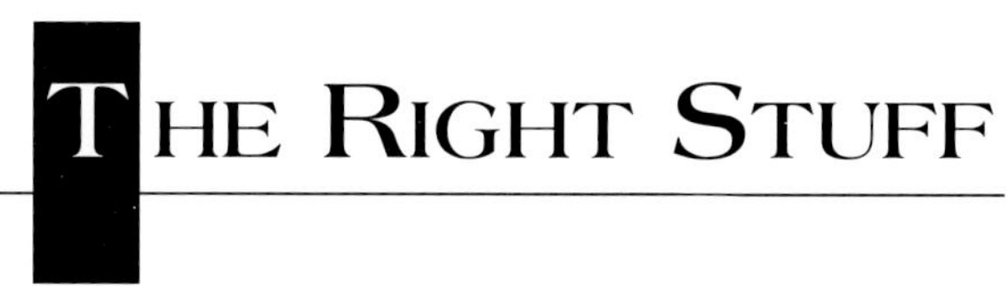

The Right Stuff

Choosing equipment if well done
Is more than half the battle won.

I have already described my early frustration with bird photography and my discovery of the Novoflex Follow-Focus Outfit, which I've used for more than a quarter of a century. It was that discovery which converted me to hunting with a camera instead of a gun.

In the early 1970's when I purchased the Follow-Focus, it had a combination of critically important features which weren't then available in any other equipment that I could find. First, it was configured like a gun which made it very easy to hold steady. Hand holding a camera with a long telephoto lens is both awkward and tiring. It is also quite awkward to carry in the field, especially when you are carrying binoculars as well.

The second, and most important, feature was the focusing system. To focus, you merely squeezed or released a spring loaded mechanism in the rear hand grip. This allowed me to focus very quickly without having to touch the lens. With practice, I found it possible to keep flying birds in focus. I could follow a small bird as it hopped from branch to branch relatively easily. If the bird stopped, even for a second, I could get its picture. Exposures were made with a cable release actuated by a trigger in the forward hand grip.

Another important feature was a bellows, placed between the camera and the 400 mm lens. Fully extended, it permitted focusing to a distance of as little as six feet. Fully collapsed, the focusing range was from about twenty feet to infinity. Coupled with a camera with an aperture-priority automatic exposure system, the Follow-Focus outfit was truly "state of the art" at that time. For twenty years or so I have used it with a Canon AV-1 camera and power winder, now almost collectors items themselves.

Important advances in cameras and lenses have contributed to the obsolescence of this equipment. The most significant is the perfection of autofocus. Great improvements have also been made in auto-exposure systems, and shutter speeds up to as high as 1/8000 of a second are now available. Many new cameras are internally motorized with picture taking speeds of several frames per second, another valuable feature. With so many excellent choices of cameras and lenses any recommendations I could make would probably be out of date by the time this book is published.

I have recently bought a Nikon N70 camera and a Nikkor AF 75-300 mm f4.5 - 5.6 zoom lens and mounted them on a gunstock of my own design which incorporates a Nikon MC 12B remote trigger (Figure 1). This new combination has exceeded my expectations. Here are some of the considerations that led to my choices:

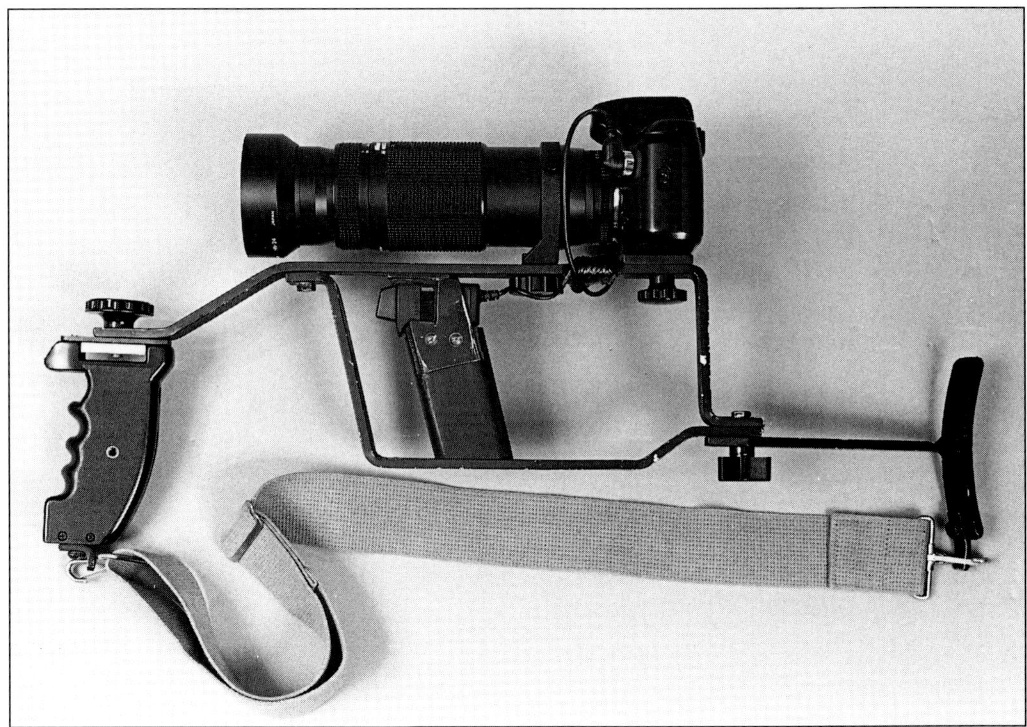

Figure 1

1. Autofocus

The camera and lens combination must provide fast and reliable autofocus. The lens I chose has the ability to focus to a minimum distance of five feet, an important feature when shooting birds. There are three different autofocus ranges; 5 feet to 10 feet, 10 feet to infinity or 5 feet to infinity. The first two options can reduce focus acquisition time when working exclusively in those ranges. The camera also has a Spot Area focus mode which uses a small focusing area in the center of the viewfinder. This can be important when the subject is surrounded or partially obscured by objects like tree limbs at different distances from the camera.

2. Auto-exposure System

The Nikon N-70 offers a wide choice of exposure modes. I normally use the Matrix Metering mode. Data on scene brightness and contrast are detected by the camera's eight segment sensor and analyzed by a built in mini-computer. The correct exposure is then calculated for many of the complex lighting situations encountered when shooting birds in their various habitats. With a center-weighted, aperture-priority exposure system like in the Canon AV-1 camera, exposure is correct only when the light reflected from the scene fits within certain average conditions. But the conditions when shooting birds are often far from average. For example, a light-colored bird in good light with a dark background such as dark foliage will fool the camera into thinking there is less light hitting the scene and over-expose the bird. Conversely, back-lit situations will cause under-exposure. Judging the correct exposure compensation is difficult enough and manually setting it often takes more time than is available. The Matrix Metering system does the job accurately and automatically.

3. Shutter Speed

The only disadvantage of faster shutter speeds is extra cost. High shutter speeds minimize the problem of camera shake, and permit using wider apertures in brighter light. Wide apertures reduce depth of field shifting background out of focus while keeping the subject in focus. In my opinion, when photographing birds, this is generally desirable.

A camera like the Canon AV-1 with a maximum shutter speed of 1/1000 second loaded with ASA 400 film often requires smaller apertures than are preferable. With the Novoflex 400 mm f5.6 lens, light conditions can require apertures as small as f16 or even f22. The majority of cases, however, call for apertures of f11 or wider. A maximum shutter speed of 1/4000 second would permit all these shots to be taken at f5.6 when using the N70's aperture-priority exposure mode. (f5.6 at 1/4000 sec and f11 at 1/1000 sec are equal exposures.) The need to change aperture settings manually is a distinct disadvantage when the amount of time available is critical.

4. Lens Focal Length

I have always considered a 400 mm lens to be an ideal focal length for the type of bird photography I do. It's long enough to get good shots at a reasonable distance and short enough to avoid serious camera shake problems. It can also be made with a combination of size, weight and speed (maximum aperture) which is within practical limits. When I purchased my lens, all of Nikon's autofocus lenses longer than 300 mm were too large, heavy and expensive for my purposes. While the 75-300 mm zoom lens I have is quite satisfactory, especially with its ability to pull back to 75 mm, I would prefer a light 400 mm lens with similar features if one becomes available.

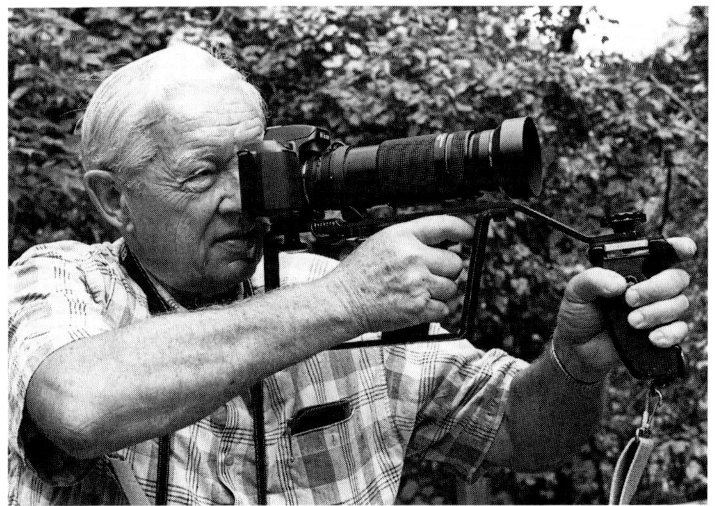

Figure 2

5. Gunstock

I mount my camera and lens on a gunstock for several reasons. First, I find it much easier to hold the camera steady (Figure 2). A general guideline for taking hand-held pictures is to use a shutter speed at least as fast as the reciprocal of the lens length. In other words, when using a 400 mm lens, the minimum shutter speed should be 1/400 sec. A gunstock lets me hold the camera steady enough to shoot at the slower speeds required when light conditions are less than ideal.

Used with a shoulder strap, a gunstock provides a convenient, comfortable and secure way to carry the camera in the field. The lens should be equipped with a mounting ring so both camera and lens can be firmly attached. You will find that by slinging the gunstock over your shoulder, you'll have freedom of movement and the camera and lens will be kept out of harm's way. And it won't interfere with your binoculars (Figure 3). I can find my target more quickly and accurately when using a gunstock, and the gun-like configuration makes the comparison with hunting even more vivid. This is not an insignificant factor for anyone who enjoys hunting as much as I did.

Unfortunately, I haven't found a commercially available gunstock that meets my specifications. I made my own using 1/4" x 1" aluminum barstock (See Figure 1, page 6). Since it was made specifically to fit my equipment, some modifications would likely be necessary for other cameras and lenses. For detailed information please write me at P.O. Box 119, Maumee, Ohio 43537.

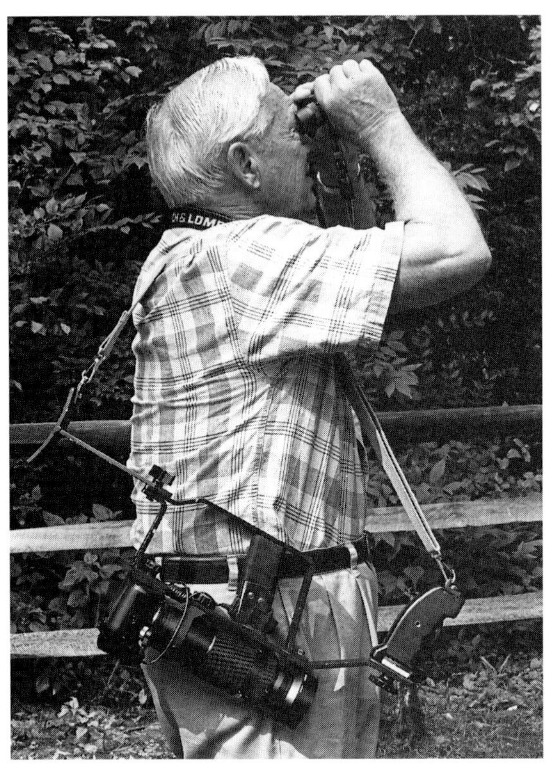

Figure 3

Since much of the beauty of birds is in their colors, it only makes sense to use color film. That leaves a choice between slides and prints. Although both have their advantages, I have always used slide film. Slides are less expensive. They take less room, are easier to file, and prints can easily be made from them. And for presentations, slides are the only logical choice.

Whether you choose print or slide film, you must decide on film speed. Color films are available in an increasingly wide range of speeds. If all other things were equal, you could simply choose the fastest one. But (as is usually the case) all other things are not equal. Generally speaking, slower films are less expensive and will produce better results under controlled conditions. Hunting birds with a camera like I do presents situations that are often not compatible with the use of low speed film for the following reasons:

- Shots are hand held. Tripods are out.
- Lenses have a long focal length and if kept within reasonable size and weight limits, they are relatively slow.
- Lighting conditions are often less than ideal.

I have always shot Kodak Ektachrome film. Until ASA 400 was introduced, I used ASA 200. Faster films are now available, but I have found 400 speed to be satisfactory for most of the conditions I encounter. I don't feel the extra speed of ASA 800 or faster films or push-processing ASA 400 film is generally worth the added cost and degradation of picture quality. I'm sure that as film technology advances, ASA 800, ASA 1600 or even faster films will become viable options. Until then, I'm sticking with ASA 400.

Contemplating the great improvements that have been made in cameras, lenses and film since I began shooting birds, I'm confident that even greater advances will be made in the next few years. Equipment will be more complex, yet easier to use and more foolproof. Film will be faster and better and may even be replaced by electronic imaging technology.

Regardless of what lies ahead, I think it is safe to say that hunting with a camera will only become easier and more fun.

Many modern high-tech tools
Will even work in the hands of fools.

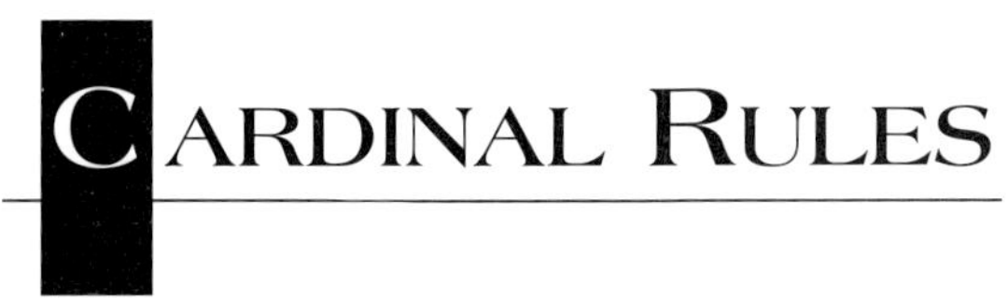

CARDINAL RULES

1. Keep it simple.

If you want to truly enjoy hunting with a camera, this is a fundamental precept. It's important to keep in mind that you're not on assignment for *National Geographic Magazine*. When in the field, take along only what you need. If it can't be easily and conveniently carried, you don't need it. Leave tripods, flash attachments and extra lenses at home or, at least, in your car. Remember, you are doing this for fun!

Keep it simple. Keep it fun.
You're not being paid by anyone.

2. Keep your camera with you.

Get into the habit of carrying your camera with you whenever you can. Many of your best photo opportunities will be completely unexpected. You won't get a picture if your camera is at home.

Modern cameras are fine and dandy,
But completely useless unless kept handy.

3. Carry spare batteries and film.

Modern 35 mm SLR cameras and autofocus lenses won't function without batteries. Don't suffer the frustrating experience of finding yourself in the middle of a wave of migrating warblers and running out of film or having your camera's batteries die with no spares in your pocket.

Not a single camera as yet designed
Can use film and batteries you've left behind.

4. Take lots of pictures. Keep only a few.

One of the great things about hunting with a camera is that no matter how many times you try, you can almost always get a better shot. There is no need to keep every picture you take. Keep only a few of each species. As you get better ones, discard the inferior ones. If you can't stand to throw away fairly good pictures, give them to friends and let them throw them out.

Shoot a lot and keep the best
Say goodbye to all the rest.

5. Practice.

Become familiar with your equipment. Read and understand the manuals. Aim at objects both close and at a distance. Learn to get the subject into the field of view and in focus as quickly as you can. Practice keeping flying birds in focus and centered in your viewing screen. If you are used to shooting a gun, forget what you've learned about leading a moving target. Camera shots travel at the speed of light. If it seems awkward at first and some of your shots go astray, don't worry. You can't hurt anyone.

6. Develop and maintain a filing system.

A big part of the pleasure of bird photography is being able to enjoy and share your pictures. A good filing system is a must. Don't wait until you have a bushel of pictures before you get started. Sort and file them as soon as they are developed.

Improving Your Odds

Even though you will be using a fairly long focal length lens, you'll often find the need to get quite close for the best shots. This is, of course, particularly true for small birds. Many of my best warbler shots have been taken at ten feet or less with a 400 mm lens. If you follow a few simple rules, you'll find that getting close is easier than it sounds.

Many species of birds seem to have very little fear of people. If you stand quietly in one place they will often come to you. It's best to avoid wearing bright clothing and to remain fairly silent, but it is sudden movement that should be particularly avoided. You will find that birds can often be more easily approached in areas that are frequented by people. You might have noticed, for example, that some birds get quite bold in picnic grounds where they become accustomed to people while on the lookout for food scraps. Birds often seem to be less threatened by a crowd than by a single person. One of my favorite birding spots is the J. N. "Ding" Darling National Wildlife Refuge on Sanibel Island, Florida (*pages 14 and 76*). Hundreds of people take the five mile drive through the refuge daily. Birds that are easily spooked in other less-traveled areas can be readily approached, either in a car or on foot.

A car can be a very effective photographic blind. Some birds that are wary of humans don't seem to have the same fear of a motor vehicle. I have gotten many good shots from my car window, by pulling over to the side of a back-coutry road.

When closer to home, there are a number of ways of attracting birds to improve picture taking opportunities. Feeding is one of the most effective. A well-placed and well-stocked feeding station should give you the opportunity for some great shots. For more about feeding stations, see page 15.

Birds can also be attracted by using a variety of calling devices, by imitating some of their calls or sounds, or by using tape recordings of their calls (*page 71*). Tape recordings of certain owls are often very effective. On several occasions during spring migration, I've encountered screech-owls being beset by scores of birds of different species, including ten or more kinds of warblers. There is something about owls that just seems to tick birds off. I suppose I'd feel the same way about someone who'd just eaten a friend of mine.

Although your camera might be equipped with the most sophisticated metering system available, proper lighting conditions are still very important. Try to have your light source behind you. When taking shots in full sun, avoid mid-day when shadows are harsh. You'll get better results when the sun is closer to the horizon. The diffused light from a bright overcast sky is often ideal for color shots.

Favor high shutter speeds and wide aperture settings. High shutter speeds will stop motion of the subject and minimize the effect of camera movement. Wider apertures result in a shallower depth of field, keeping the subject in focus while blurring the background.

Try to anticipate where you expect to make your next shot. Aim your camera and focus your lens at something close to that spot or close to the same distance. If you've guessed right, your lens should snap right into focus without having to hunt for the proper range. If a bird is approaching, try to keep it in focus in the viewing screen as it nears. When it gets close enough for a recognizable picture, start shooting. Even if it doesn't get as close as you'd like, you still might have something worth keeping until the opportunity for a better shot comes along.

The most effective way to improve your shooting odds is to take lots of shots. That's also the best way to become thoroughly familiar with your equipment and improve your skill. You'll find that just plain luck is a factor in some of your best shots. The more you shoot, the luckier you'll get.

For anyone seriously contemplating the pursuit of birding or bird photography, I would recommend considering a membership in the American Birding Association, P.O. Box 6599, Colorado Springs, Colorado 80934-6599. It offers many valuable services including a directory of names and addresses of its thousands of members. Many of these folks are willing and anxious to share local birding information. And the American Birding Association/Lane Birdfinding Guide Series provides detailed, accurate directions and maps to birding sites throughout the United States and Canada, along with other helpful information.

Happy Hunting Grounds

The 110-acre parcel of land where I have lived for all but the first four years of my life has had a great influence on my interest in birds. Our land is just within the western limits of the city of Toledo and is only a short drive from some of the premier birding areas in northwestern Ohio, itself one of the great birding regions in the country.

Over a span of a few years, an experienced birder might see almost 300 species within an hour's drive from Toledo. Our son Matt, an avid and accomplished birder, identified more than 220 species on or flying over our land in the fifteen years before he left home. The variety of habitats—the Oak Openings on the west, the marshes and open water of Lake Erie on the east, and the waters and banks of the Maumee River and its tributaries which traverse the area—account for single-day species counts which commonly reach 150 or more during the peak of spring migration in May.

The most popular birding spot in the area during spring migration is the Magee Marsh Bird Trail (often referred to as the Crane Creek Bird Trail because it is reached through Crane Creek State Park). Magee Marsh Bird Trail is located on the southwestern shore of Lake Erie about 20 miles east of Toledo. The access road from U.S. Route 2 runs along a causeway with marshes on both sides which are productive during several months of the year. The main entrance to the trail is at the west end of the parking lot which lies just south of the beach. The trail itself is a boardwalk through about seven acres of scrubby and marshy woods.

When weather conditions cooperate, this small area can be teeming with thousands of birds of many species including thirty or more kinds of warblers. Many of these are migrating birds that have flown from Central and South America. By the time they reach Lake Erie their energy reserves are depleted, so they stop to rest and feed before making the crossing. Under the right conditions, huge numbers will pile up along the lake shore. Witnessing such a phenomenon is an unforgettable experience.

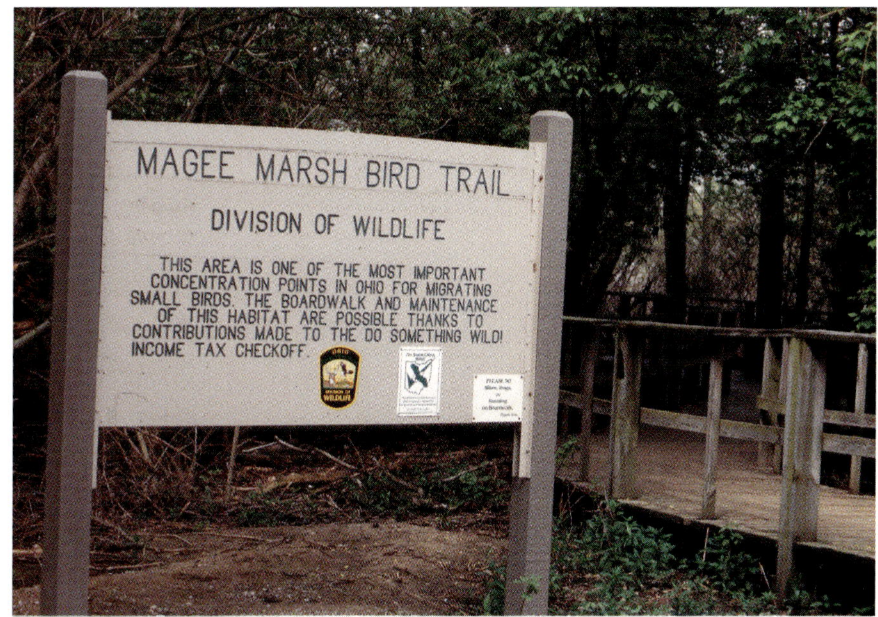

Entrance to Magee Marsh Bird Trail

There are a number of other good birding areas along the southwestern shore of Lake Erie and the Maumee River corridor. Most of the Toledo area Metroparks are also productive. Oak Openings Preserve Metropark, a tract of about 3500 acres in the Oak Openings area west of Toledo is noted for its many breeding bird species and a few species not seen commonly anywhere else in the region.

For the past few years, Mary Pat and I have been spending the month of April on Sanibel Island near Fort Myers, Florida. This is the home of the renowned J. N. "Ding" Darling National Wildlife Refuge, which features a five mile wildlife drive that provides great opportunities for close-up shots of many species of birds, particularly waterfowl, wading birds and shorebirds. Many of them have become so accustomed to people that they can be approached very easily. There are a number of other good birding spots on the island and within an hour's drive on the Florida mainland.

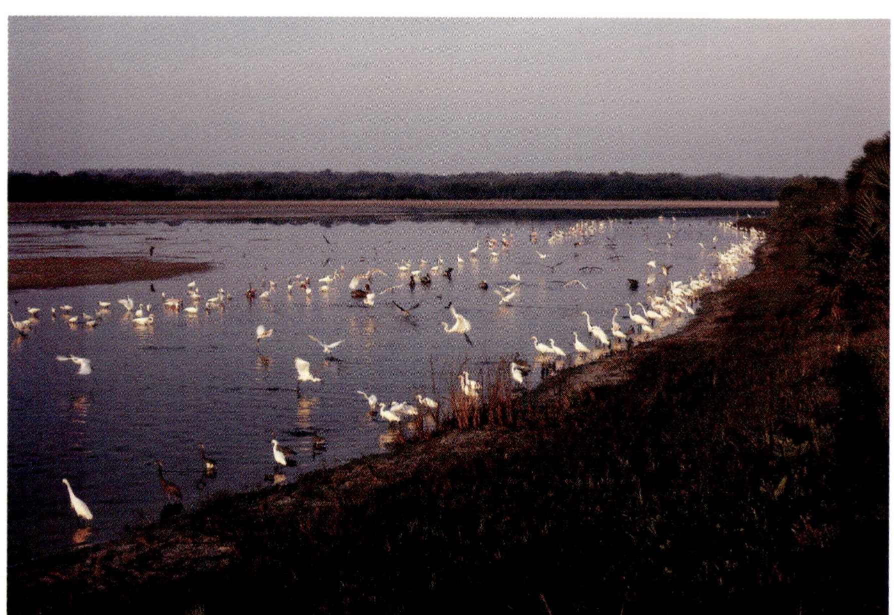

View from Wildlife Drive—J. N. "Ding" Darling Wildlife Refuge

Whenever we travel, particularly in the United States, I bring along my camera. Not only has it added immensely to my enjoyment, it has also contributed significantly to my growing collection of slides. Obviously, some spots are better than others, but no matter where we have gone, I've always found plenty of birds to keep me interested. I hope the photographs on the following pages will help to capture some of the allure of a hobby that has given me so much pleasure and excitement—hunting birds with a camera.

The first three sections that follow, *At Your Feeding Station, Spring In Northwest Ohio* and *Water, Marsh and Shore Birds,* contain photographs of birds that are either residents or visitors to northwest Ohio. Many of them, of course, can also be seen in other areas including the vicinity of Sanibel Island where some of the pictures were taken.

The next section, *Sanibel Island* features birds that are residents or visitors in April on or near Sanibel Island. Several of these species are also seen regularly, or at least seasonally, in the Toledo area.

In the *Winter Visitors* section, you will find shots of a few birds that might show up in northwest Ohio during the late fall or winter.

Screech-Owl Encounter includes some interesting night photos of a pair of screech-owls bringing food to their nest.

The pictures in the final section, *On The Road,* were taken on trips we have taken to the southwestern part of the country.

At Your Feeding Station

A good place to begin shooting is at your feeding station. If it is properly oriented, you may not even have to leave your house. It's best if you can locate it near shrubbery or brush which will provide some protection from predators. Make sure also that there are plenty of perches nearby so you can get pictures without including any of your feeders. A picture of a bird on a feeder has, in my opinion, about as much appeal as a shot of one in its cage at the zoo.

Providing a variety of feeds will attract a larger number of species. The addition of a bird bath will bring even more. Sunflower seeds, particularly the small dark variety called oilers, are a favorite of most seed eating birds as well as woodpeckers. Other seeds such as millet, thistle seed and cracked corn are also good, both in feeders and spread on the ground. A suet feeder will appeal to many species, especially woodpeckers. Sugar water will attract Ruby-throated Hummingbirds (*page 52*) and Baltimore Orioles (*page 48*).

A few of the regular, year-round visitors you might expect at a northwest Ohio feeder, depending on location and surrounding habitat are shown on pages 16 through 22.

As the seed attracts smaller birds, the feeding birds may attract raiding hawks. It's not uncommon for a feeding station to be raided by a hawk. Two of the most likely marauders, American Kestrel and Cooper's Hawk, are pictured on pages 23 and 24.

Depending on location, type of feed furnished and time of year, dozens of other species could make an appearance including several that are pictured elsewhere in this book:

Eastern Towhee	53
Red-headed Woodpecker	54
Red-winged Blackbird	49
Evening Grosbeak	95
Rose-breasted Grosbeak	47
Indigo Bunting	46
Fox Sparrow	53
White-crowned Sparrow	53
Common Redpoll	95

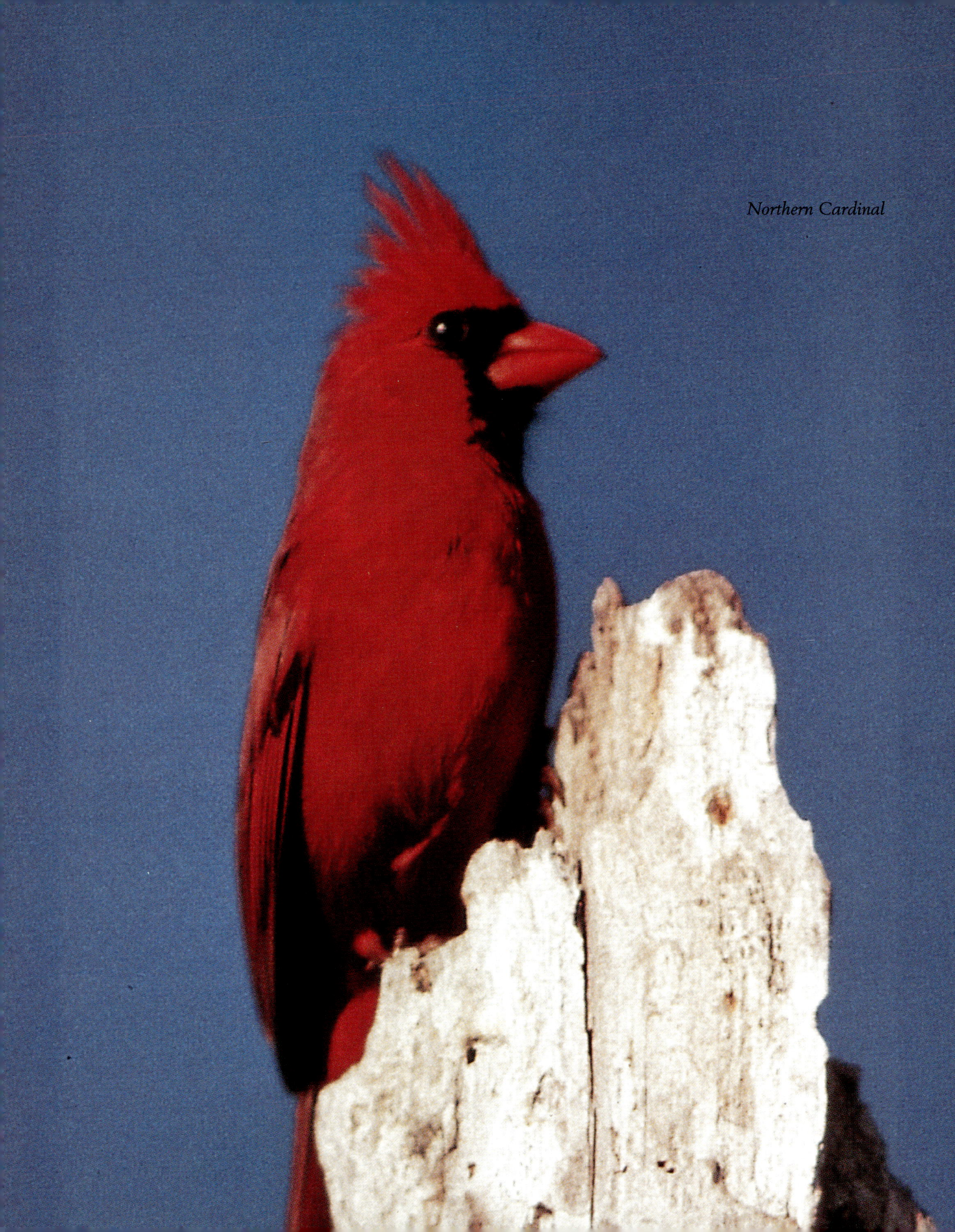
Northern Cardinal

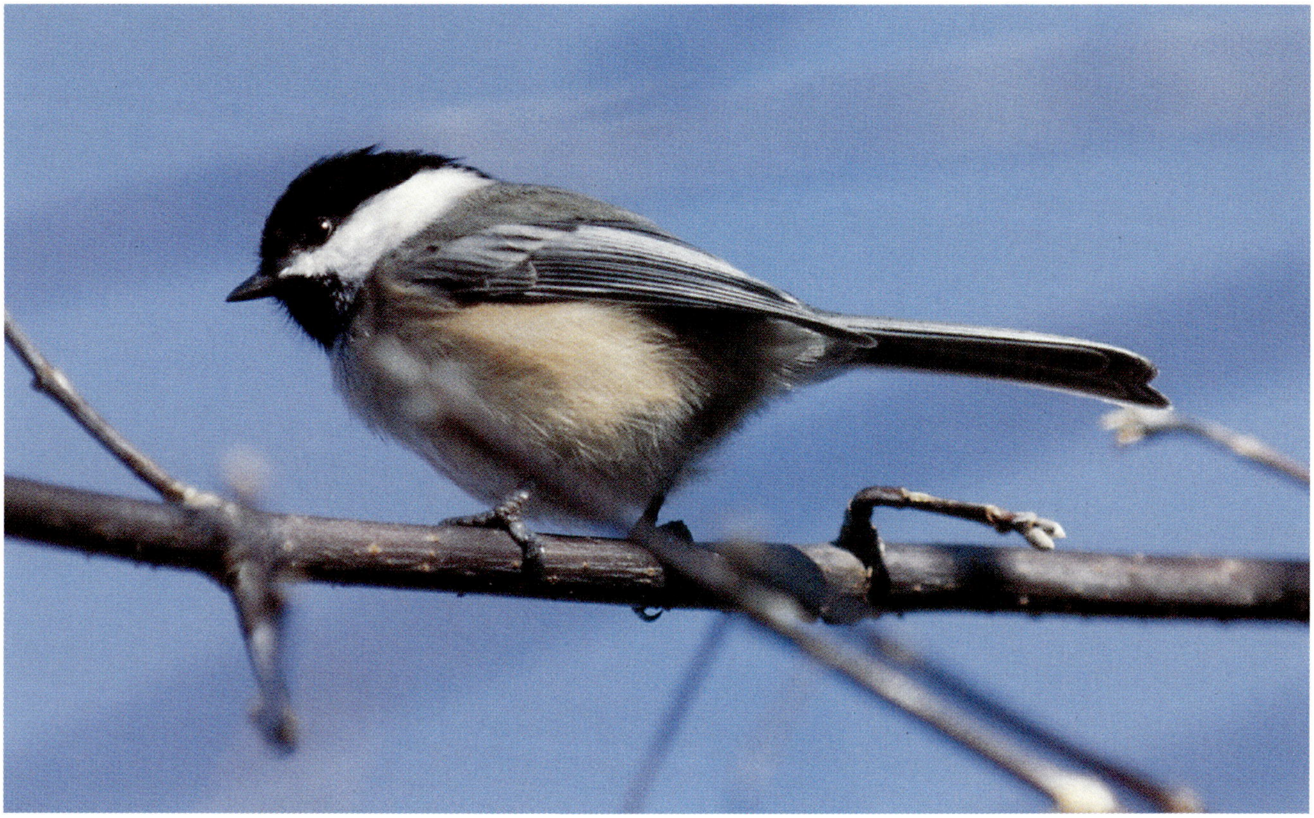

Black-capped Chickadee

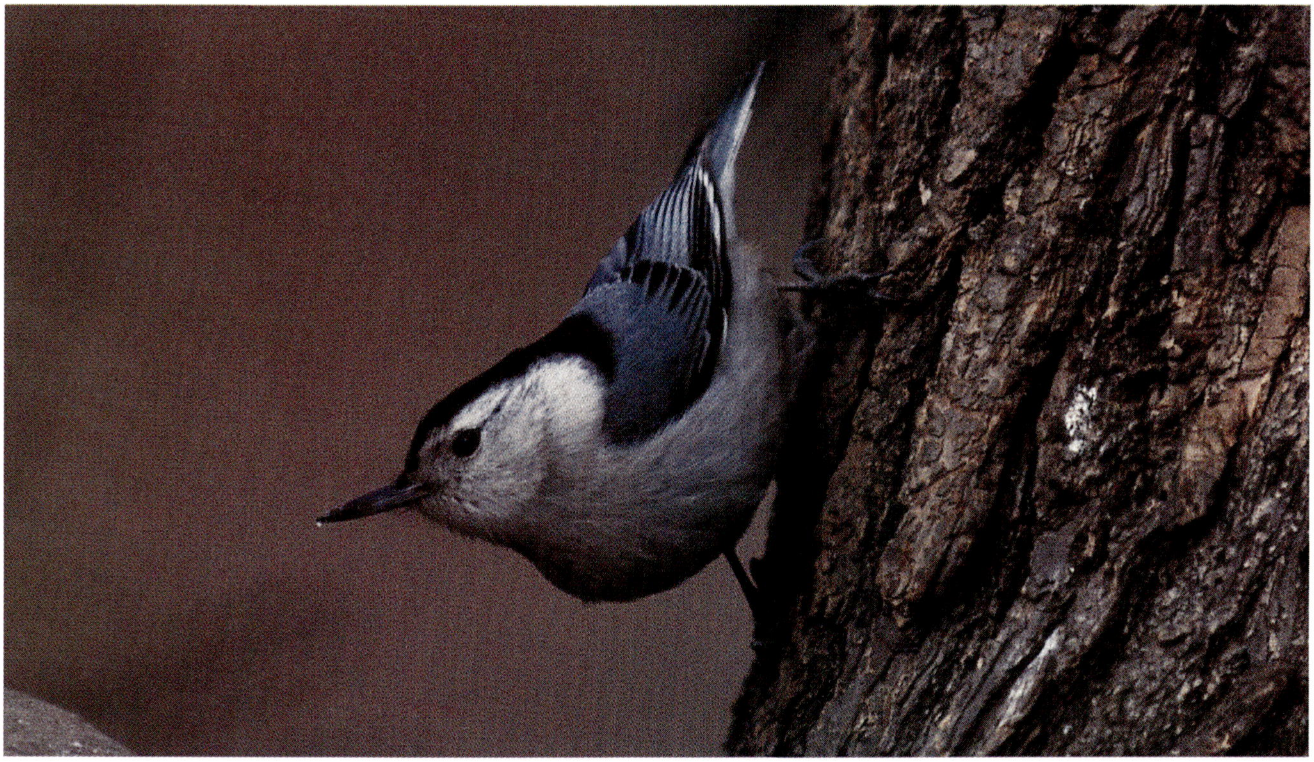

White-breasted Nuthatch

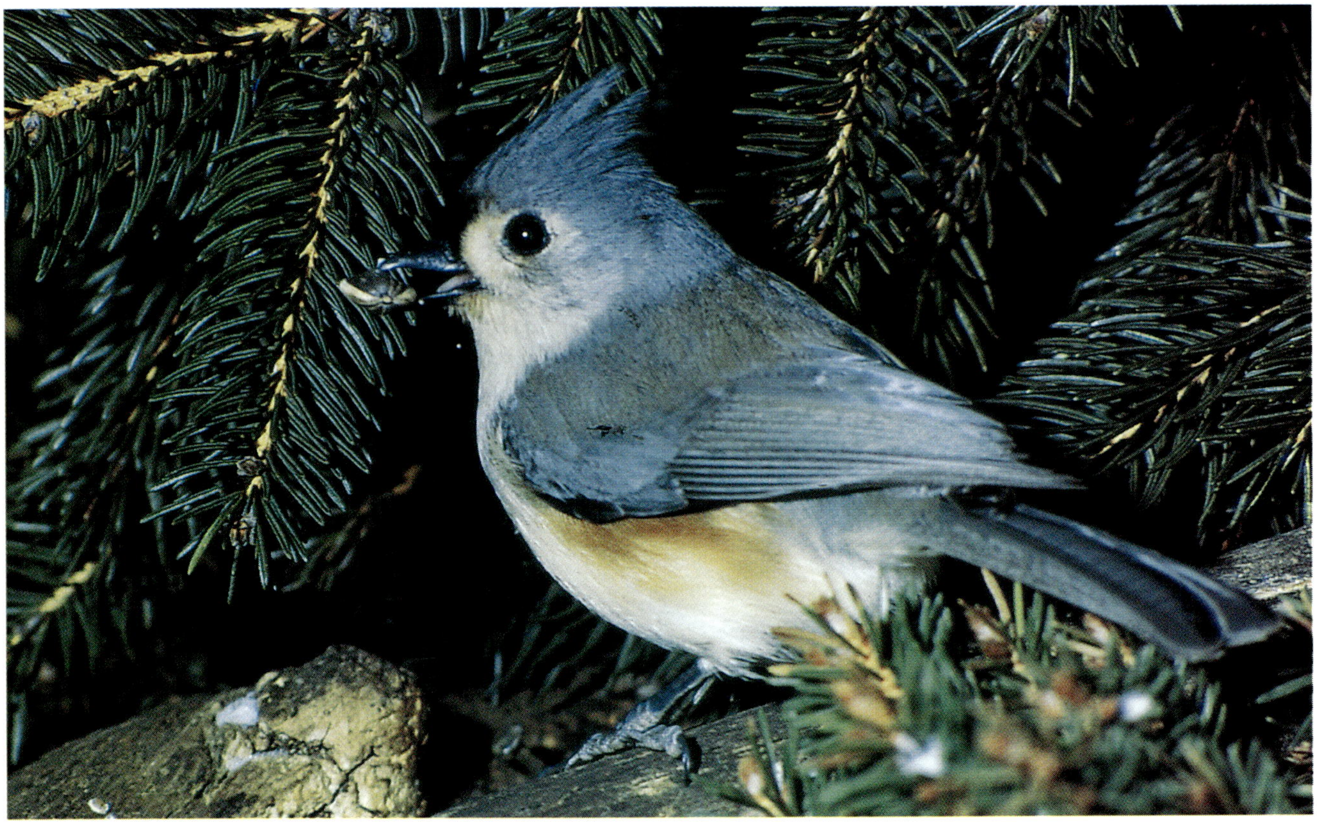

Tufted Titmouse

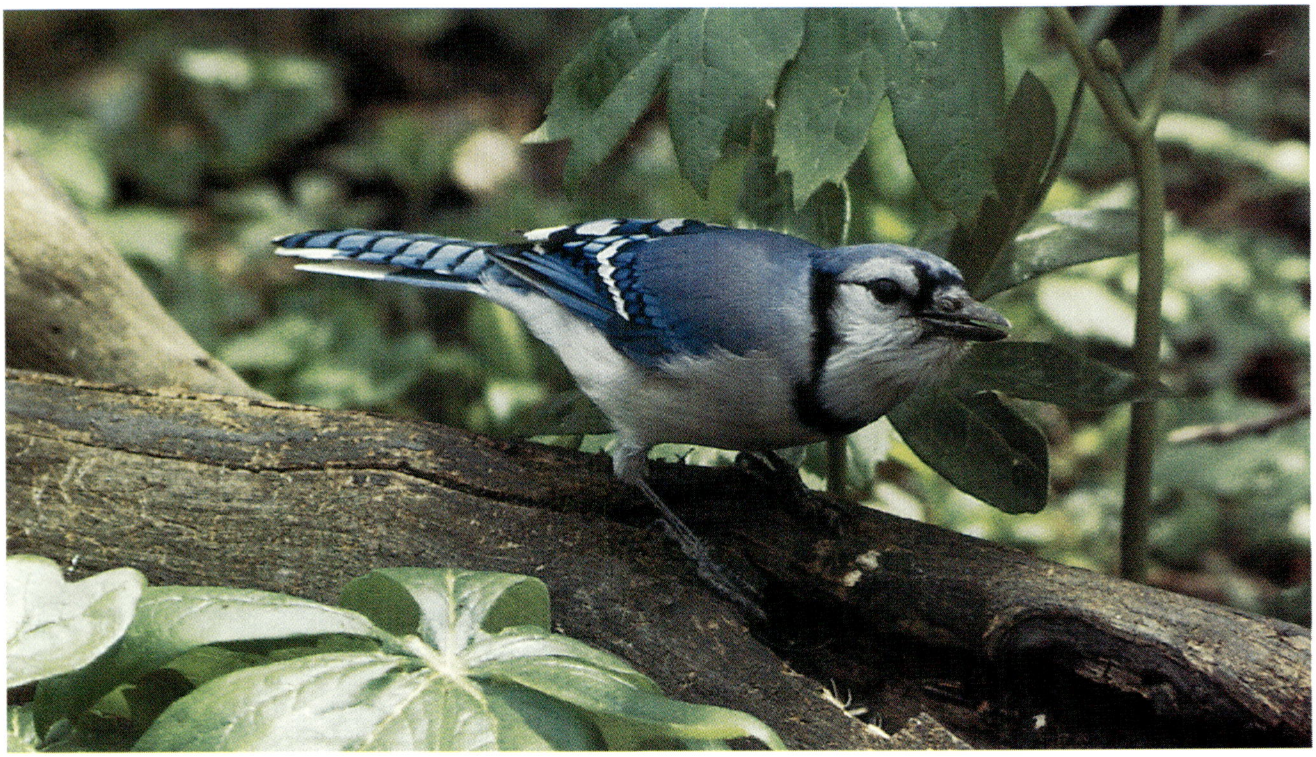

Blue Jay

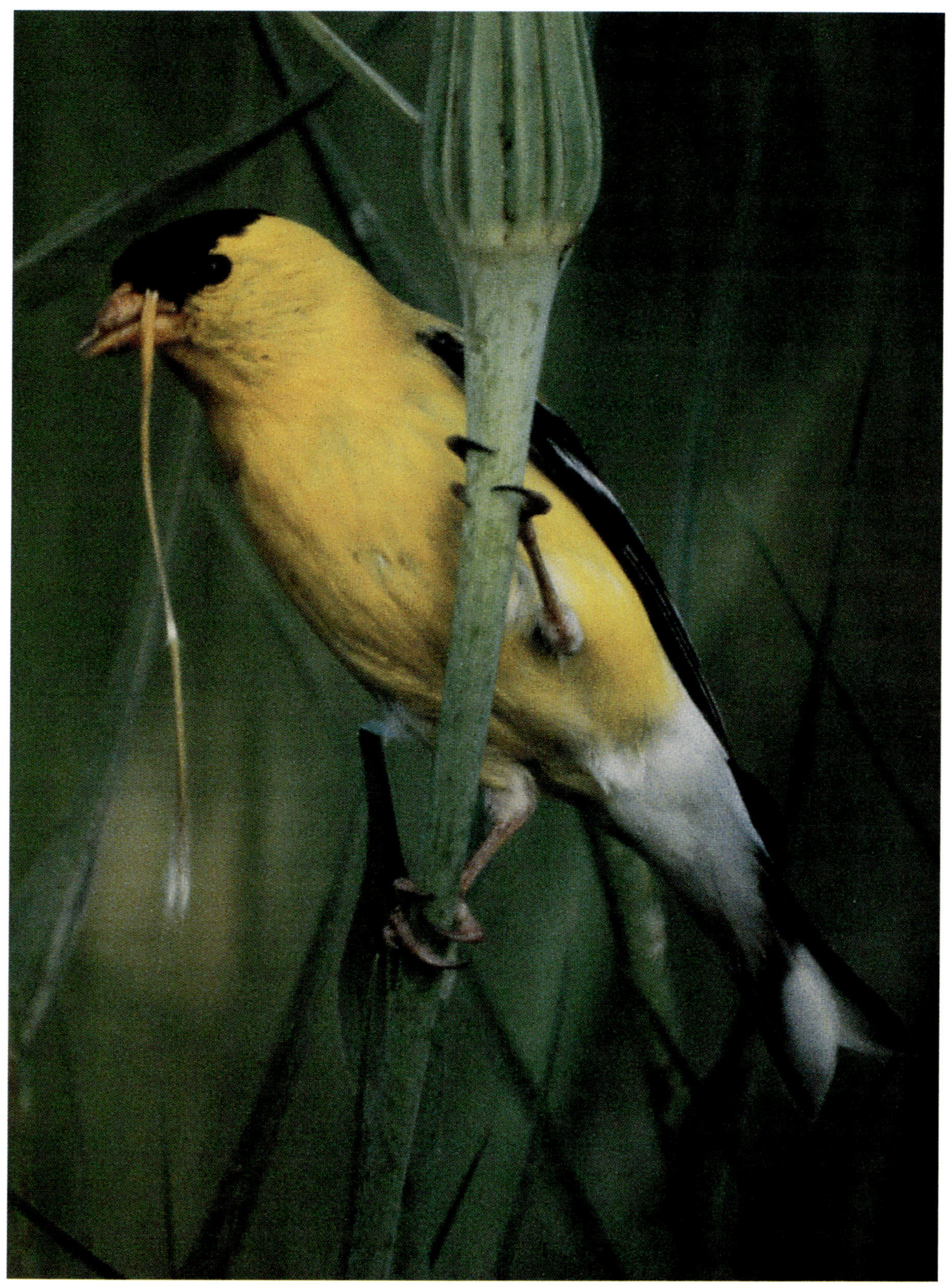

American Goldfinch

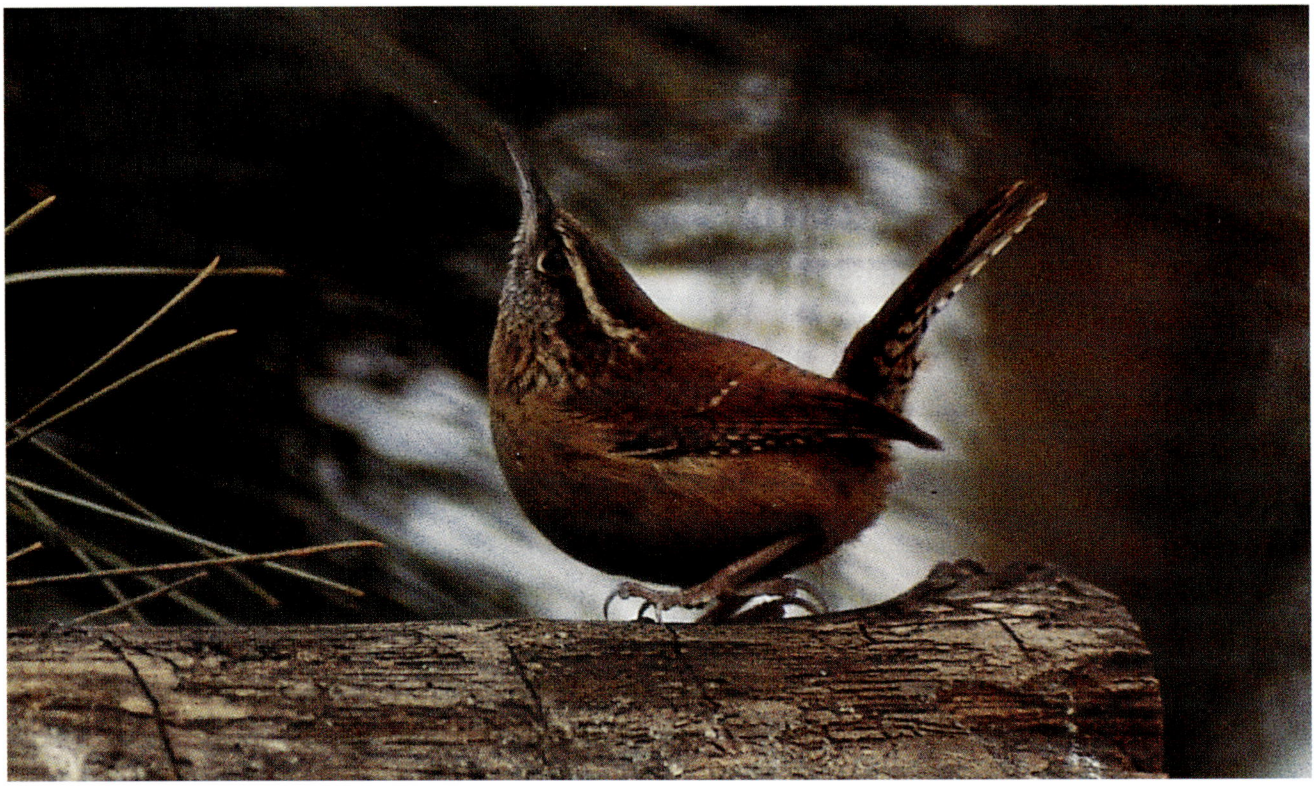

Carolina Wren

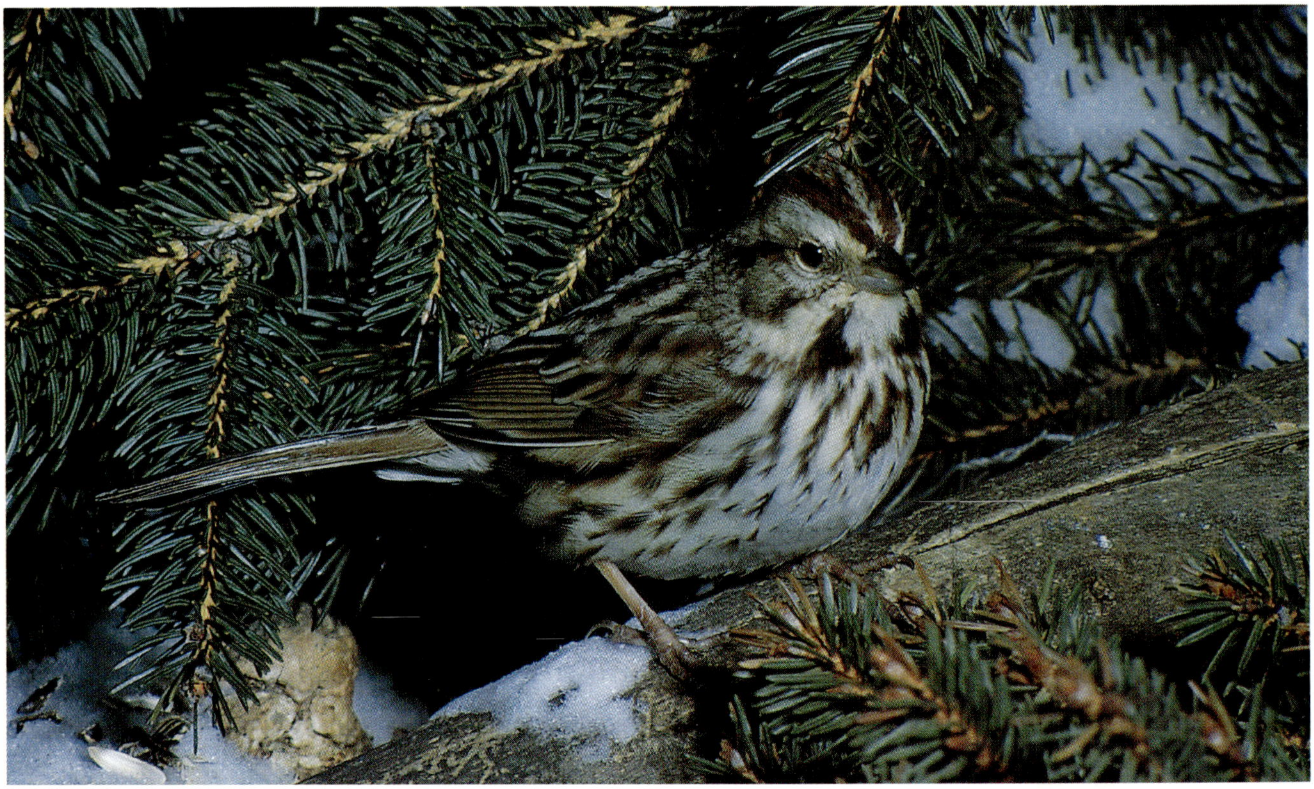

Song Sparrow

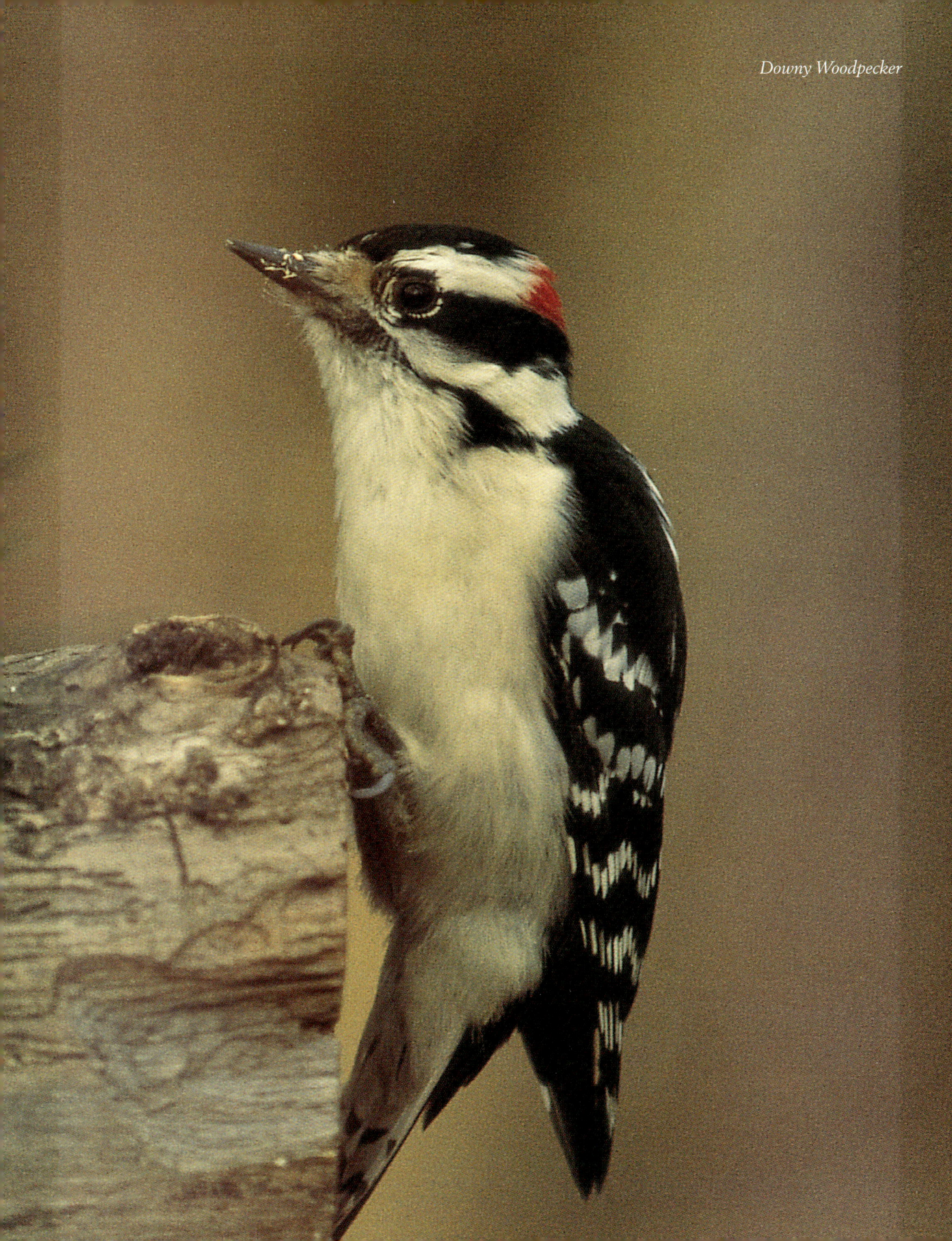

Downy Woodpecker

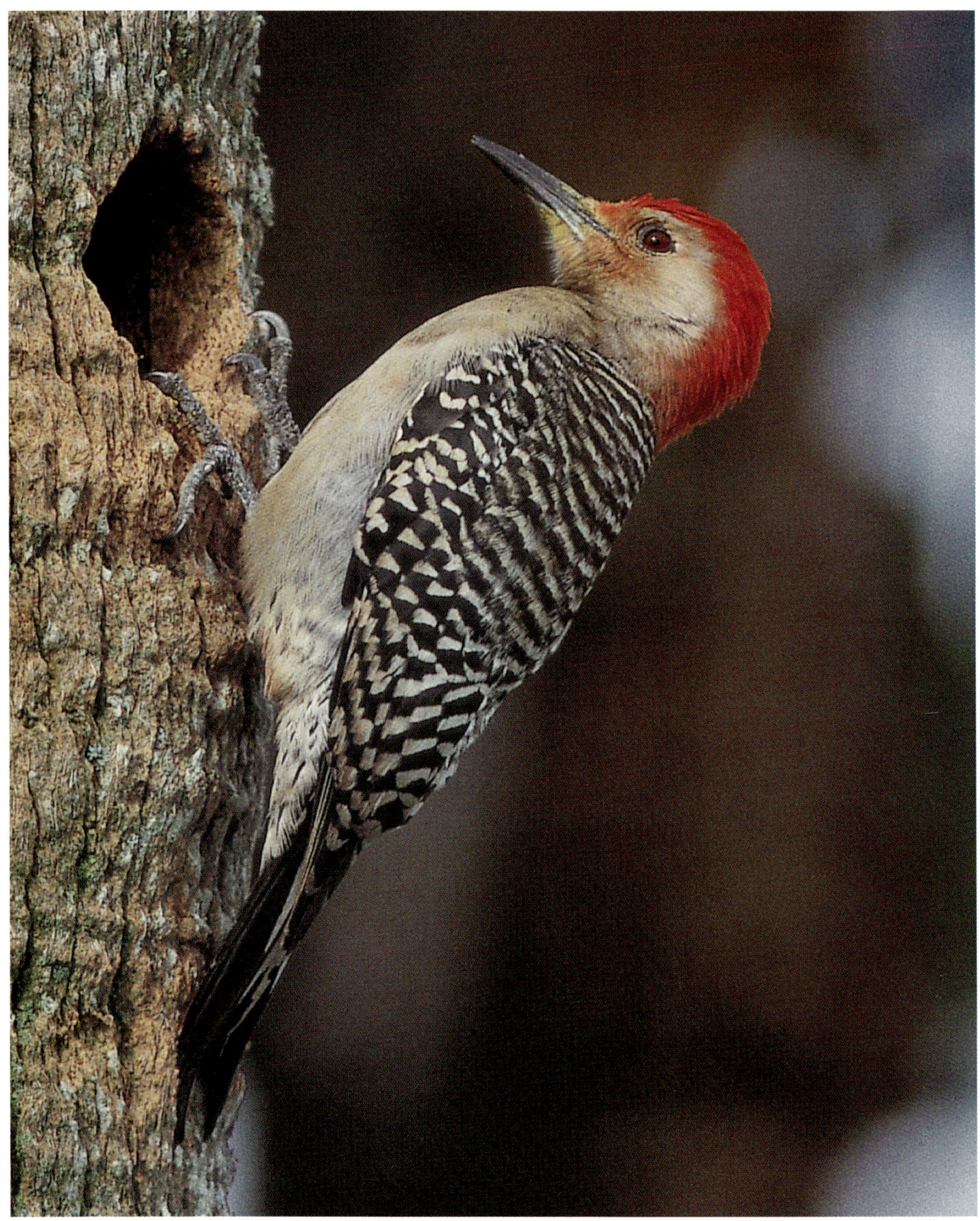

Red-bellied Woodpecker

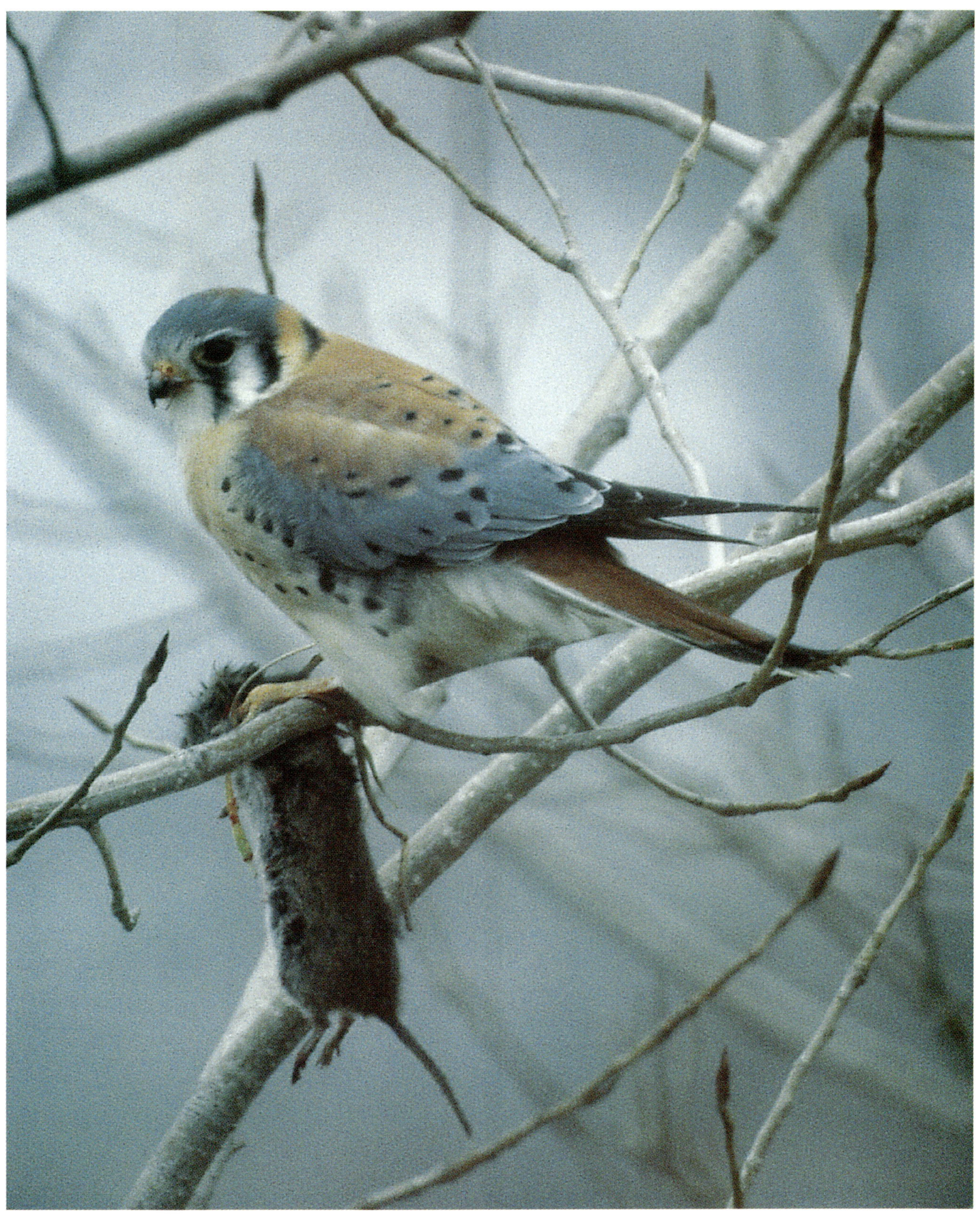

American Kestrel

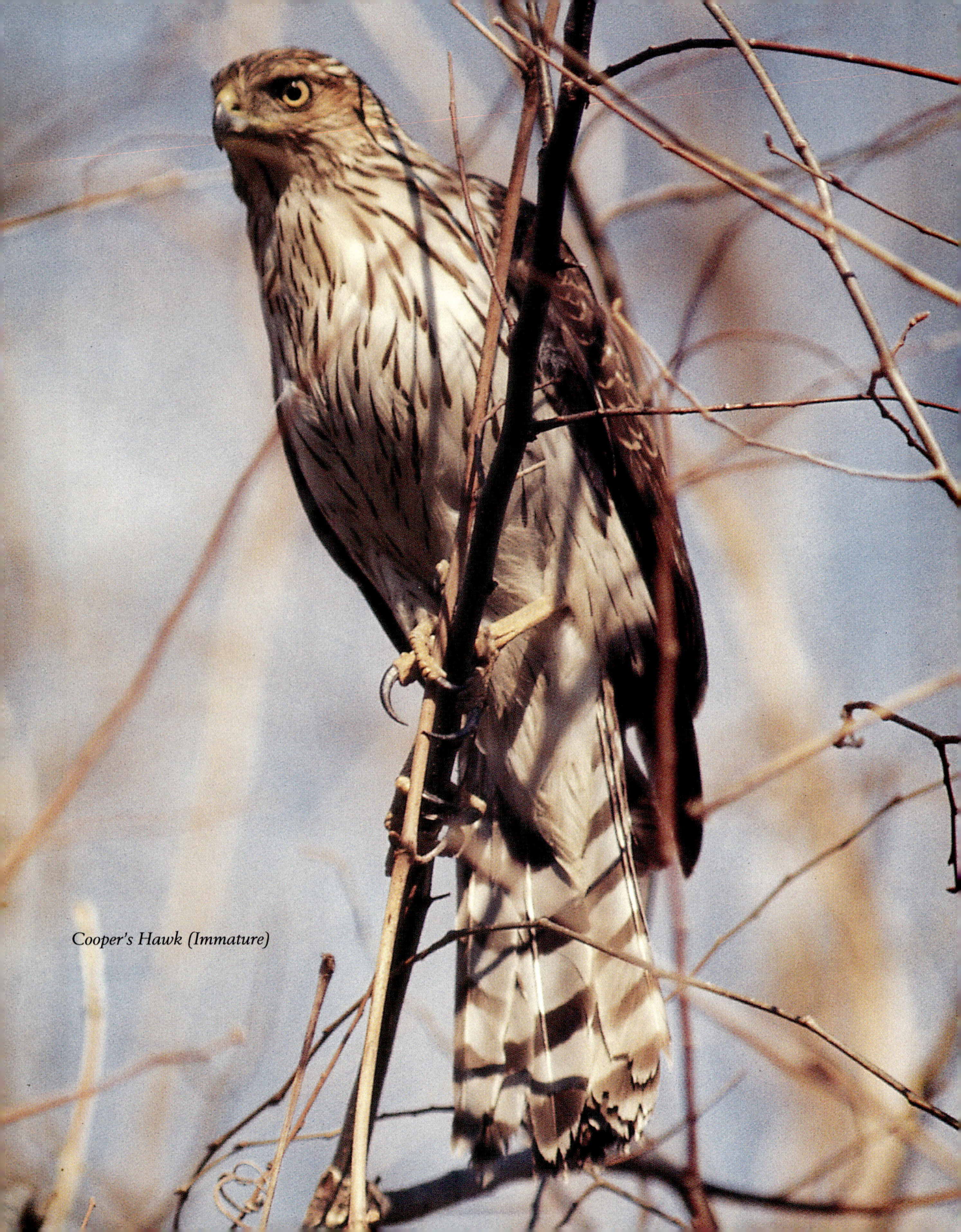

Cooper's Hawk (Immature)

Spring in Northwest Ohio

Bird migration occurs throughout much of the spring and fall in northwest Ohio, but it is in May that the heaviest movement of the most species occurs. That's when birders from far and wide converge on the Magee Marsh Bird Trail.

One day in early May, 1983, I arrived at the Bird Trail at about 7:30AM. As I approached the parking lot, I knew it was going to be an exciting day. Birds were flying and singing everywhere. They were in the trees, in the bushes, on the ground—even all over the parking lot. Not only were they everywhere, but many of them weren't a bit disturbed by the growing number of birders that were congregating. Some even perched *too close* for pictures.

I took more shots in less time that morning than at any time before or since. To my great chagrin, however, I had violated Cardinal Rule number 3 (*page 9*). I had brought only three spare rolls of 36 exposure film with me. Normally, that would have been enough, but I ran out in less than two hours. I jumped into my car and headed back toward Toledo (breaking a few more rules on the way) in search of a store that might have film. After driving almost twenty miles, I found one that had three rolls of high speed Ektachrome. I raced back and finished the last roll before noon. By that time, however, many of the birds had departed for Canada and there were almost as many birders as birds. For the birders it was a bird-watching experience never to be forgotten, and for the birds, I'm sure it was one of their best birder-watching days ever.

During the peak of migration in May more than 130 species of birds can be seen in the immediate vicinity of the Bird Trail. This includes all of those pictured in this section through page 55 and, of course, many more.

My favorites are the warblers. There are approximately fifty species of warblers that are seen in the United States. About three quarters of them pass through northwest Ohio during their migration. Twenty-three of those are pictured on pages 26 through 41 and on page 89.

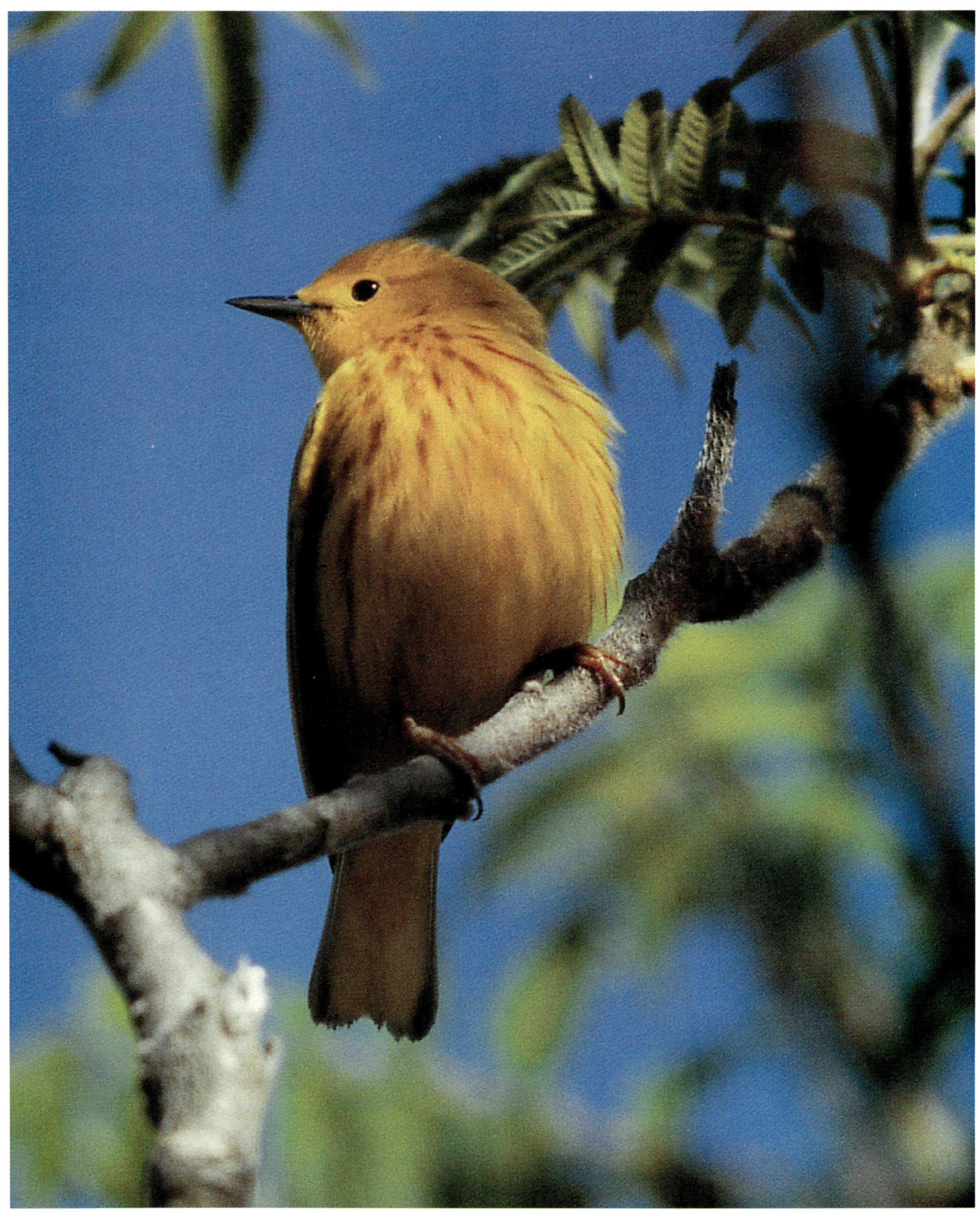

Yellow Warbler

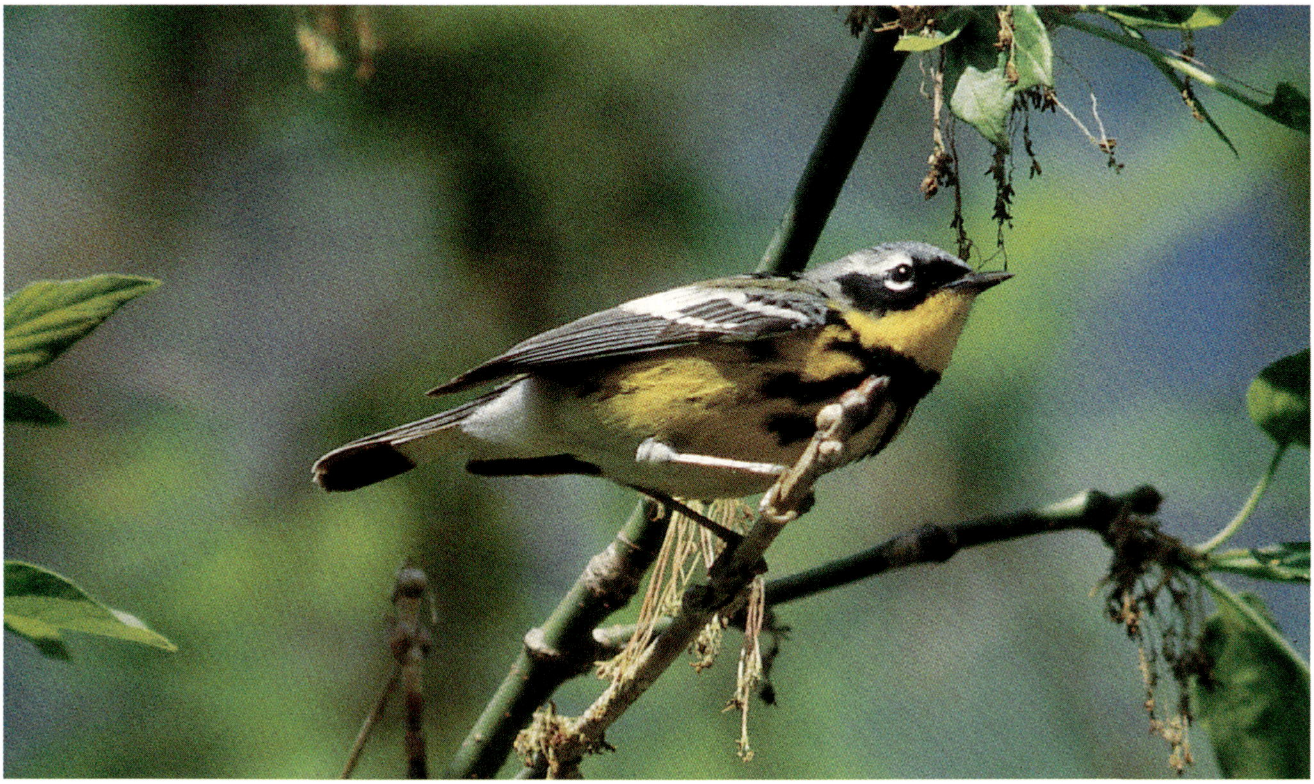

Magnolia Warbler

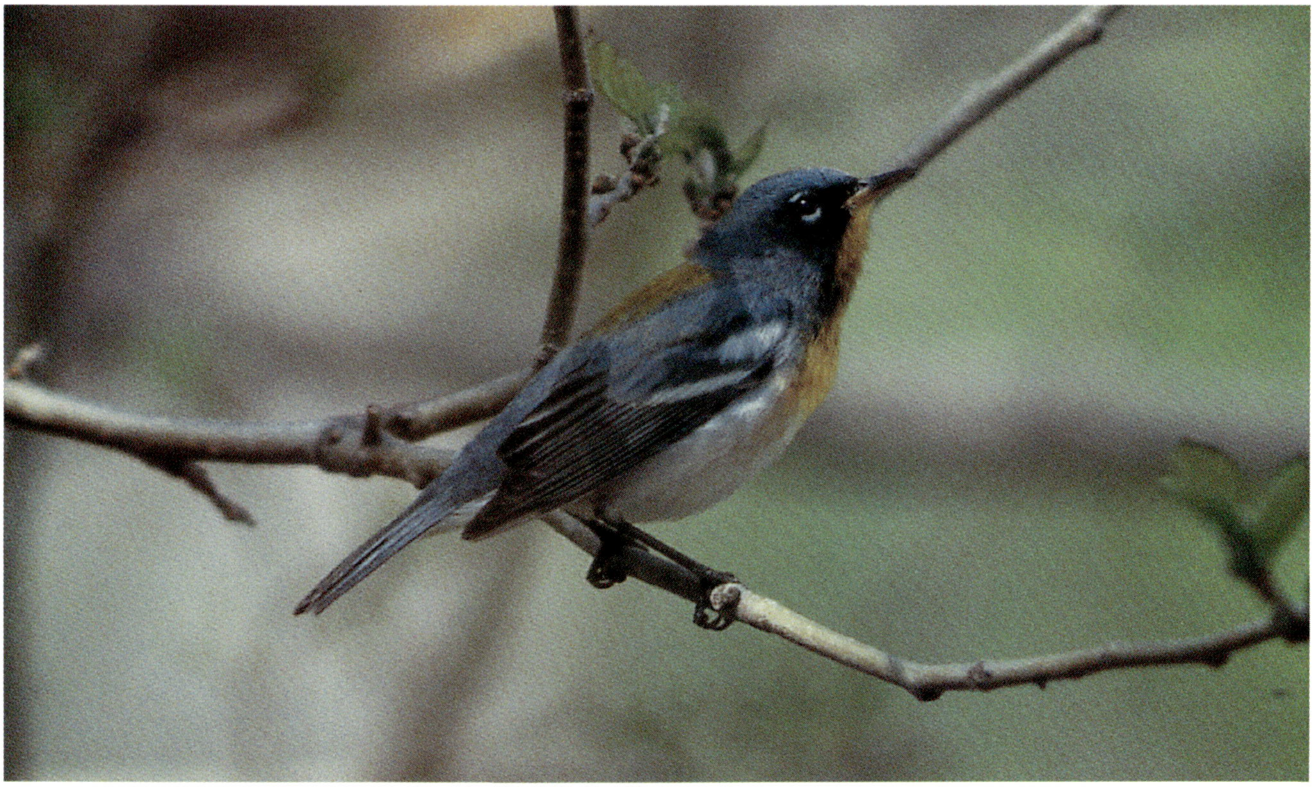

Northern Parula

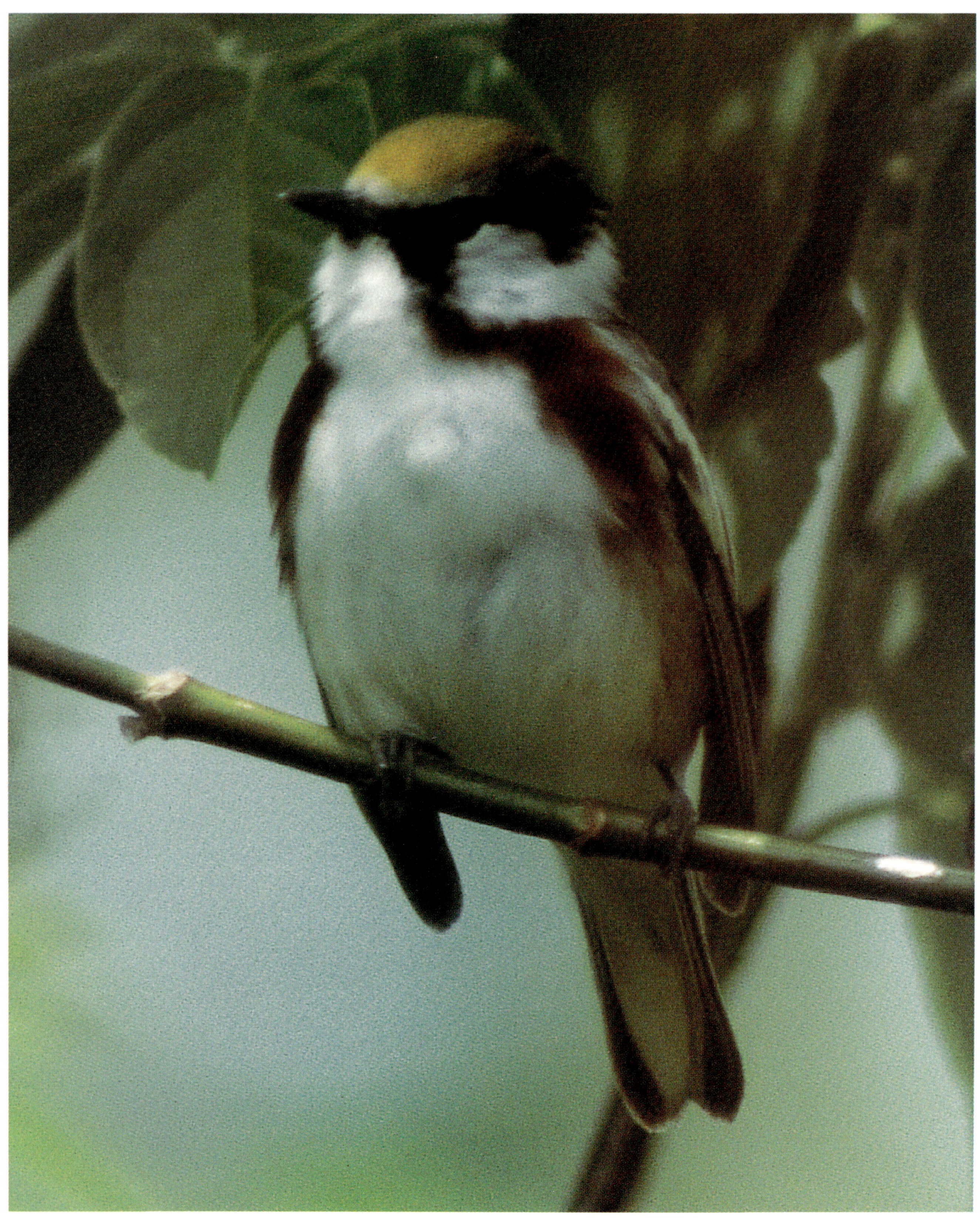

Chestnut-sided Warbler

Some warblers are known to hybridize.

Golden-winged and Blue-winged Warblers can produce two different hybirds depending on which species is the male and which is the female. One of the hybrids, known as the *Brewster's Warbler*, is shown below. This was a rather lucky shot since it's the only one I've ever seen and it wasn't overly cooperative. Pictured on the following page is a *Golden-winged Warbler*. Below it is another lucky shot of the same bird with a *Blue-winged Warbler*. The opportunity for this photo lasted no more than a couple of seconds. At the time it was taken, autofocus had not been perfected, and the photo would have been nearly impossible without the Novoflex Follow-Focus outfit.

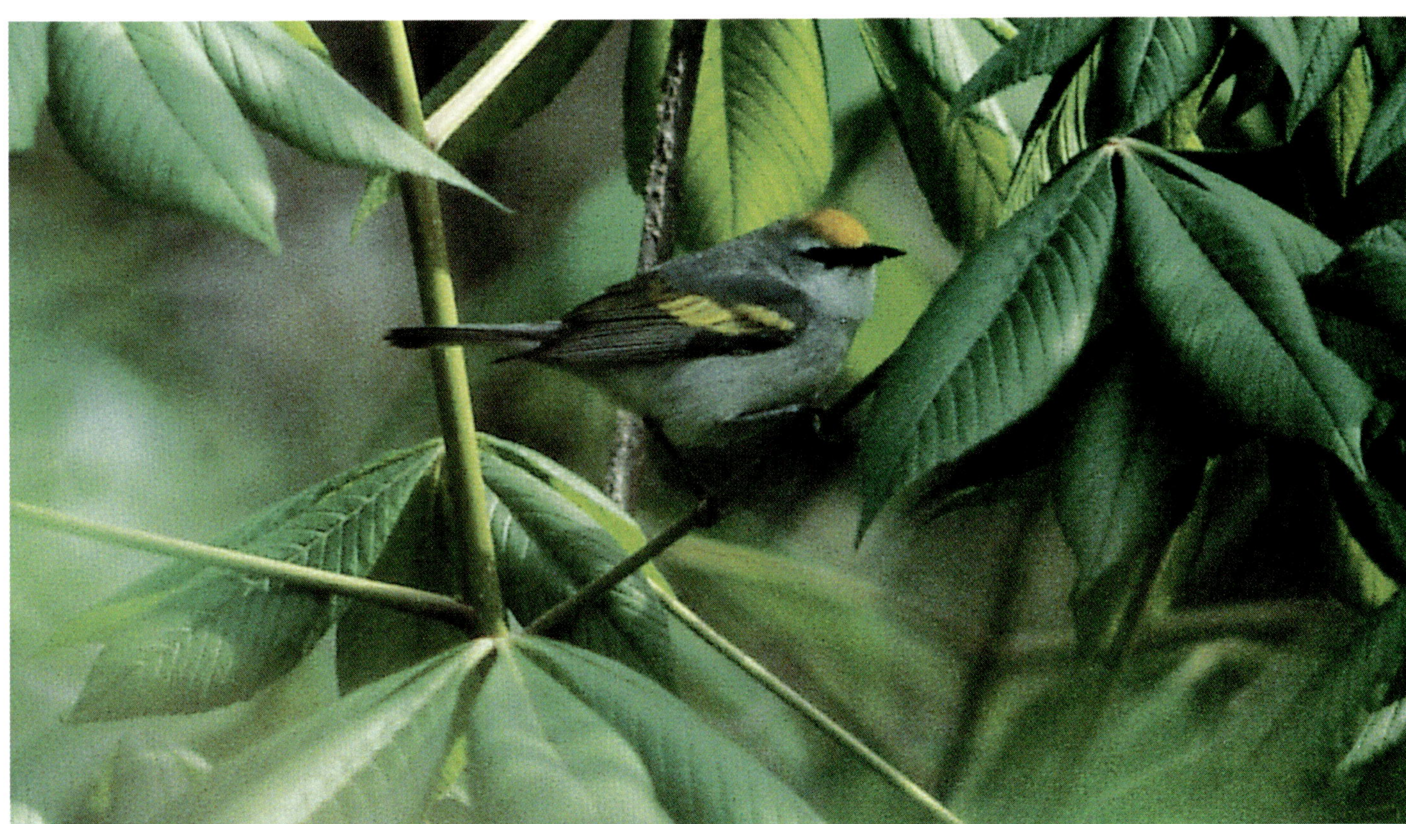

Brewster's Warbler

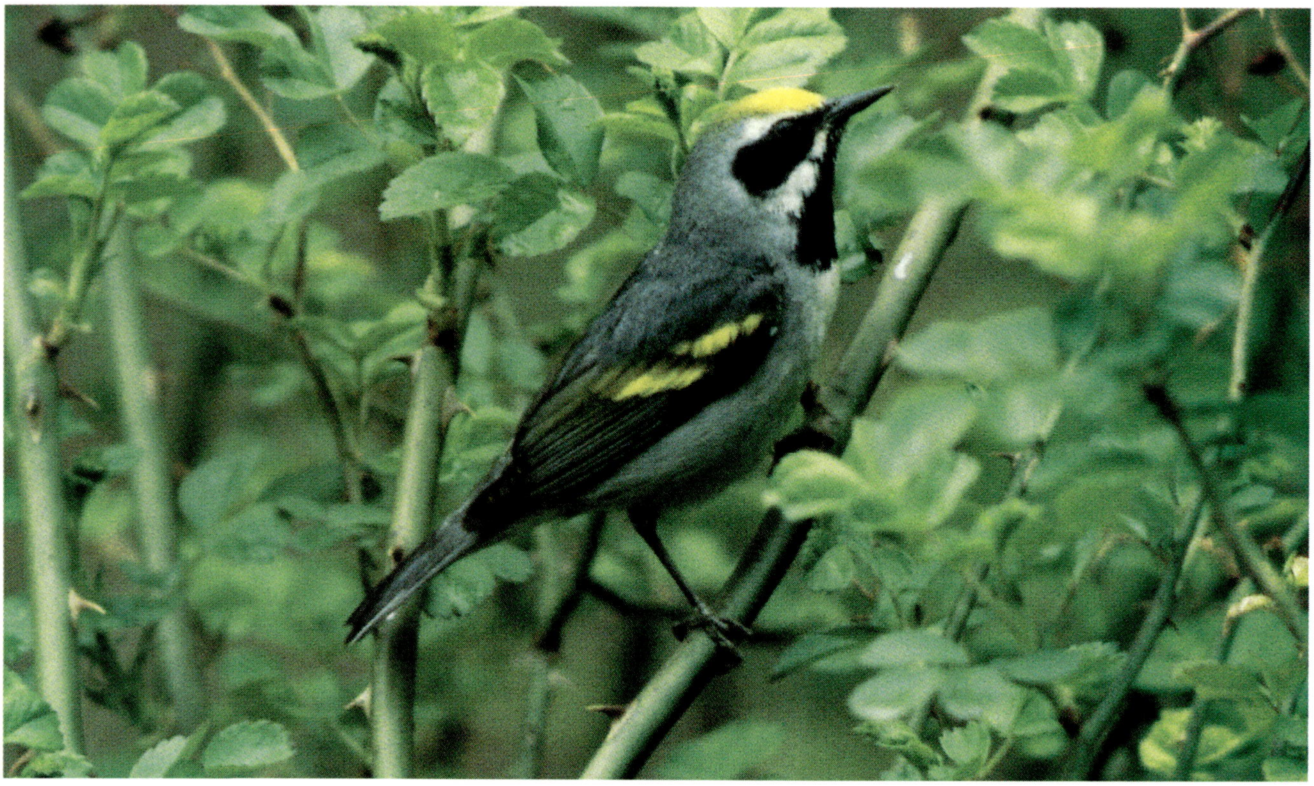

Golden-winged Warbler

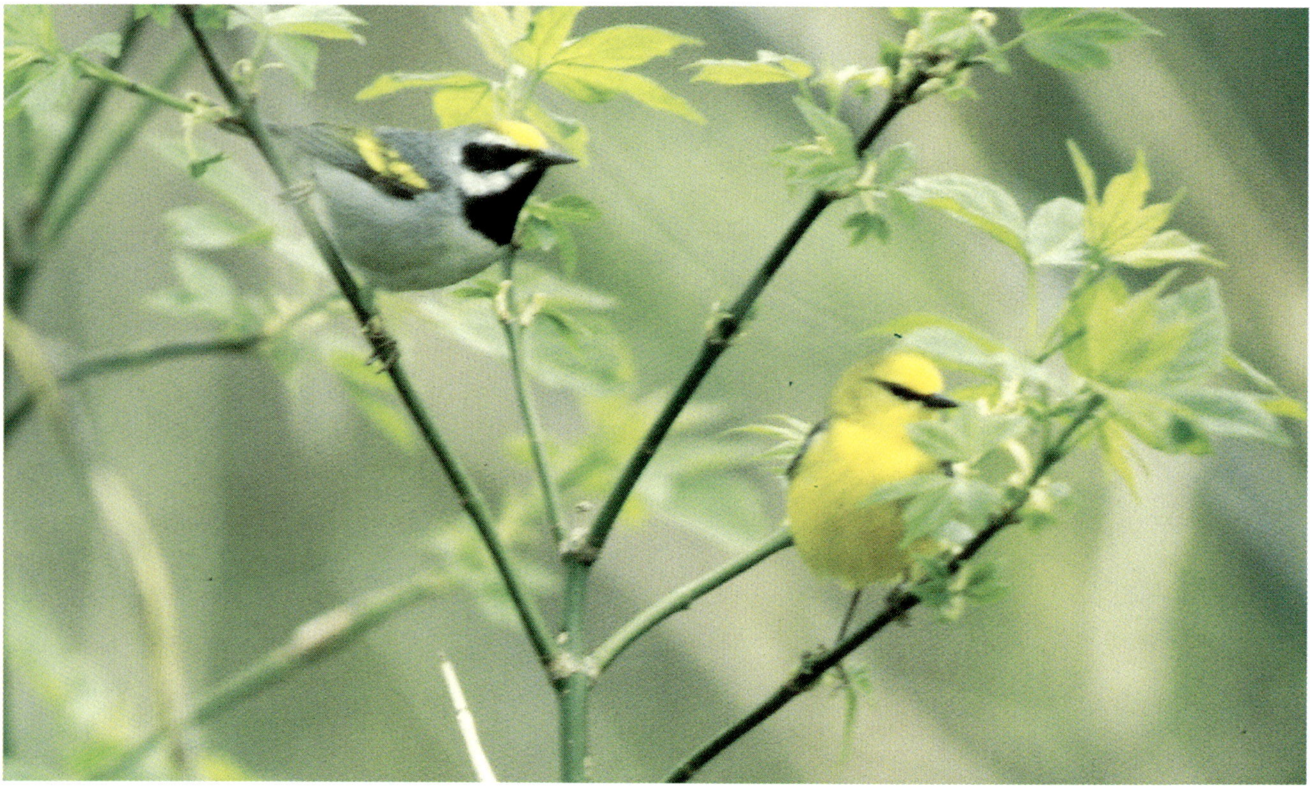

Golden-winged & Blue-winged Warblers

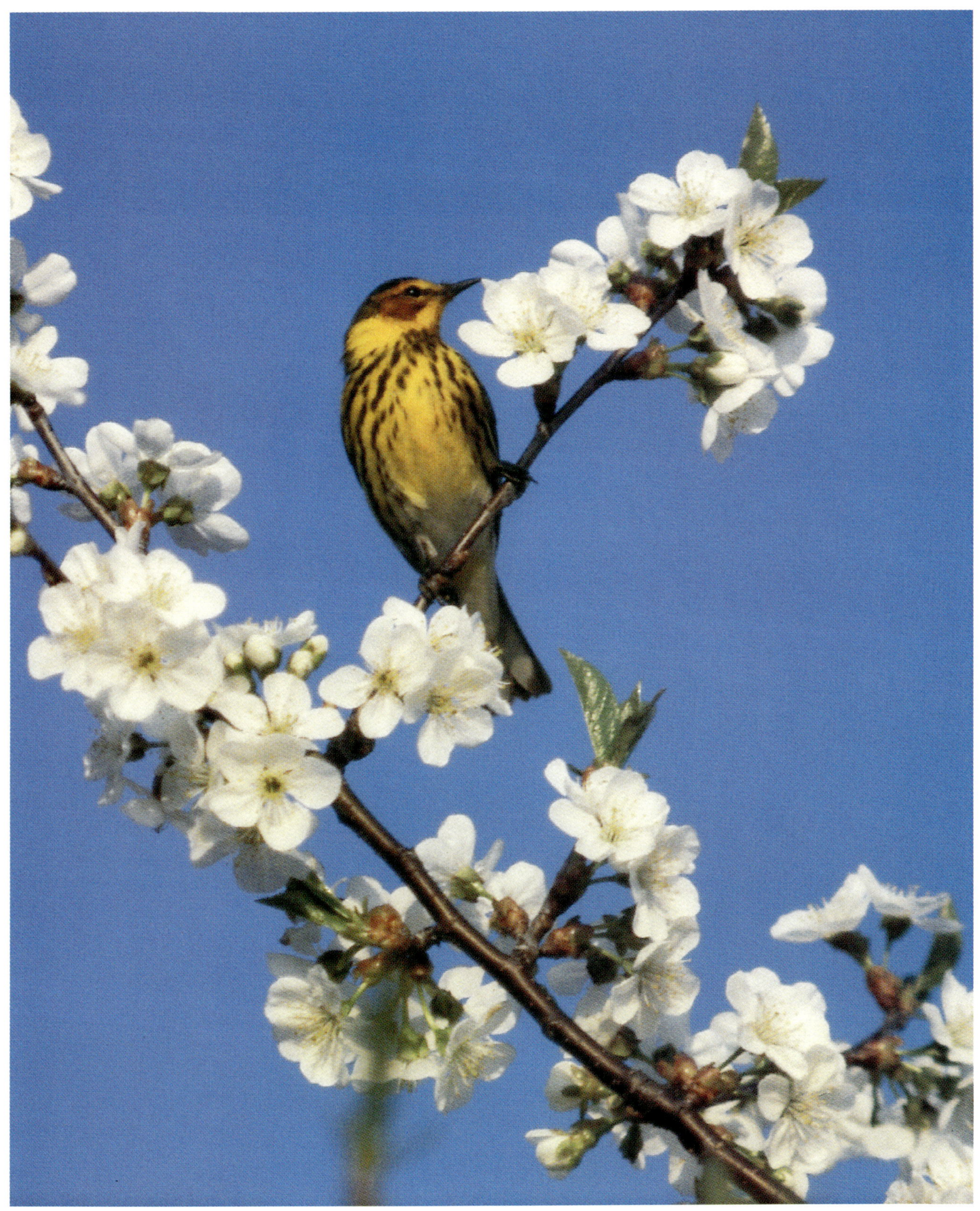

Cape May Warbler

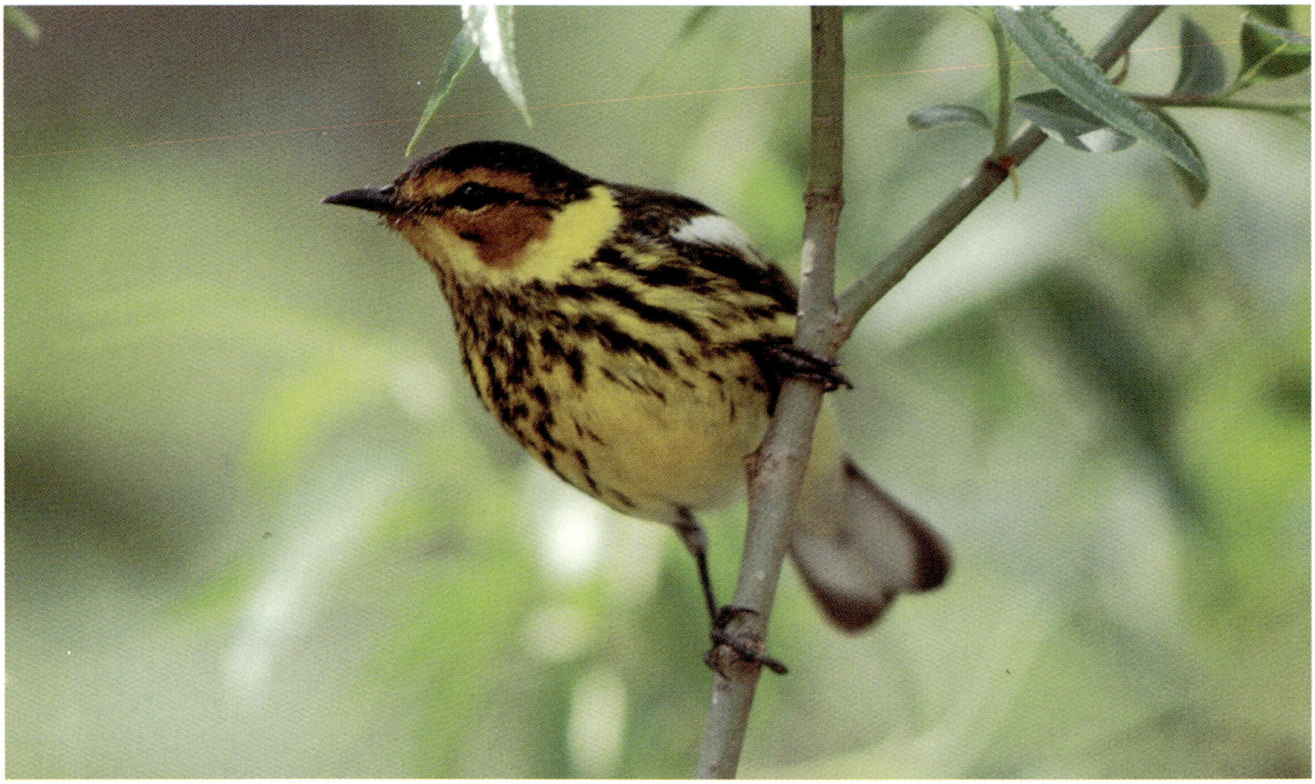

Cape May Warbler

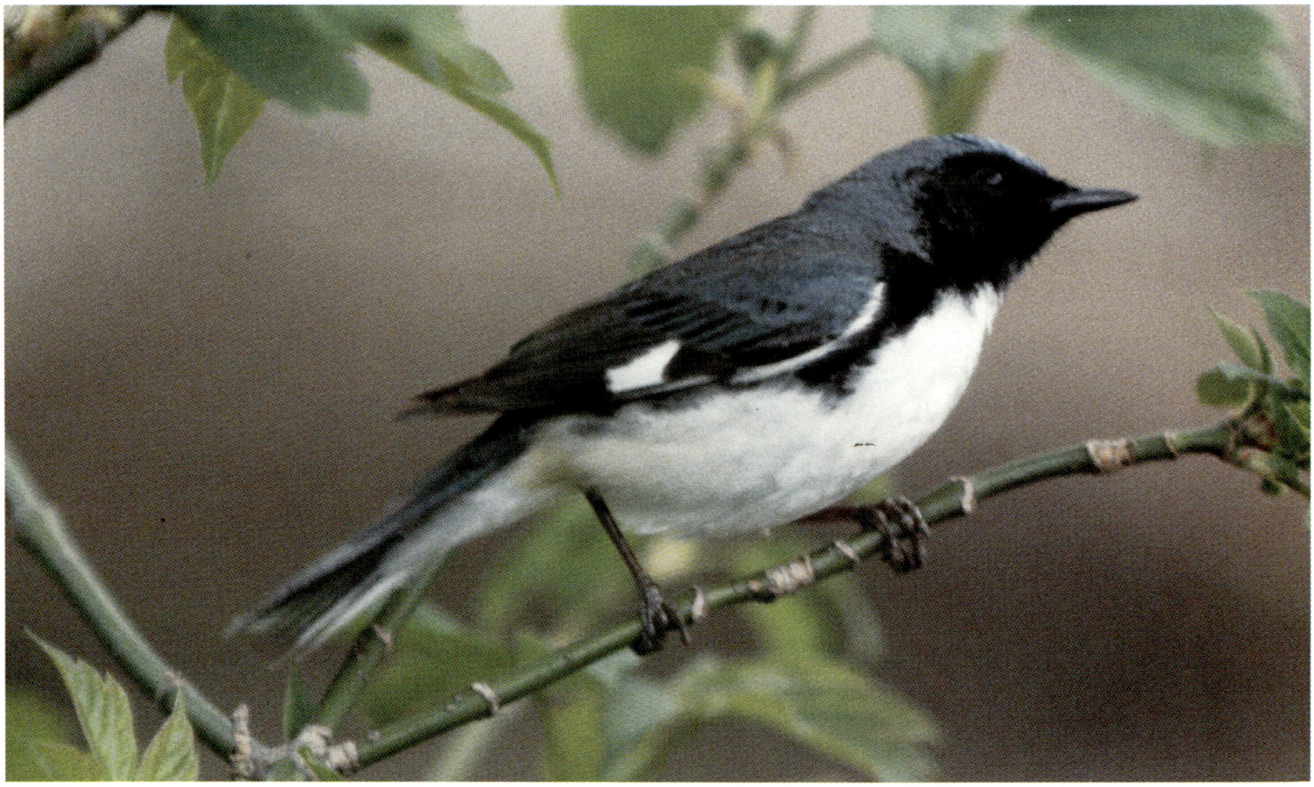

Black-throated Blue Warbler

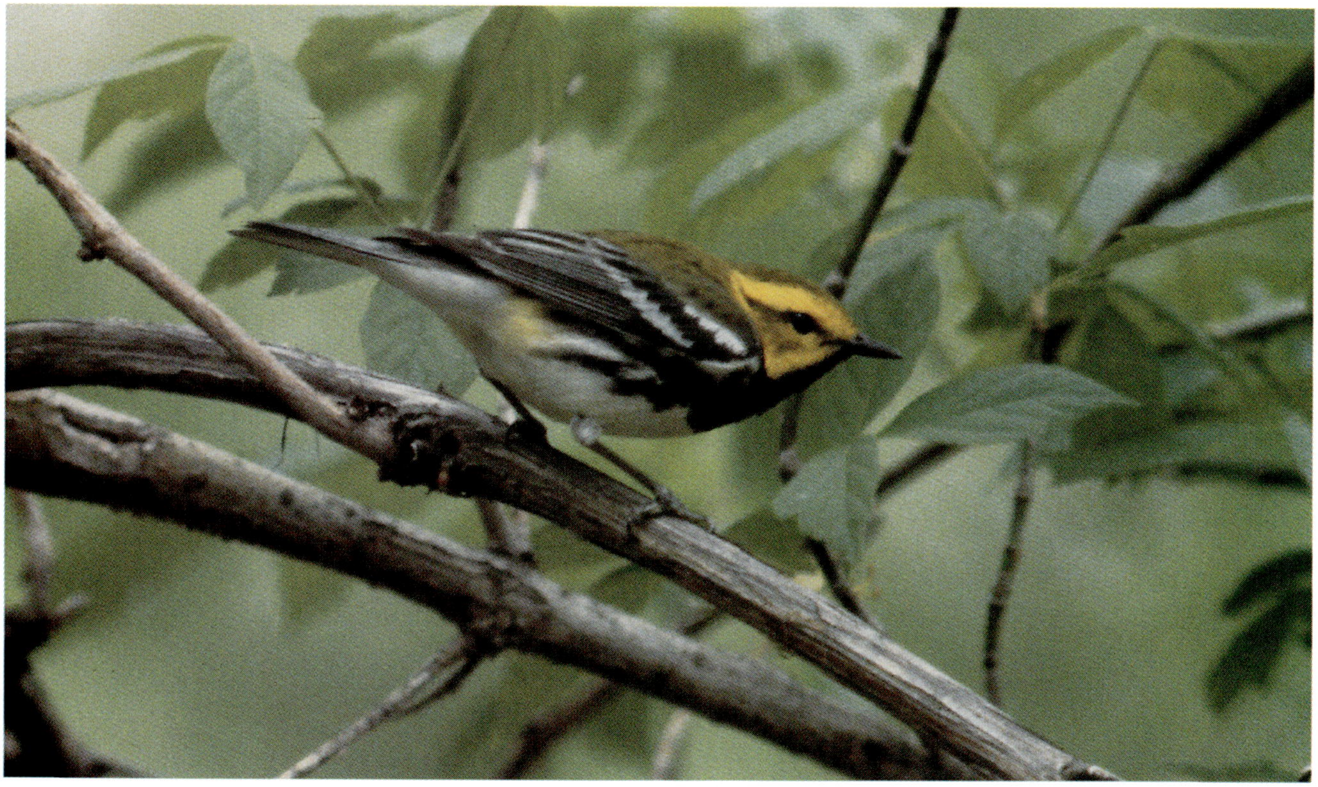

Black-throated Green Warbler

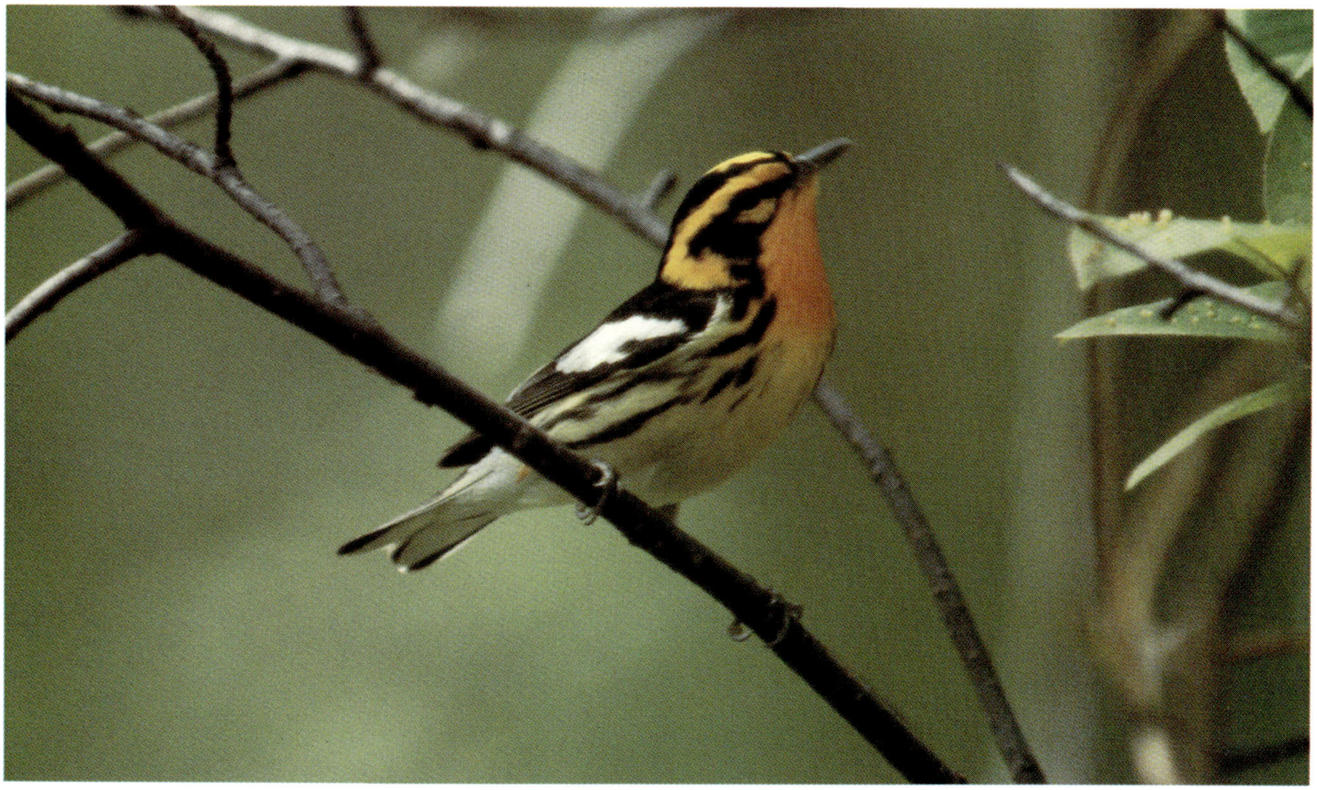

Blackburnian Warbler

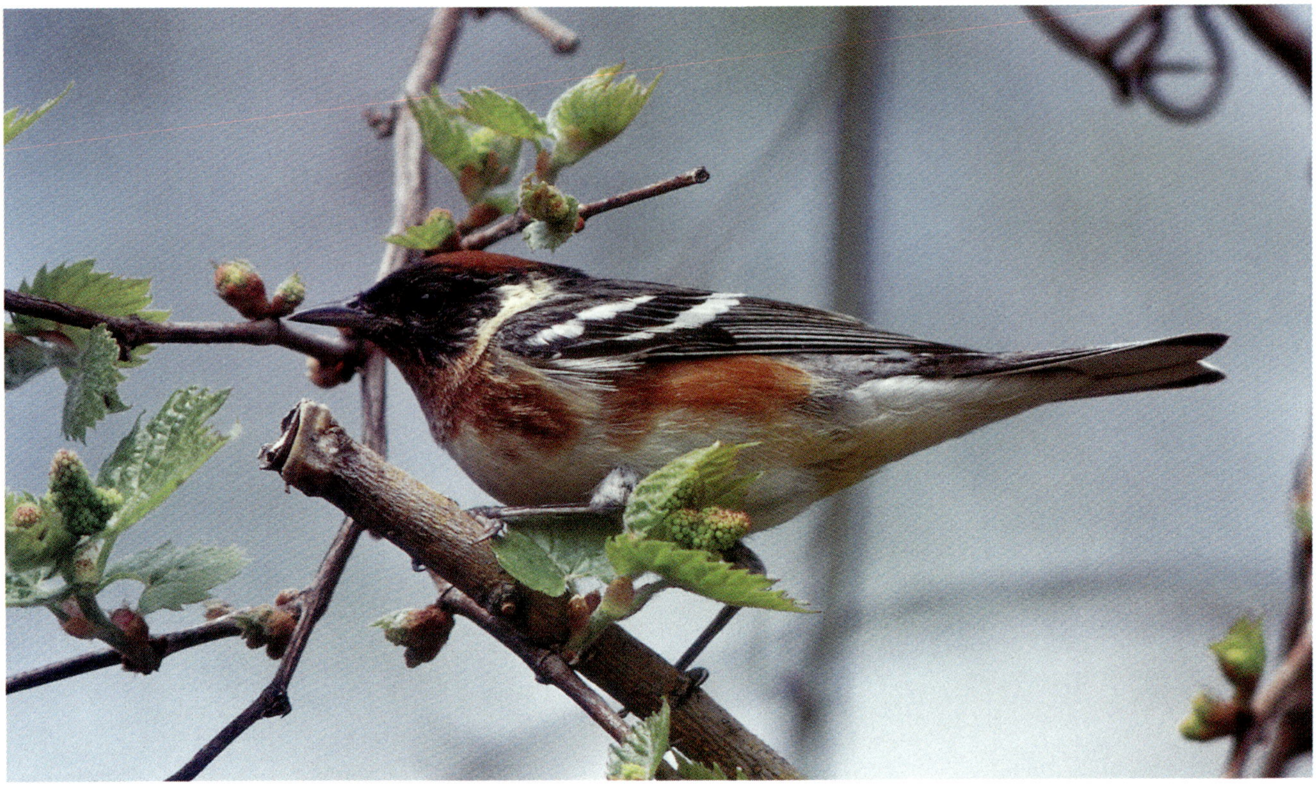

Bay-breasted Warbler

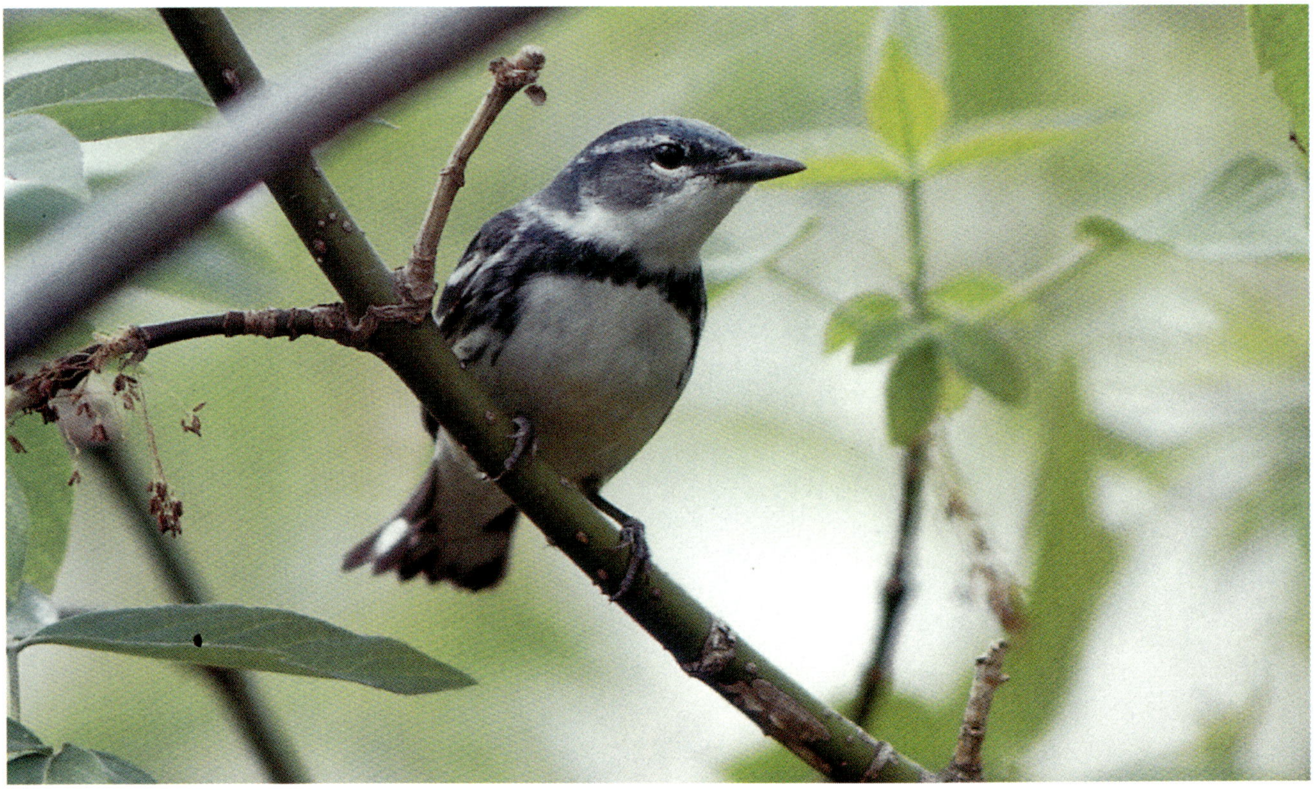

Cerulean Warbler

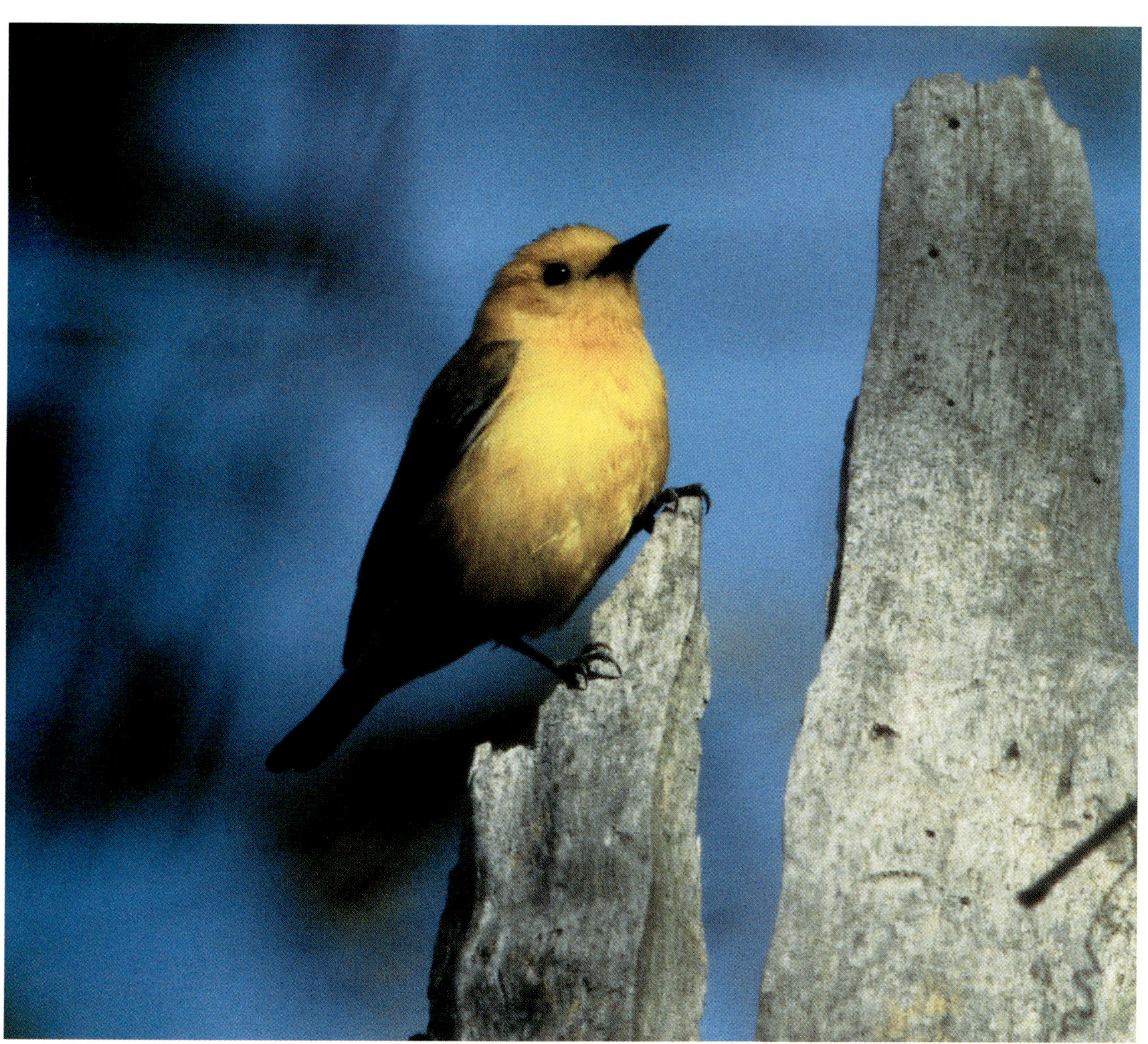

Prothonotary Warbler

The Kirtland's Warbler is extremely rare.

Only a few hundred pairs remain. Extensive conservation efforts have made some progress, but they are still classified as endangered. They nest in burned over jack pine forests, primarily in the northern part of the lower peninsula of Michigan. Seldom seen outside of their nesting area, there have been, however, a few sightings during migration at the Magee Marsh Bird Trail and at Point Pelee, Ontario which juts into Lake Erie from the Canadian shore.

The top photo on the opposite page was taken in May of 1979 at Point Pelee with my Novoflex. It was a somewhat scruffy looking specimen, but it was extremely cooperative, paying little attention to me as I snapped pictures from only a few feet away.

The other picture was taken eight years later in May of 1987 at the Bird Trail. This one made its appearance on a beautiful weekend day when hundreds of birders were present. Most of them got a good look at it. Once again the bird didn't seem to be at all disturbed by the constant crowd that surrounded it.

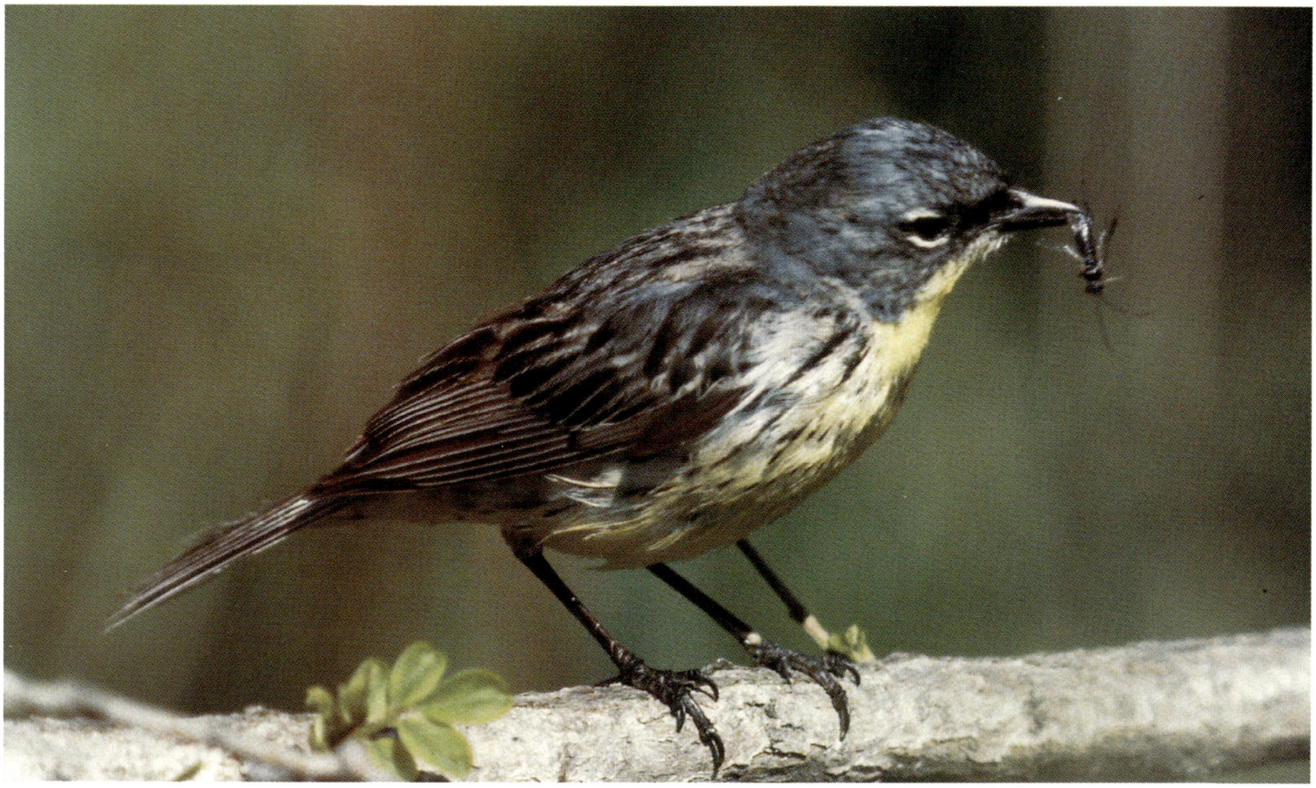

Kirtland's Warbler

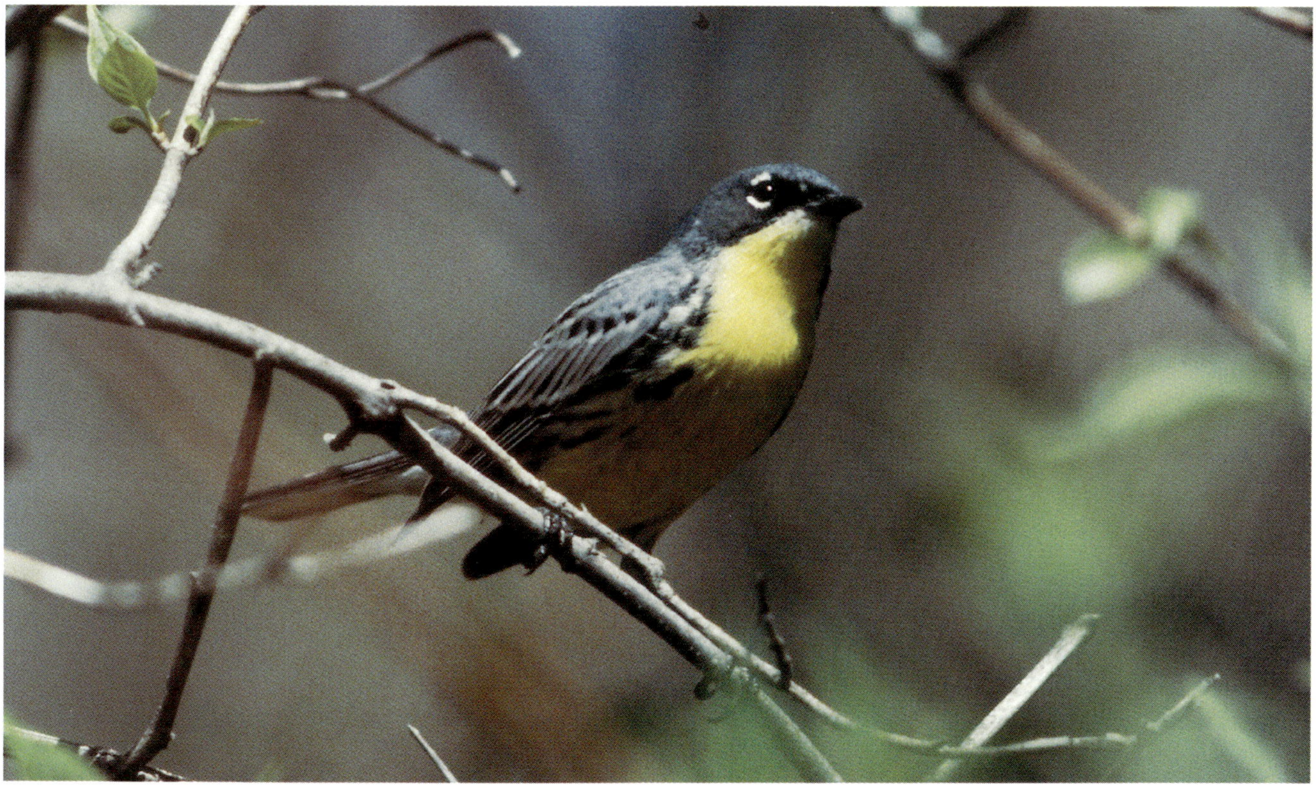

Kirtland's Warbler

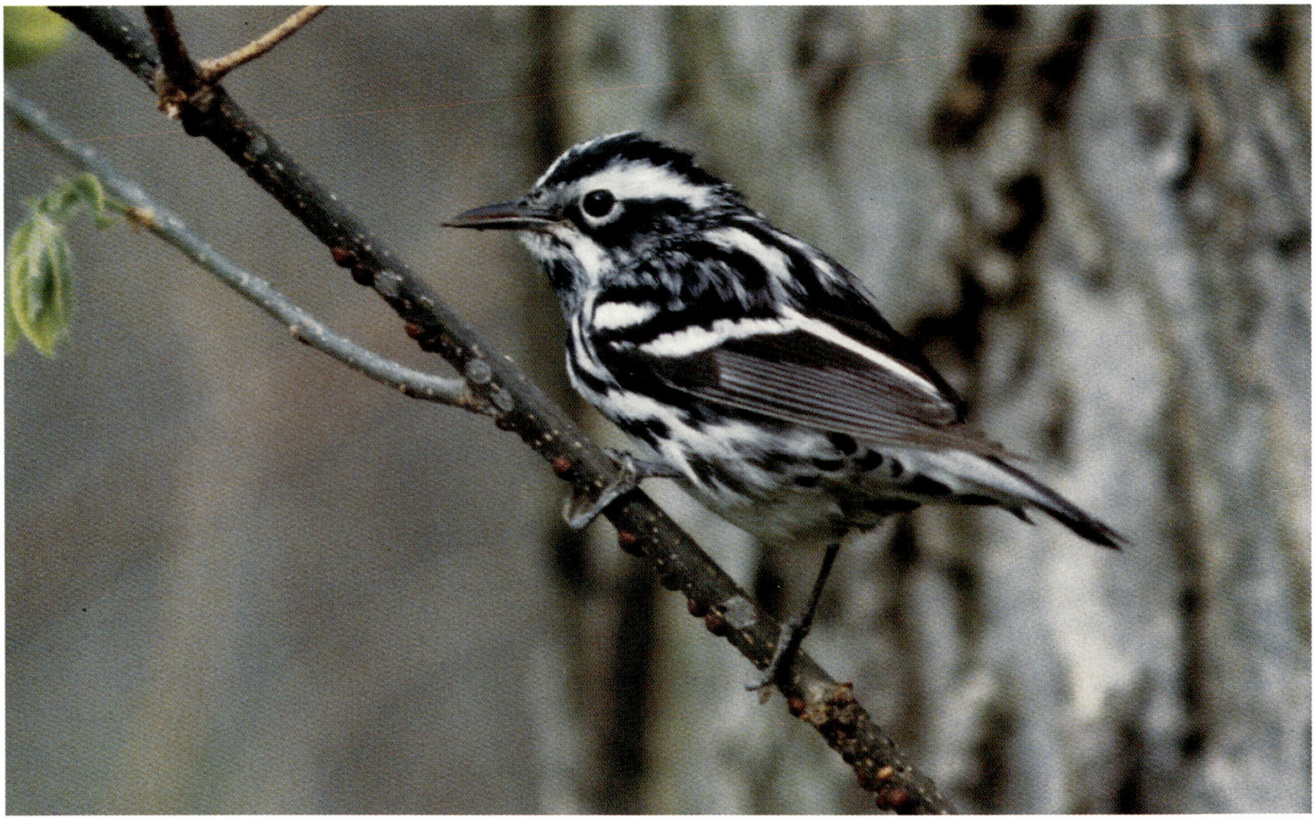

Black-and-white Warbler

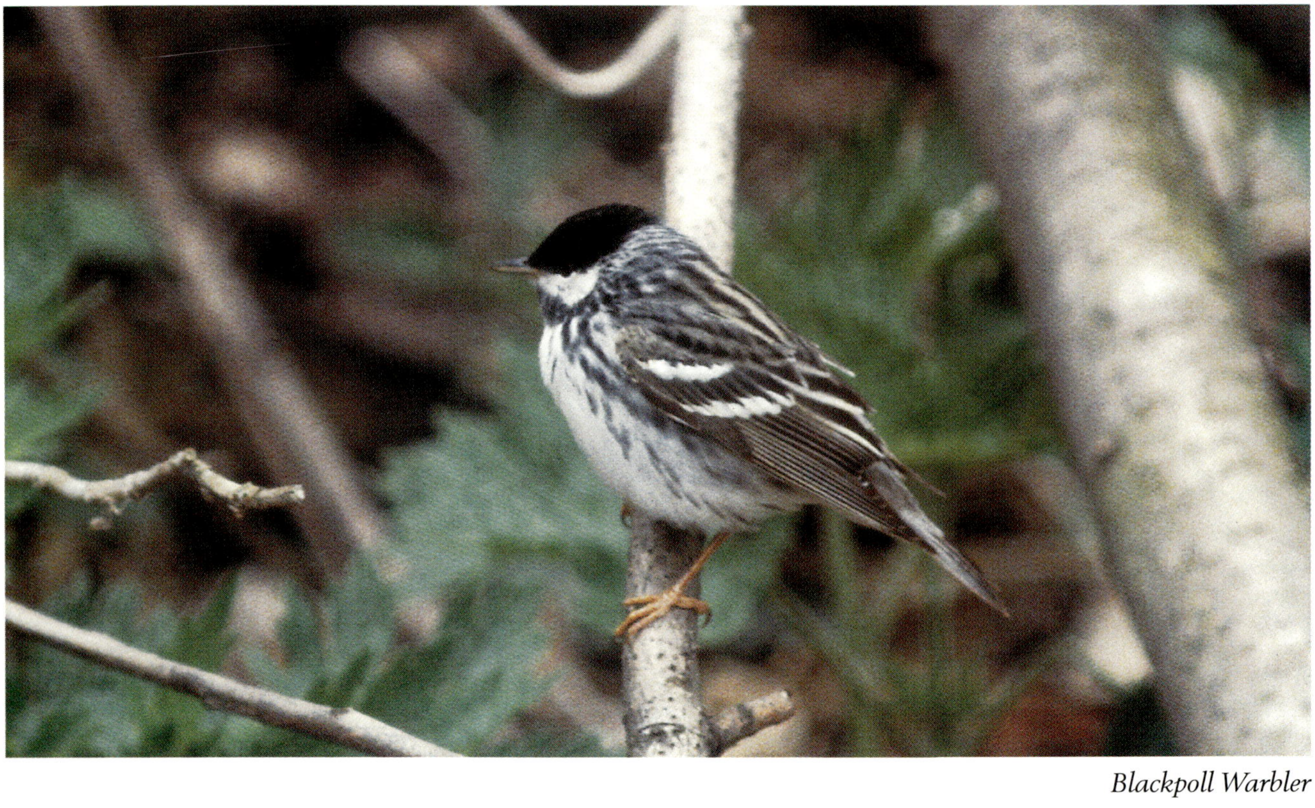

Blackpoll Warbler

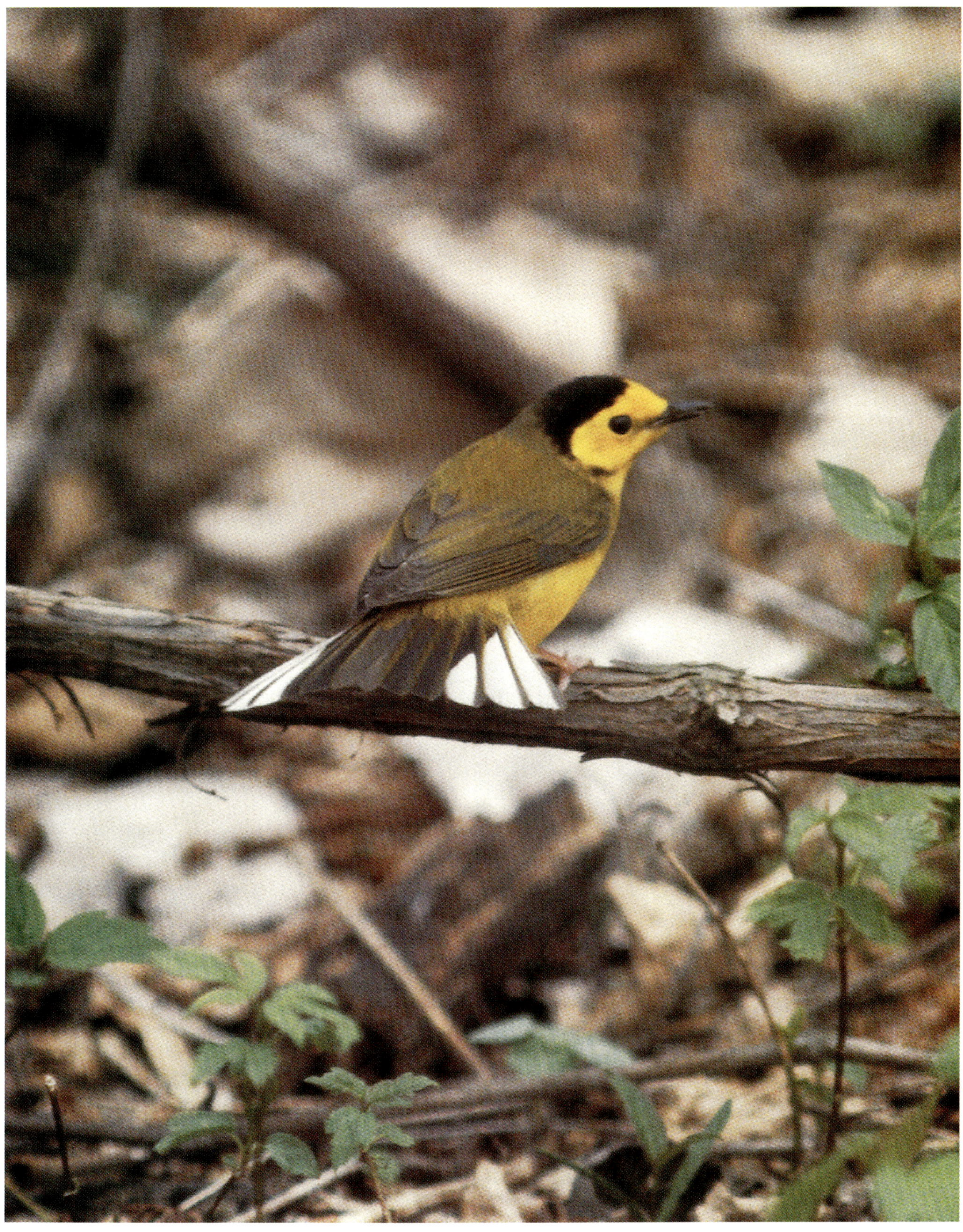

Hooded Warbler

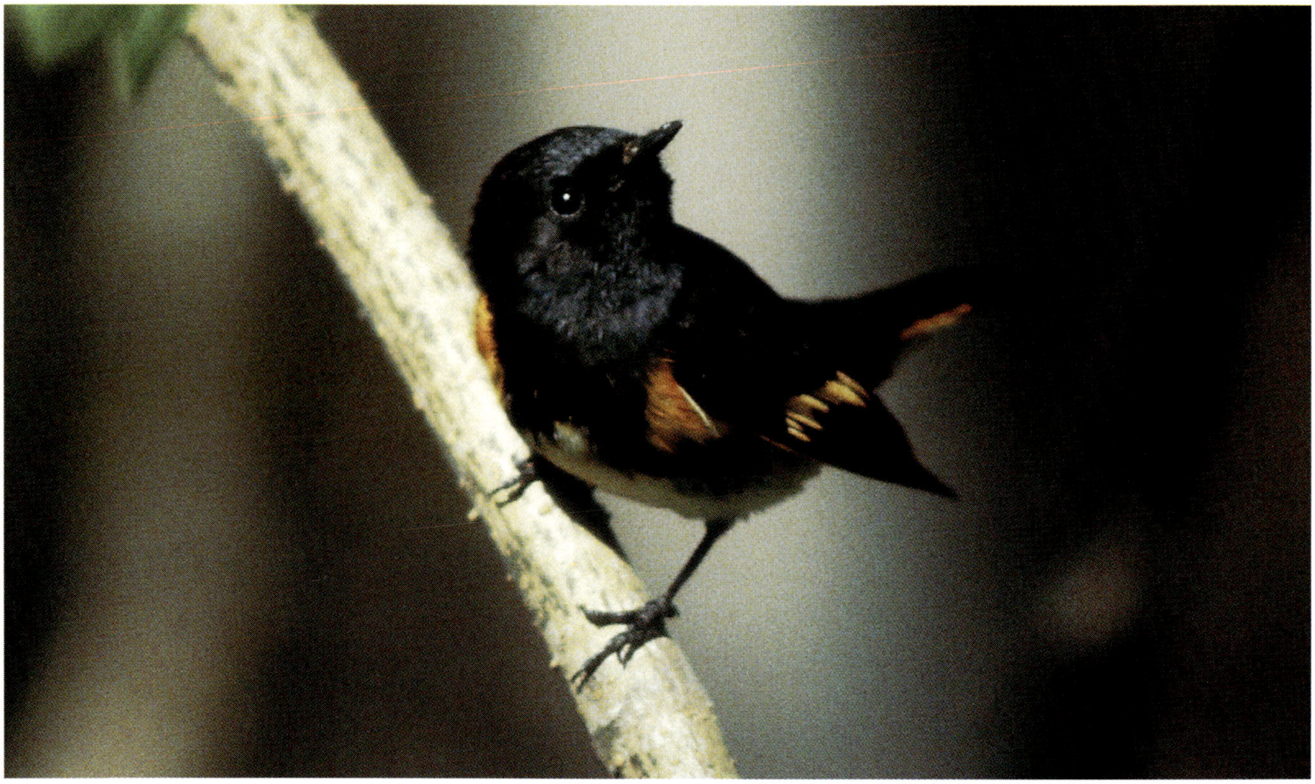

American Redstart

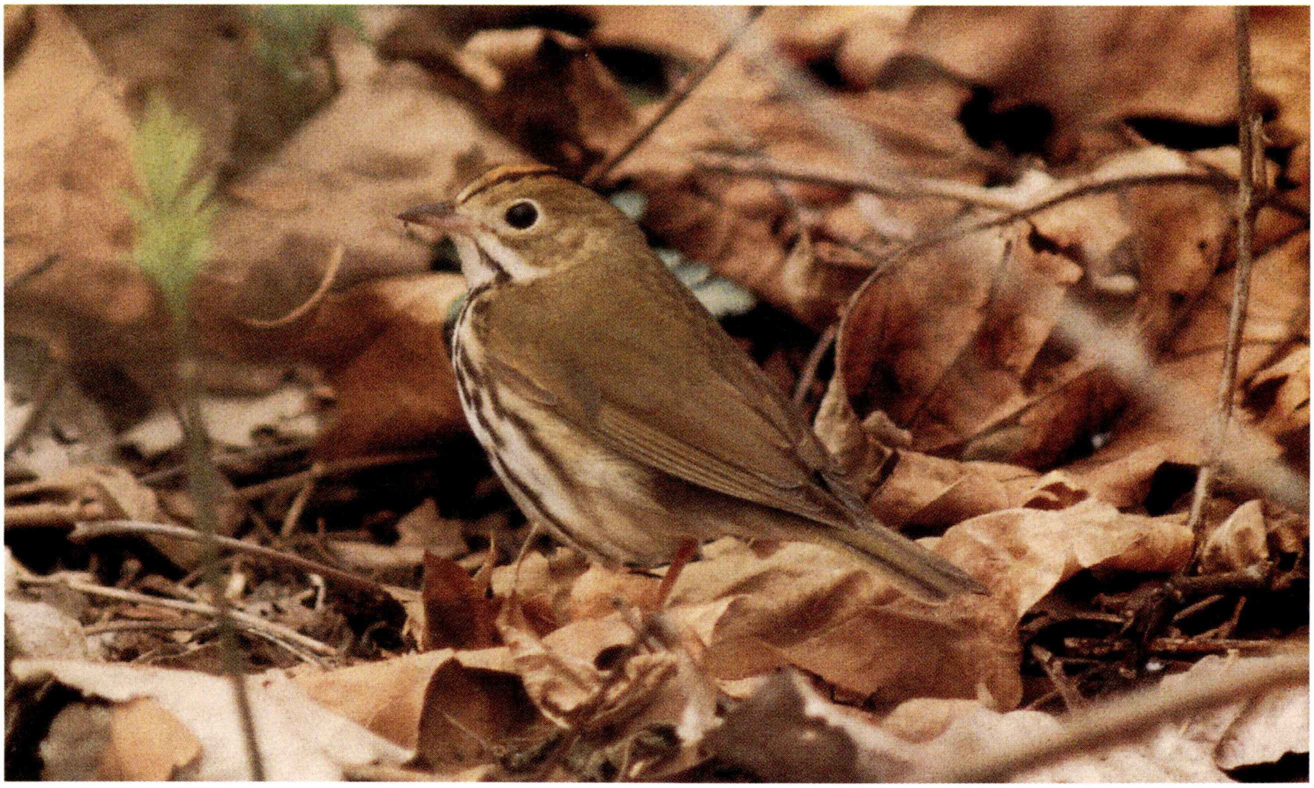

Ovenbird

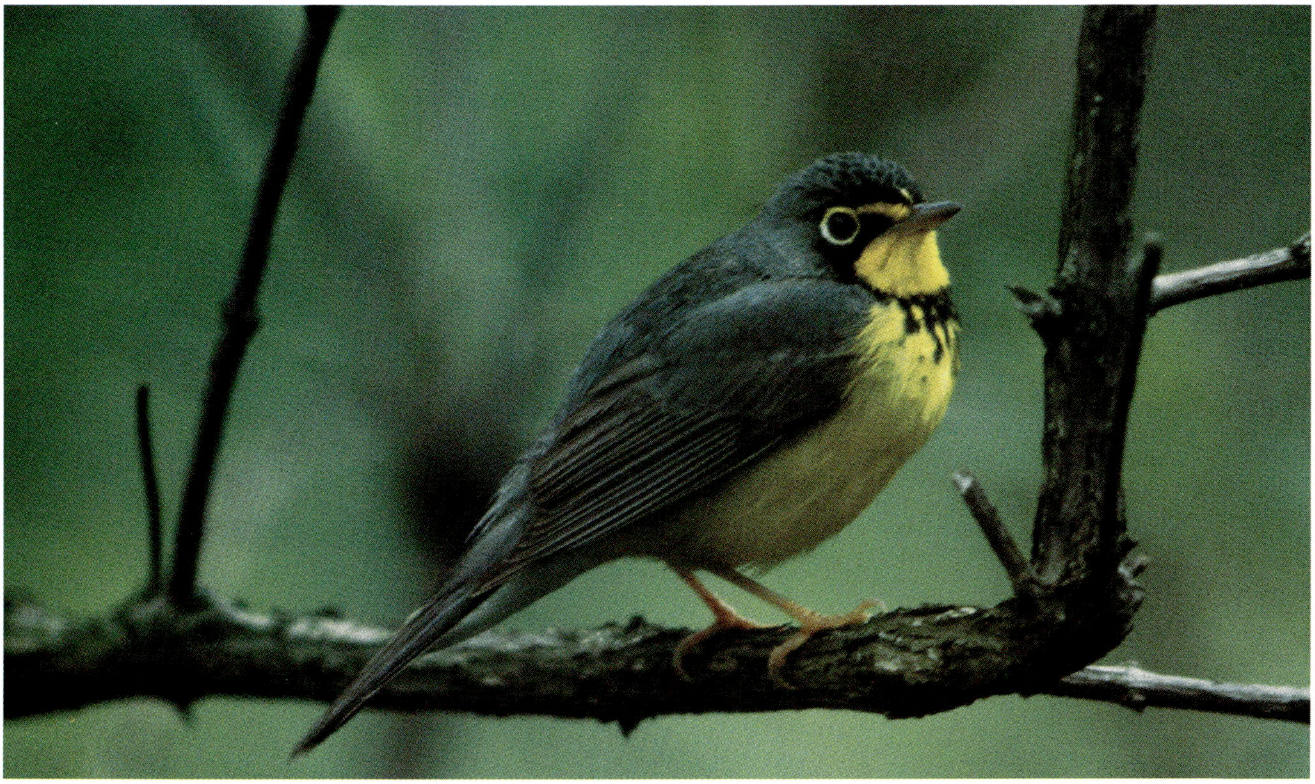

Canada Warbler

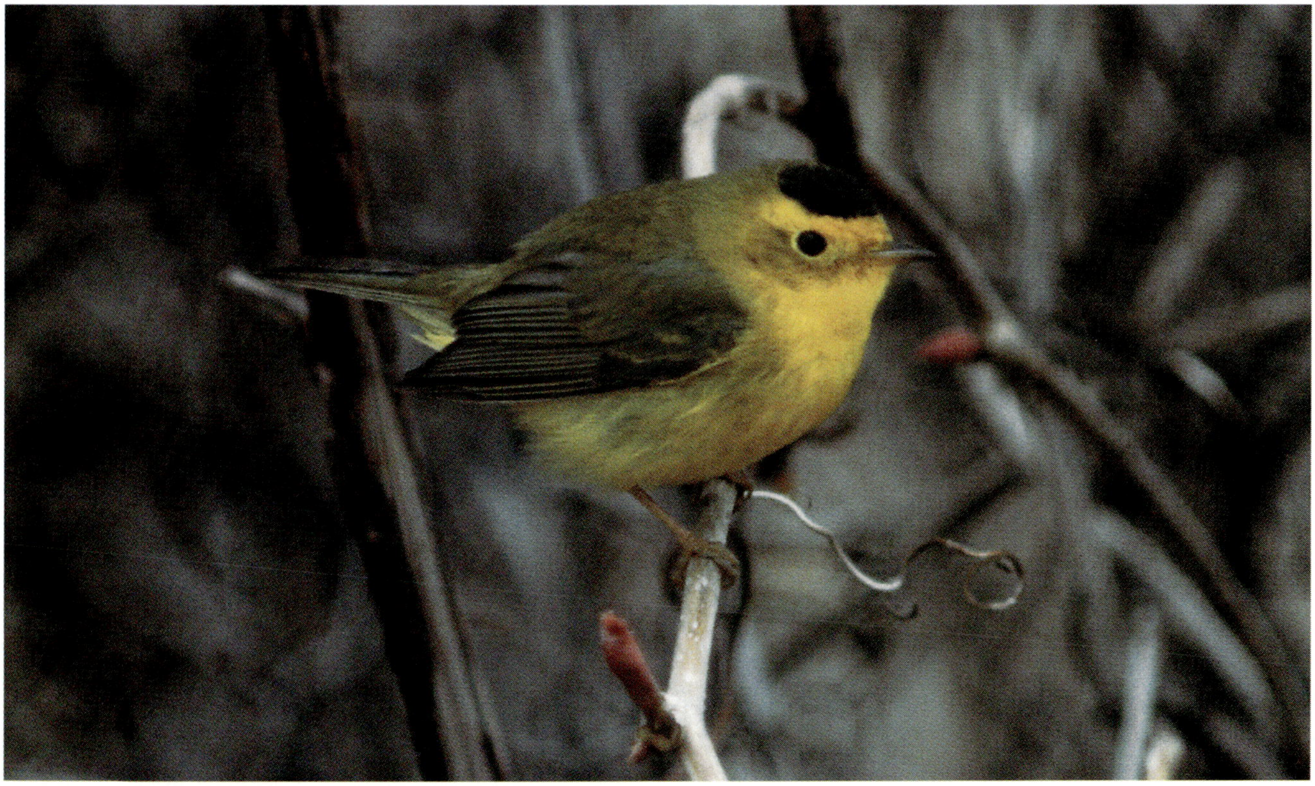

Wilson's Warbler

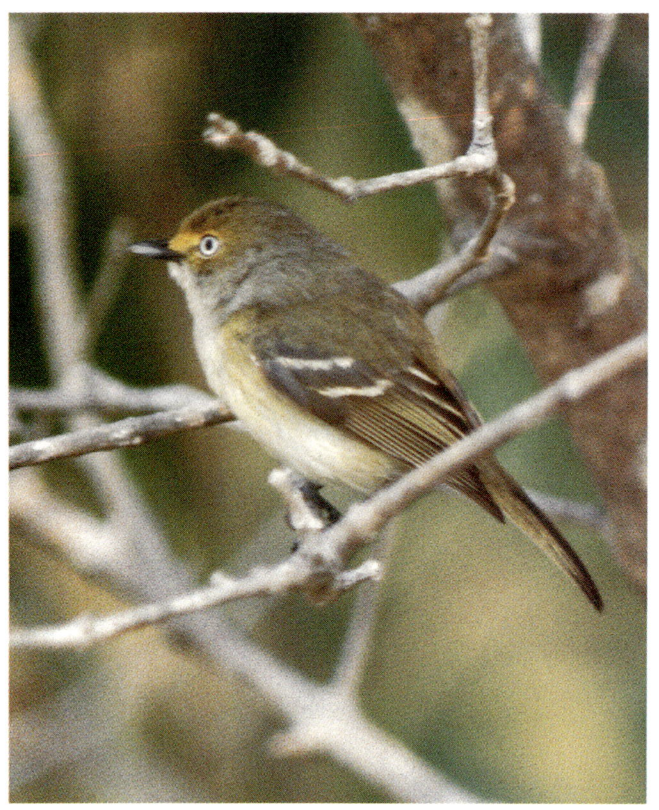
White-eyed Vireo

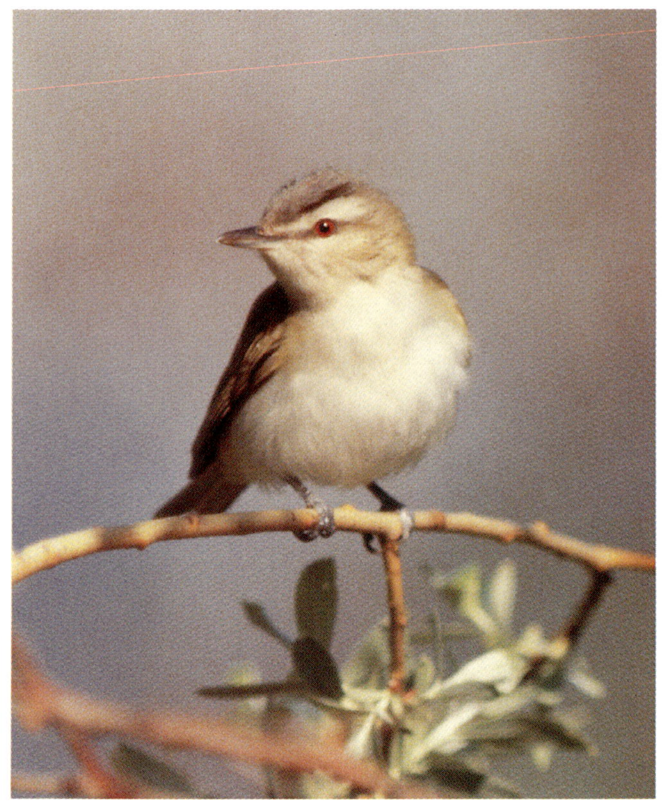
Red-eyed Vireo

Philadelphia Vireo
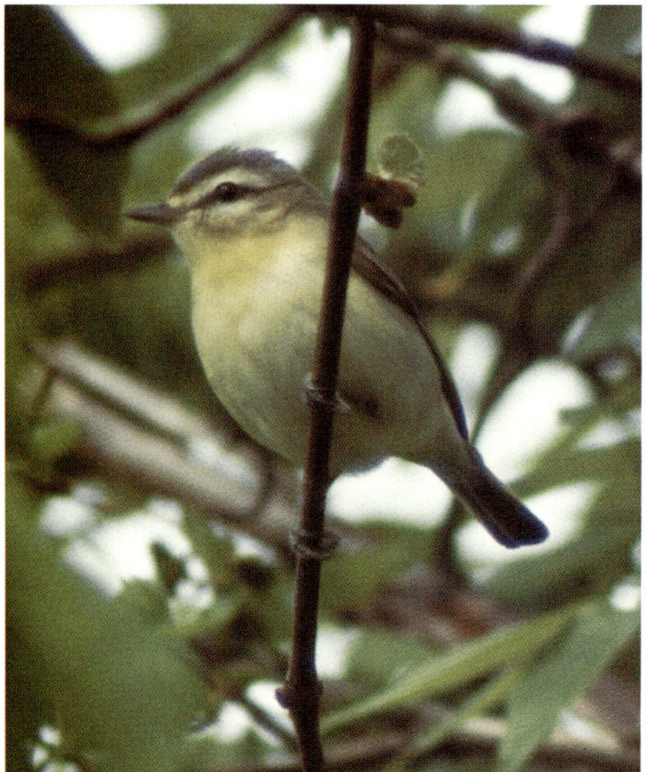

Warbling Vireo
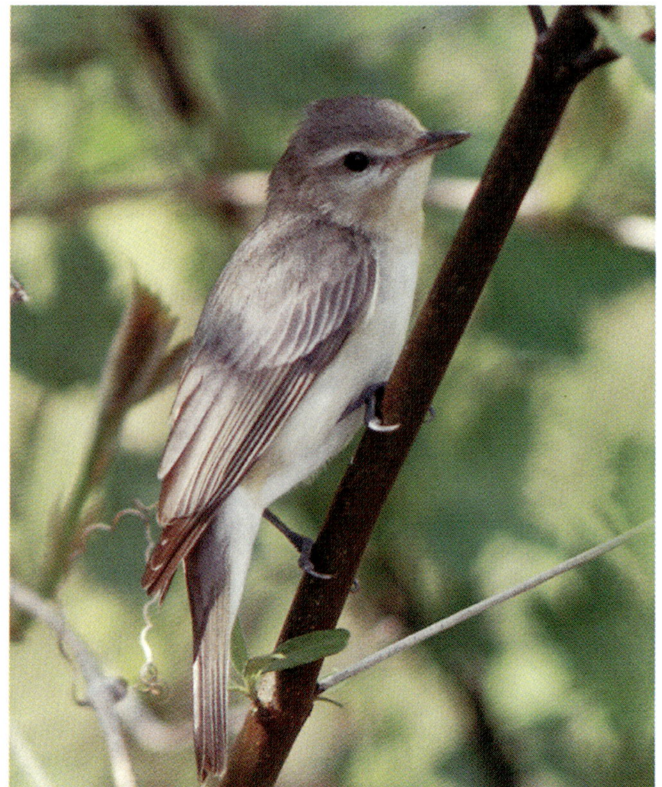

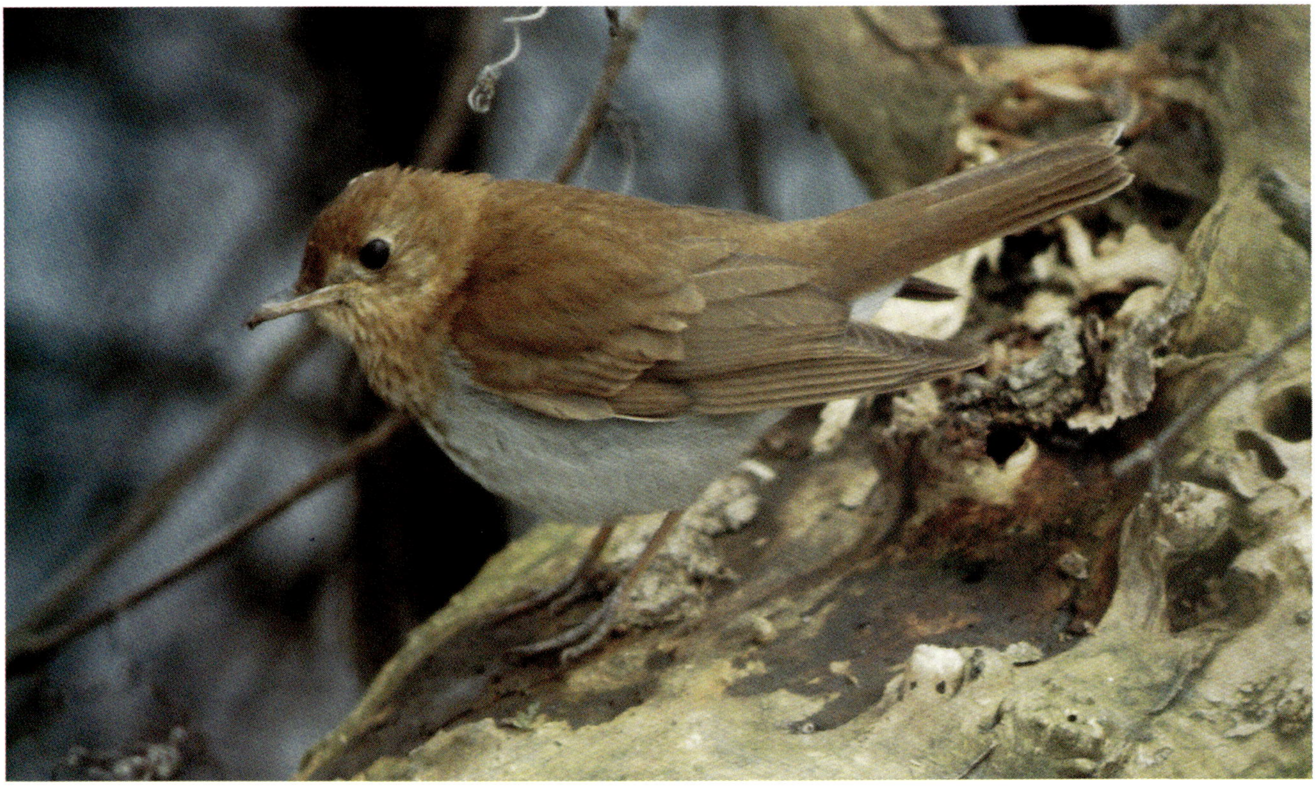

Veery

Hermit Thrush

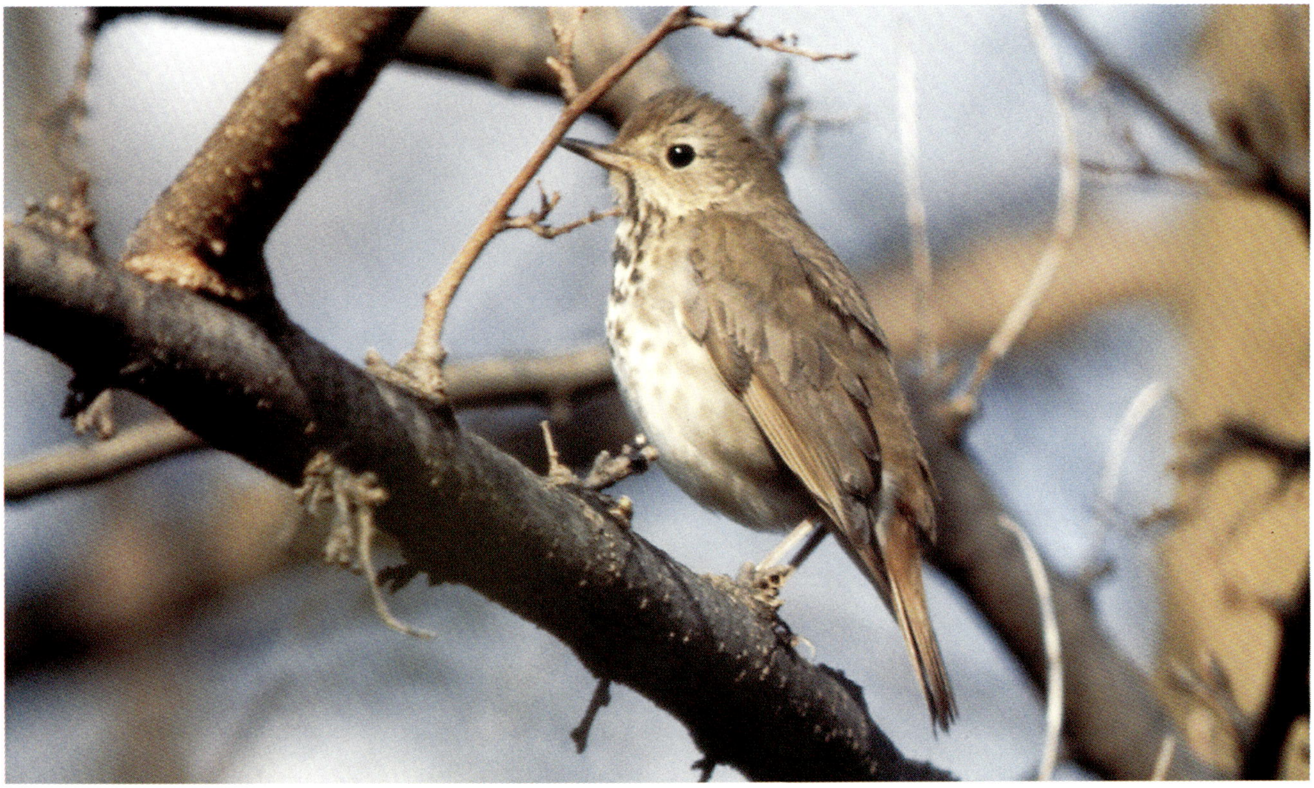

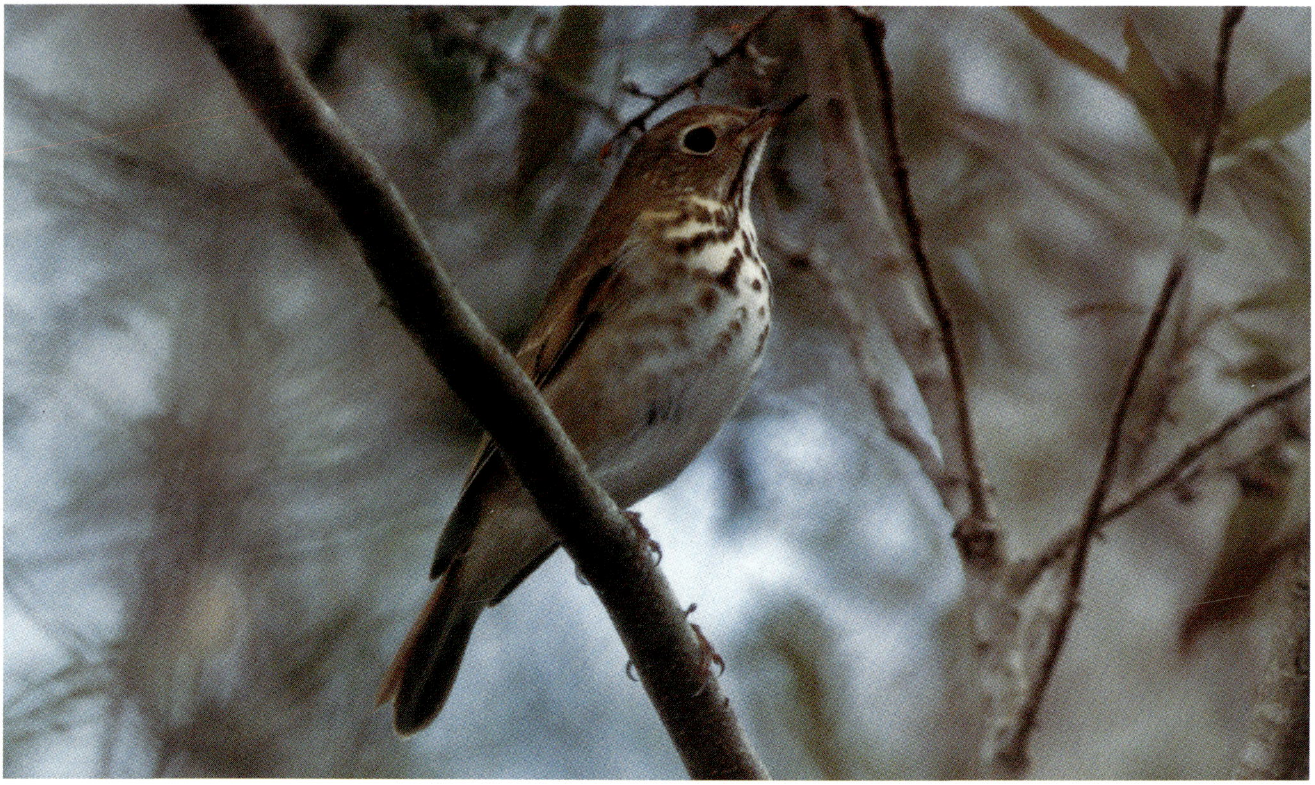

Swainson's Thrush

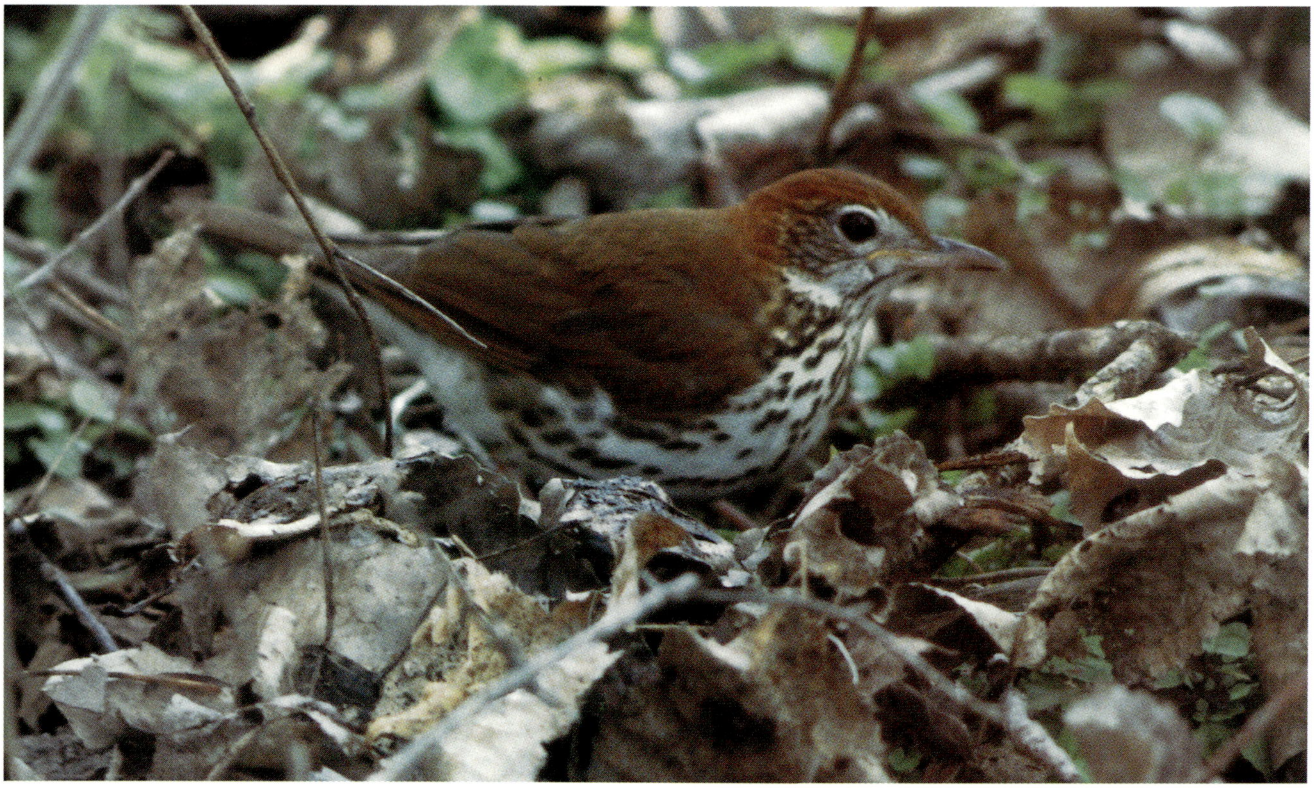

Wood Thrush

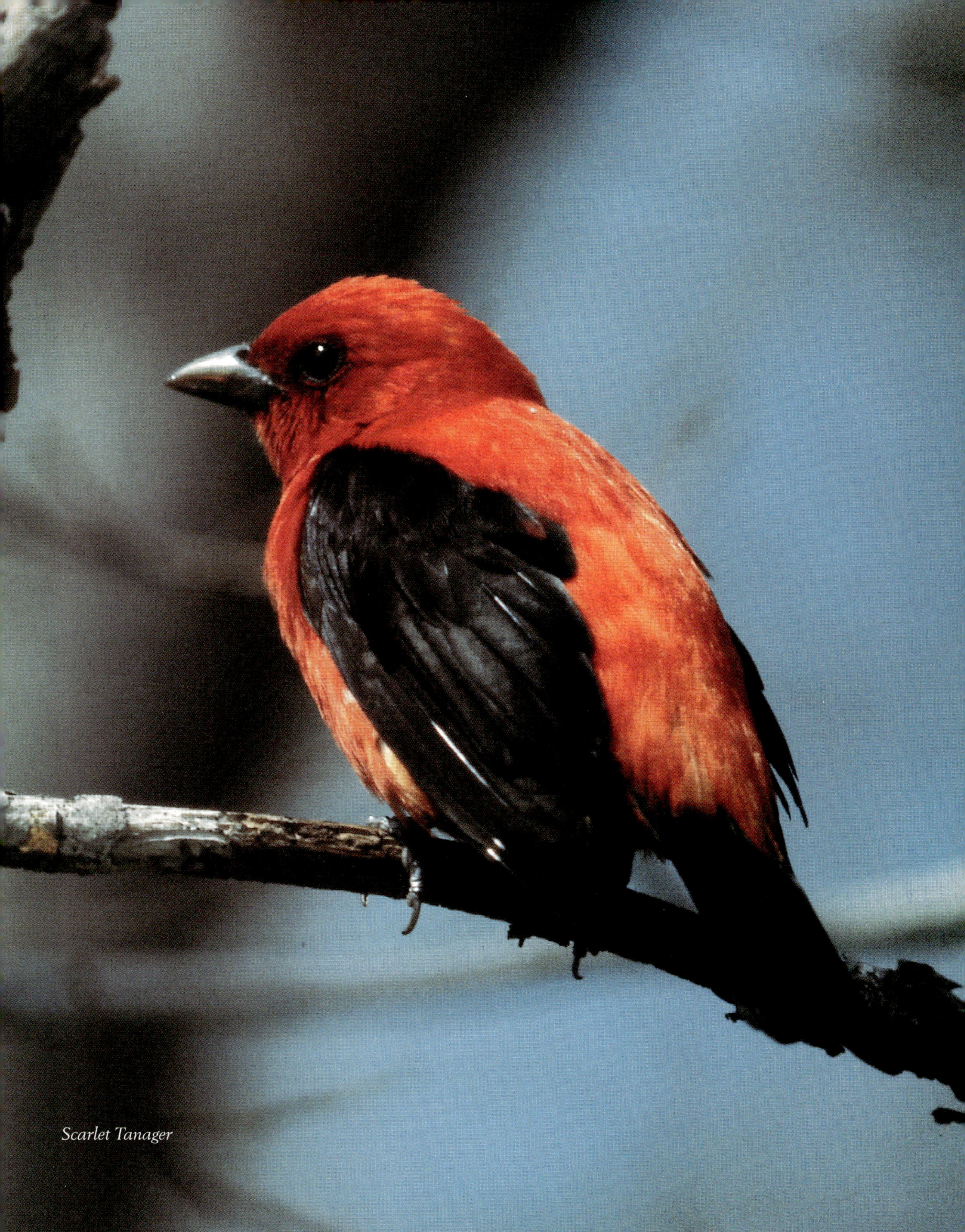

Scarlet Tanager

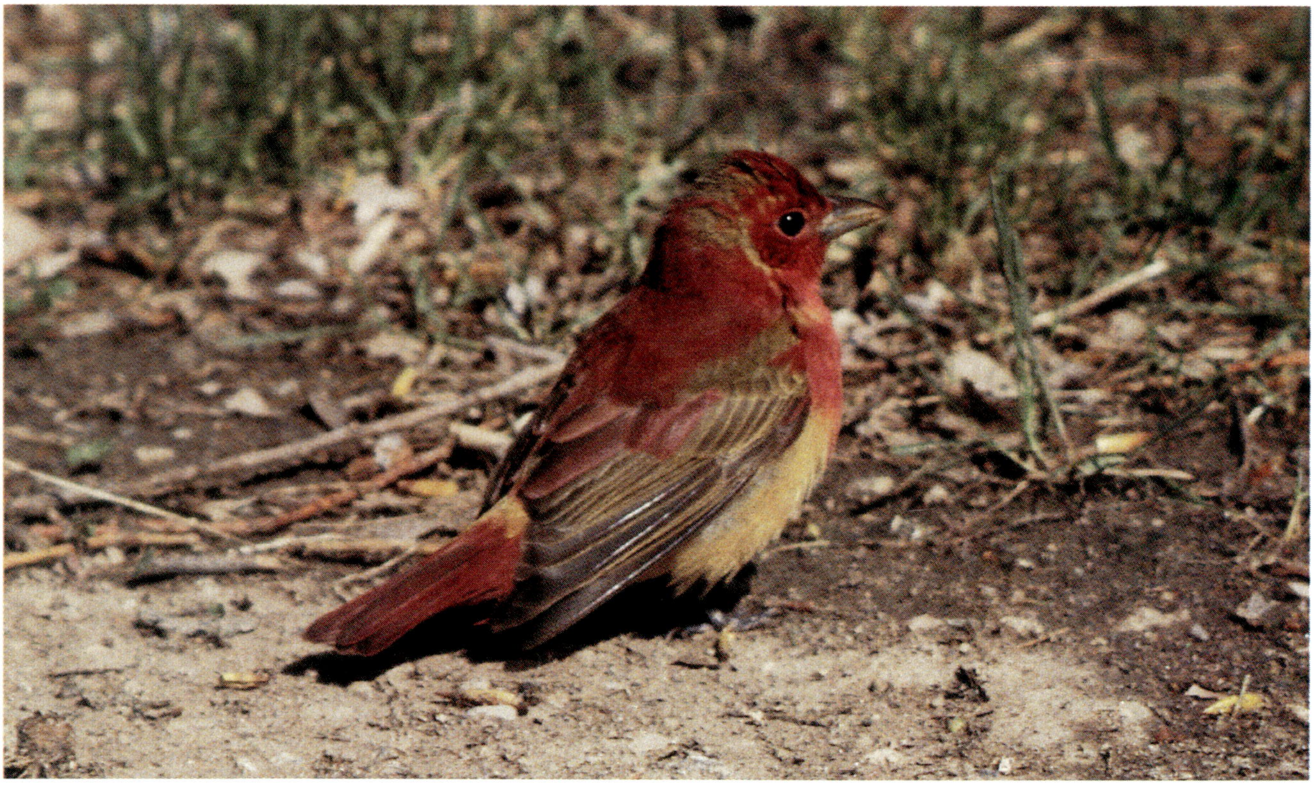

Summer Tanager (Molting)

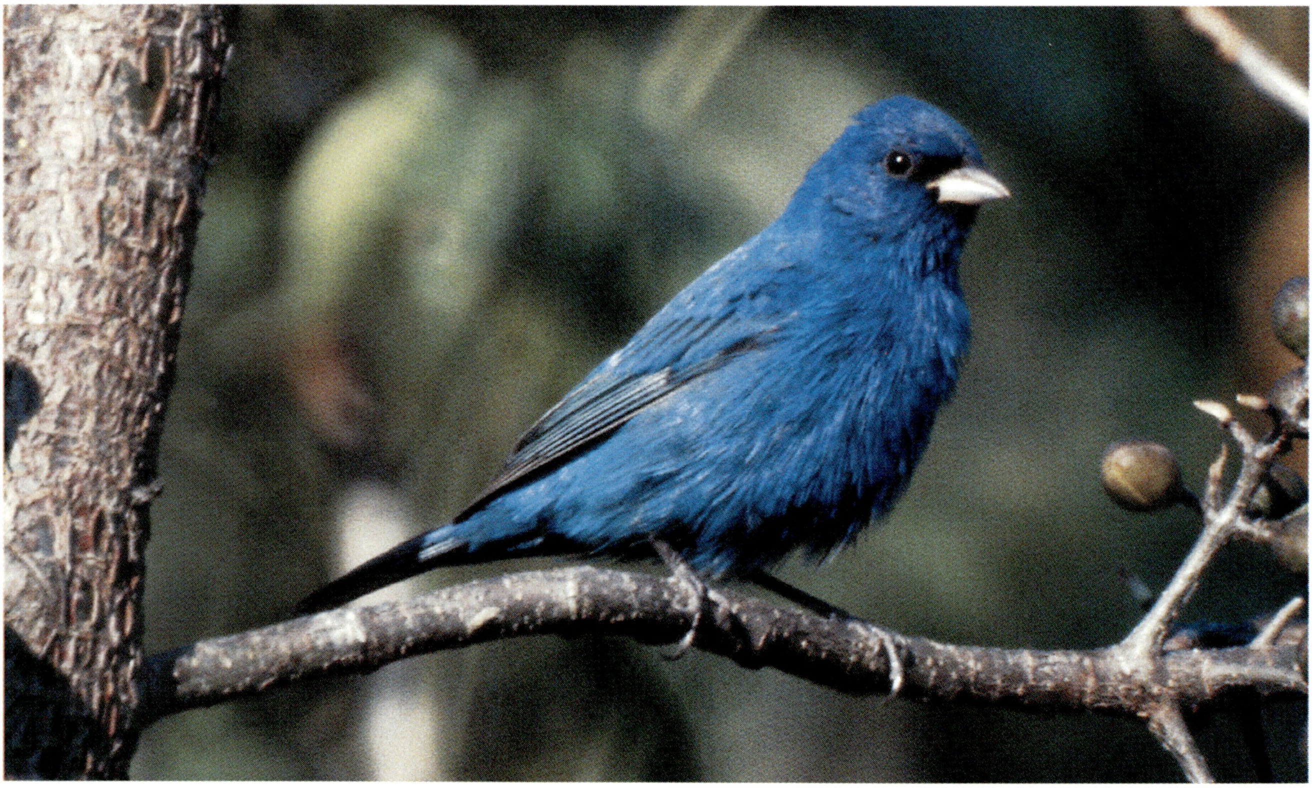

Indigo Bunting

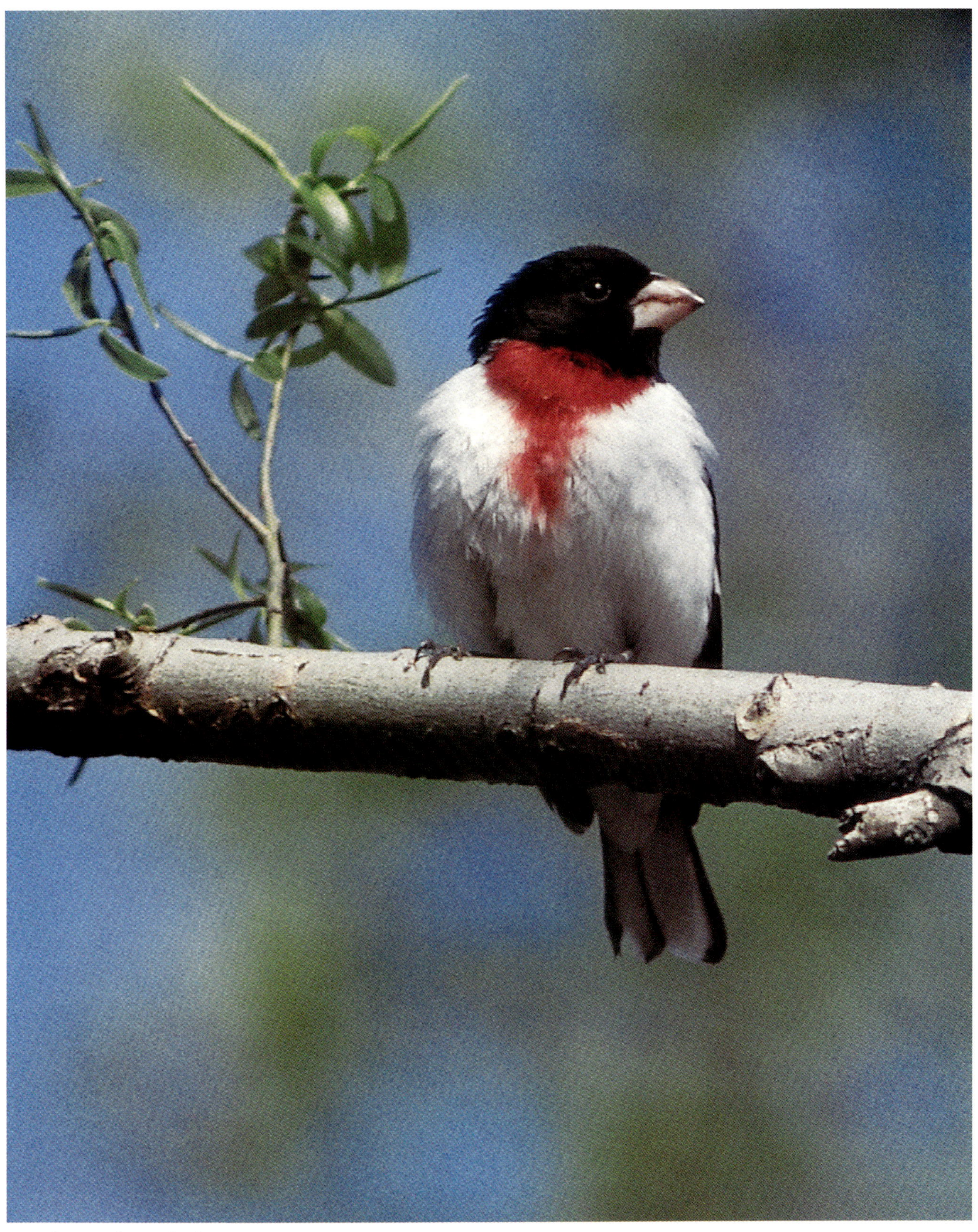

Rose-breasted Grosbeak

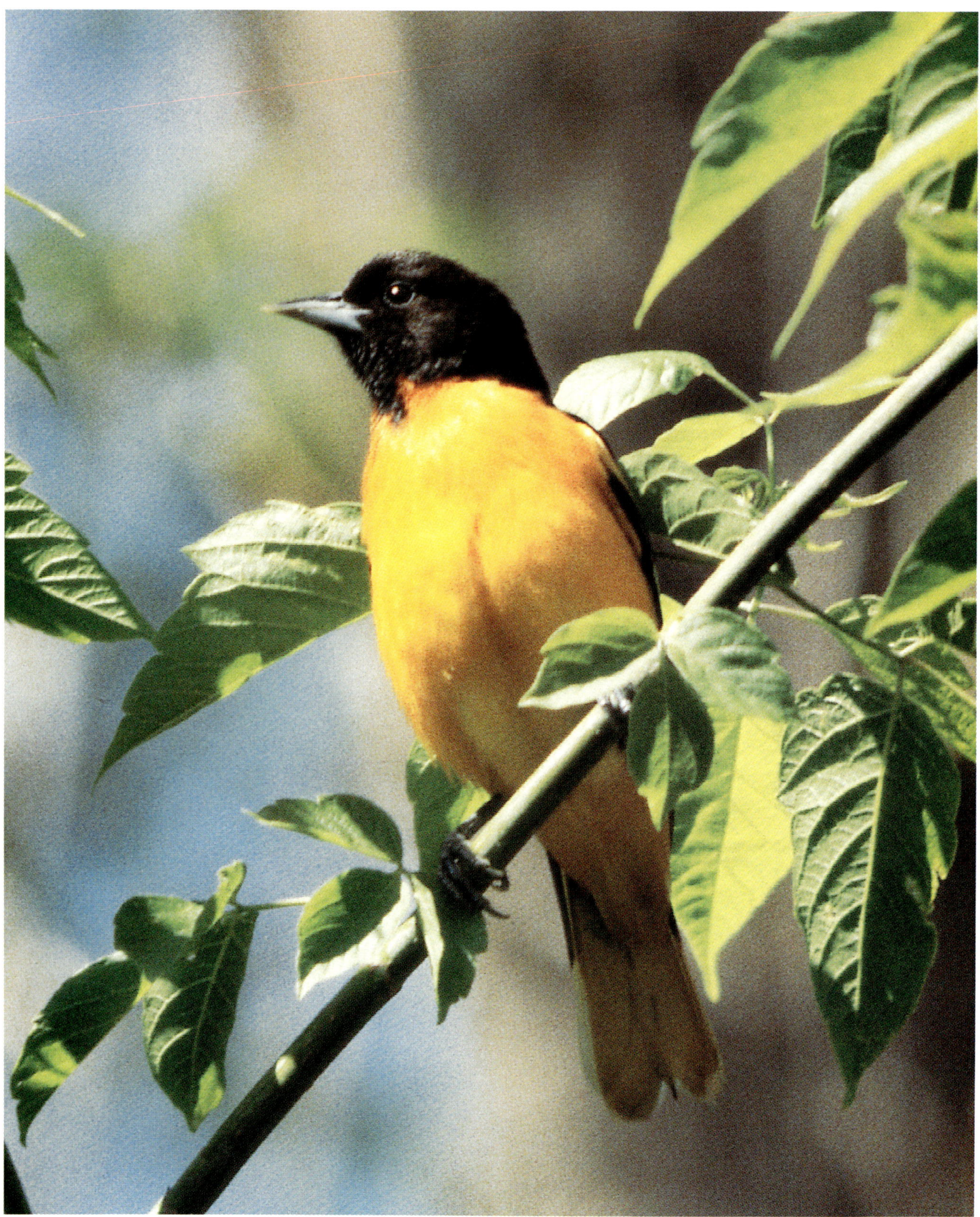

Baltimore Oriole

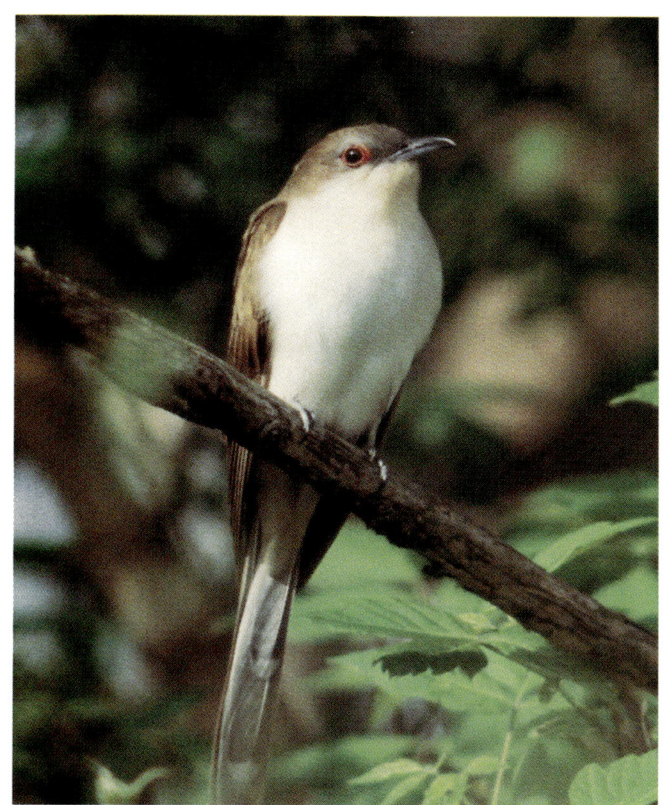

Black-billed Cuckoo

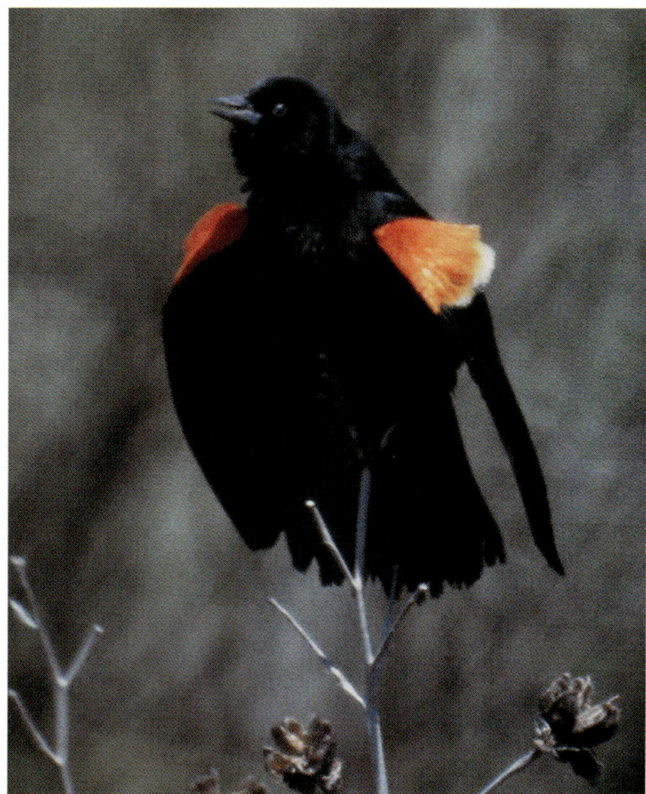

Red-winged Blackbird

American Woodcock

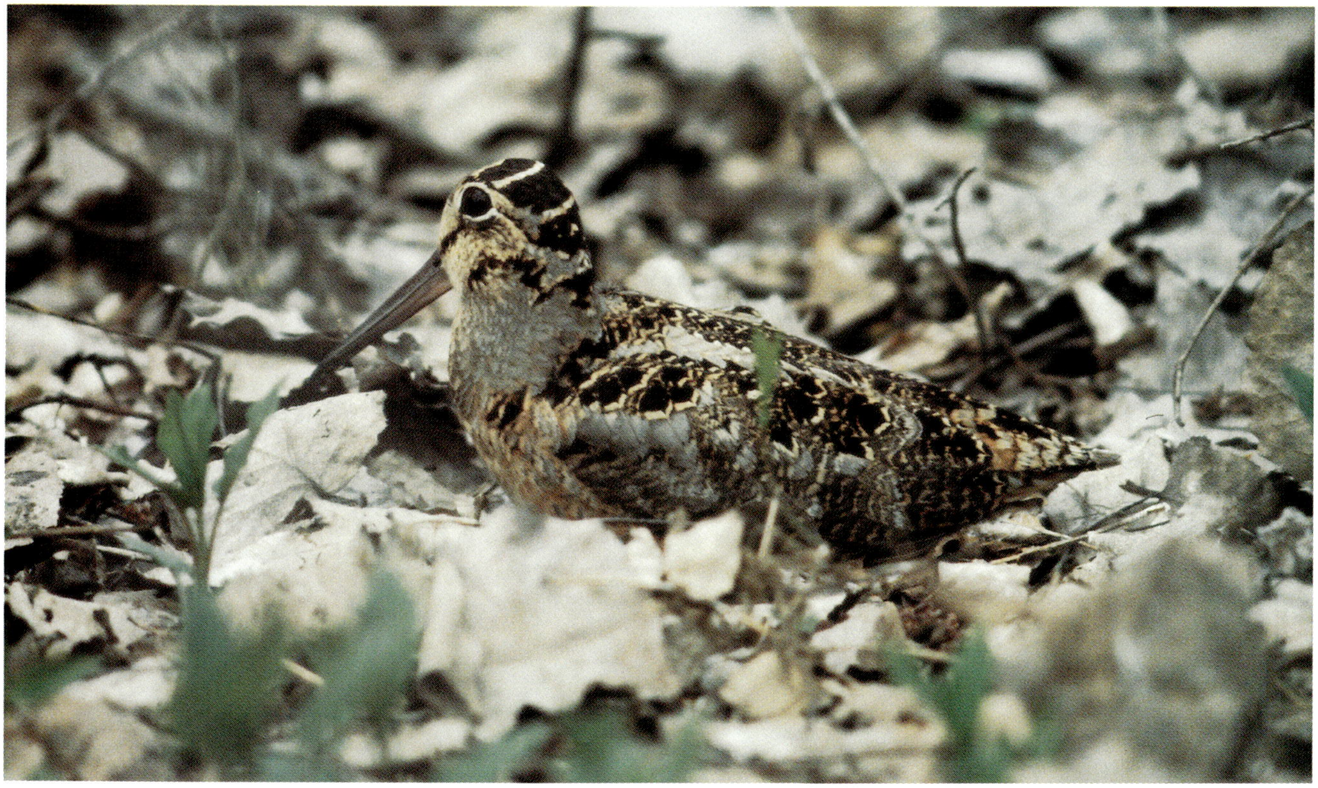

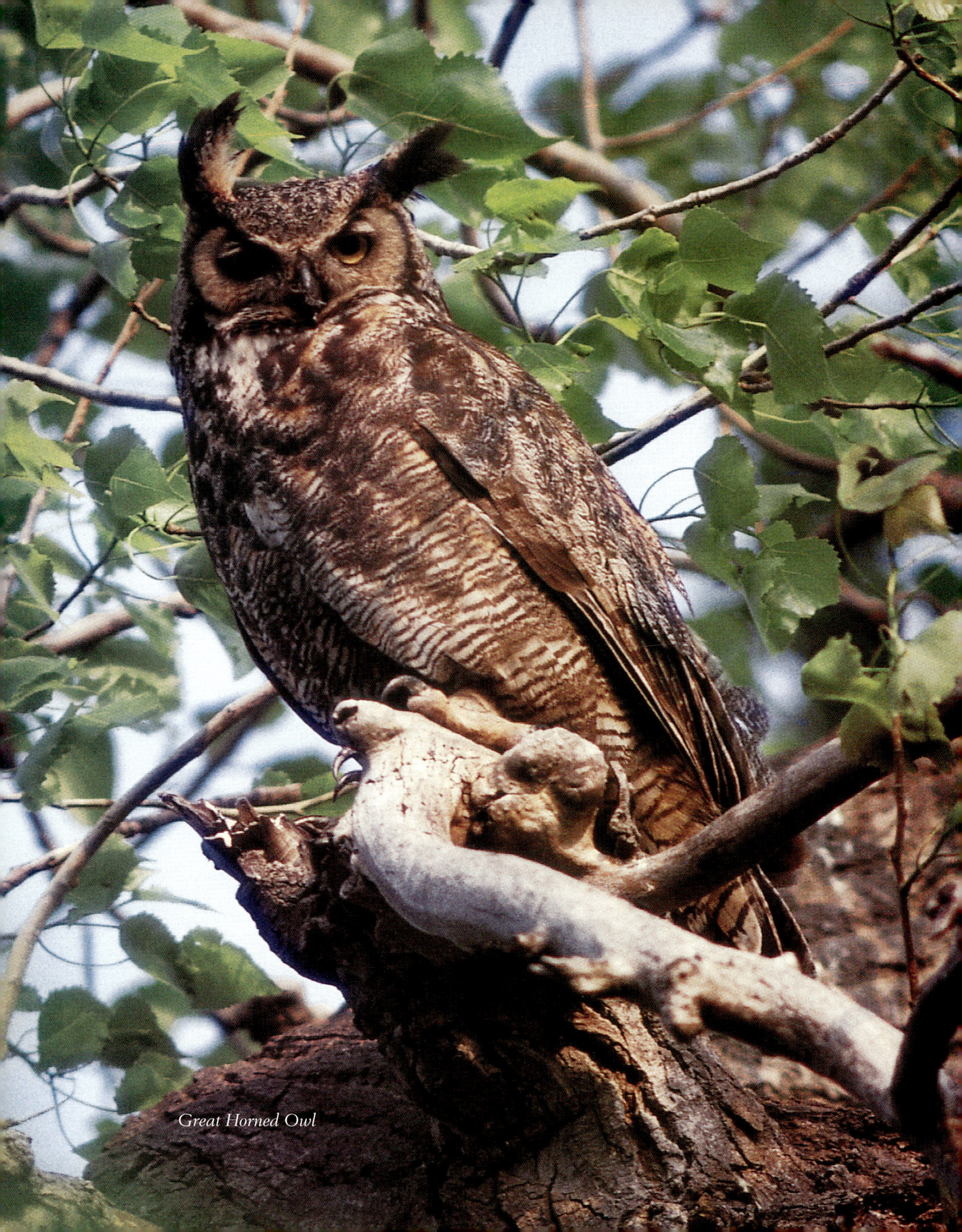

Great Horned Owl

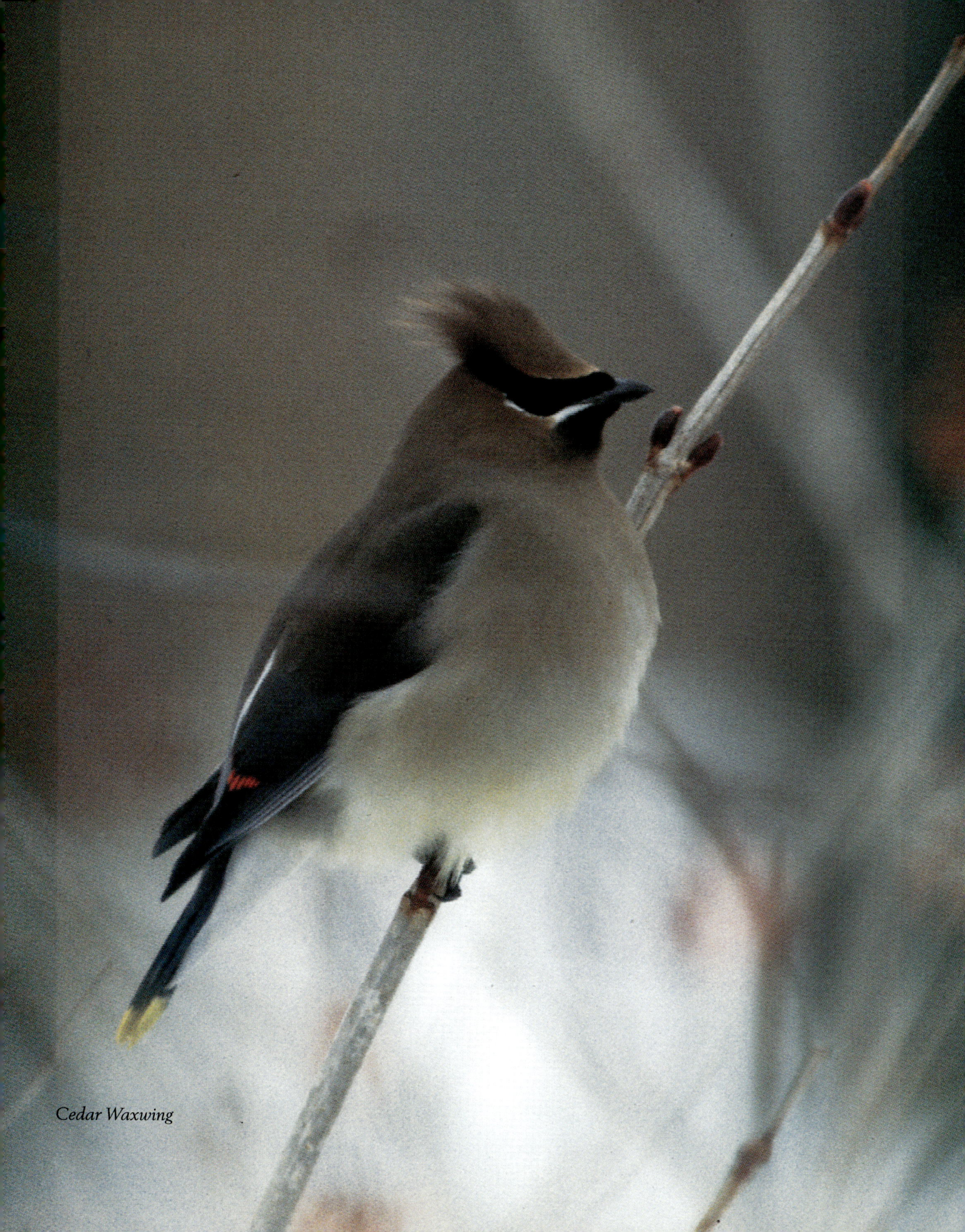

Cedar Waxwing

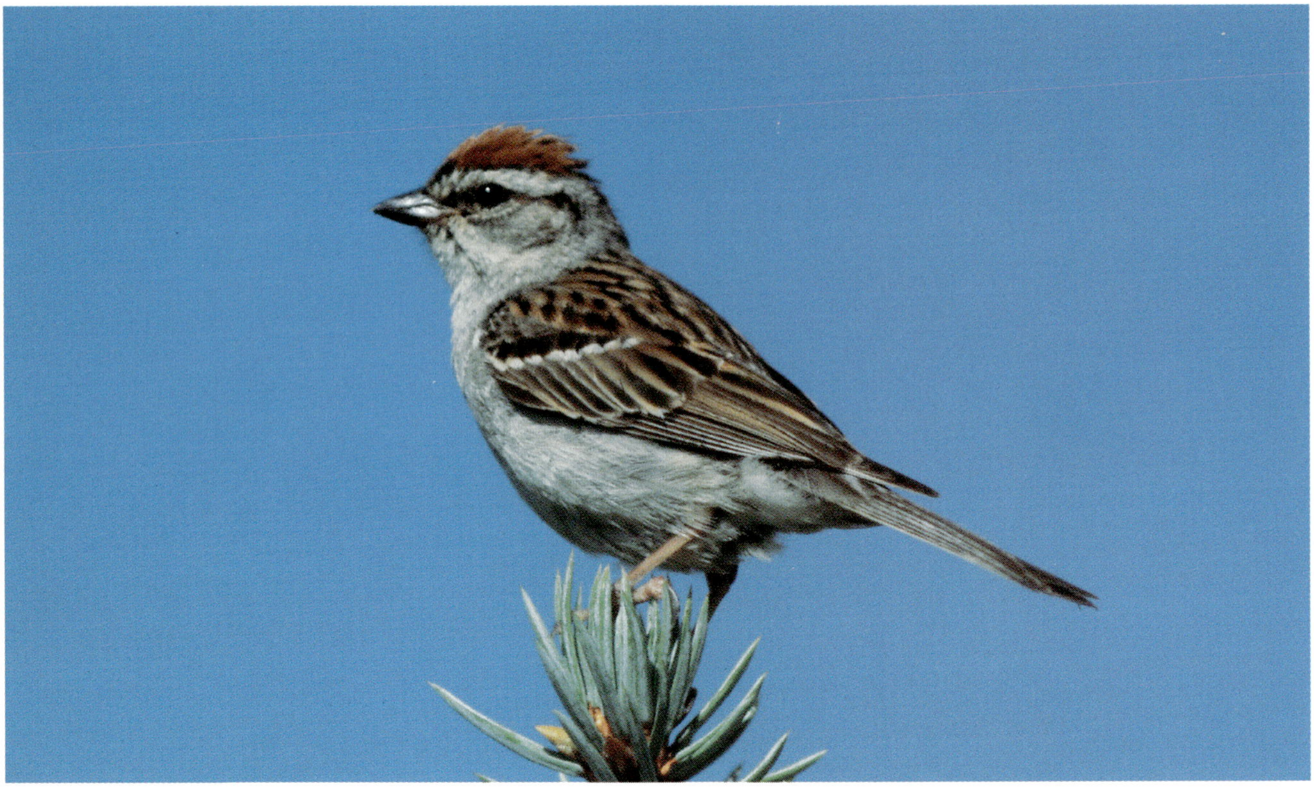

Chipping Sparrow

House Wren

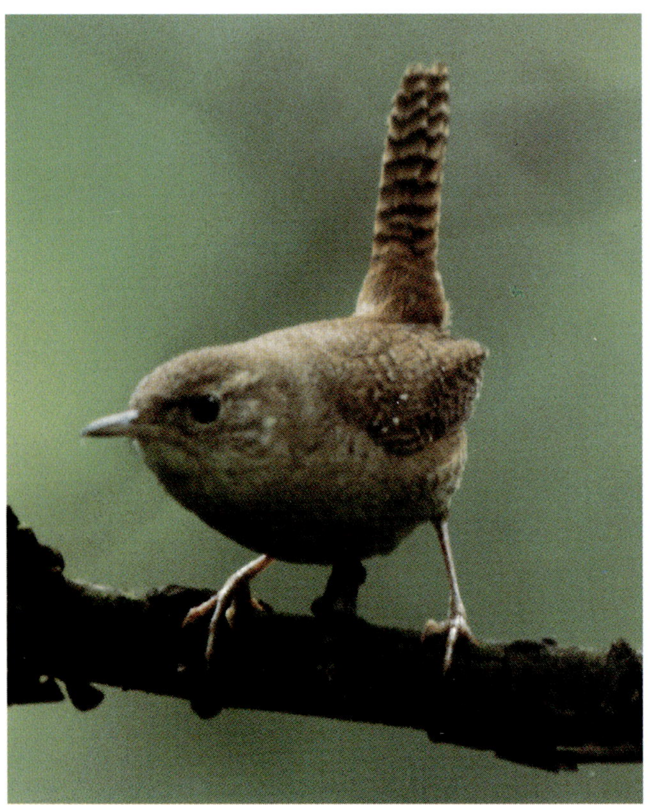

Ruby-throated Hummingbird

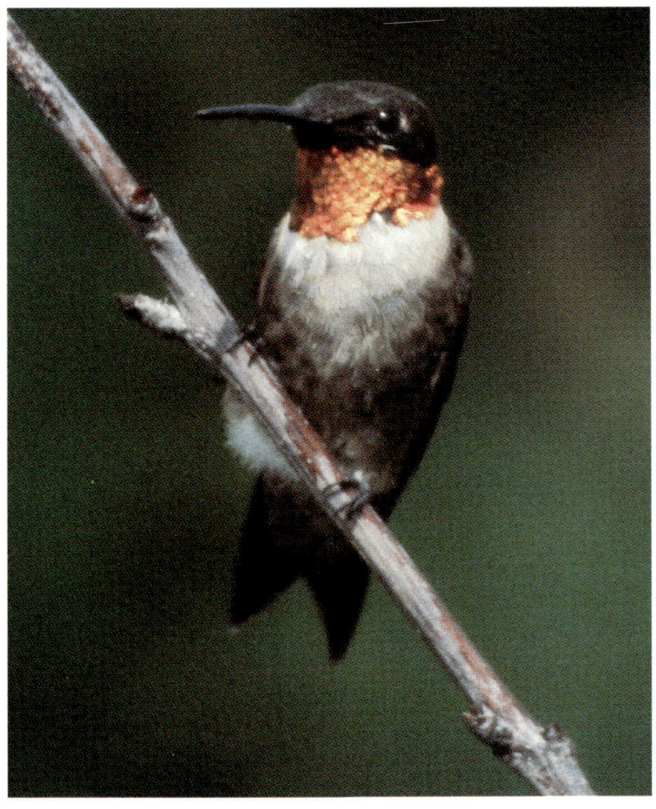

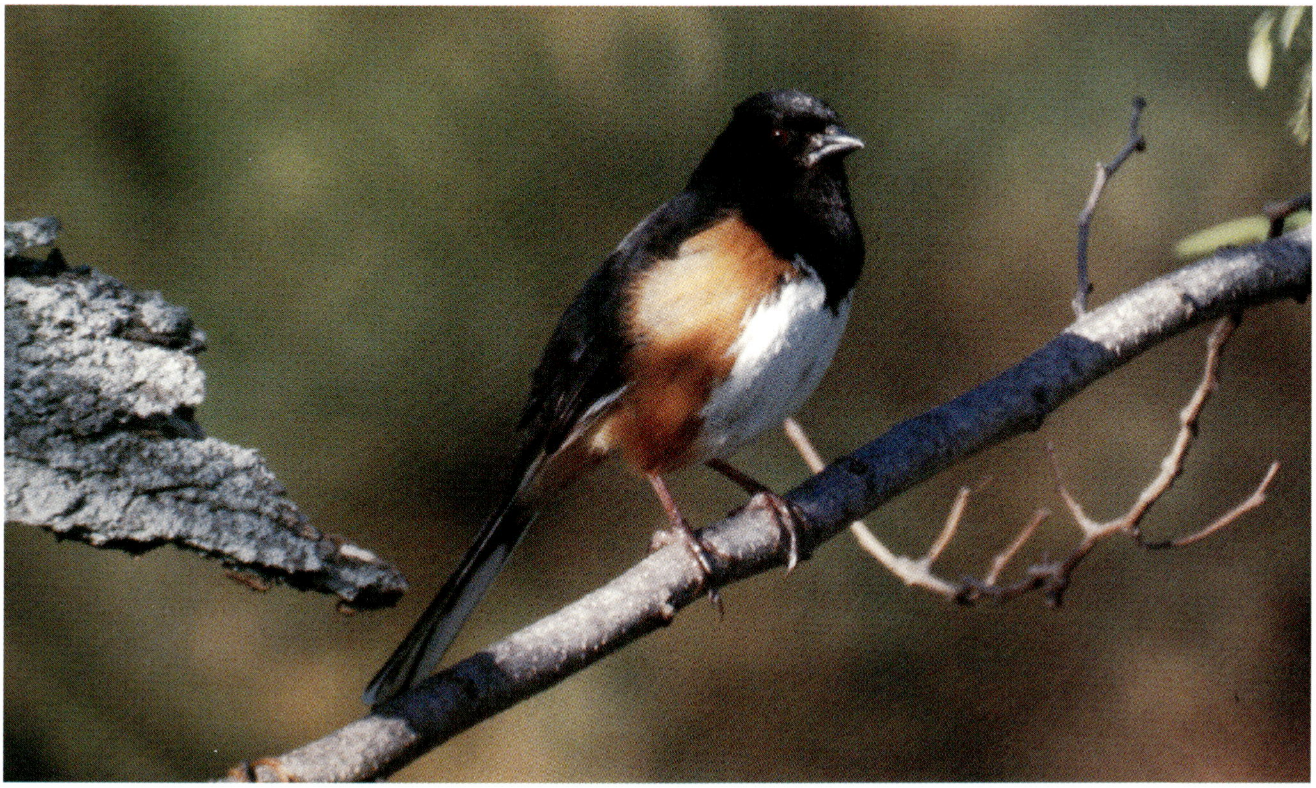

Eastern Towhee

Fox Sparrow

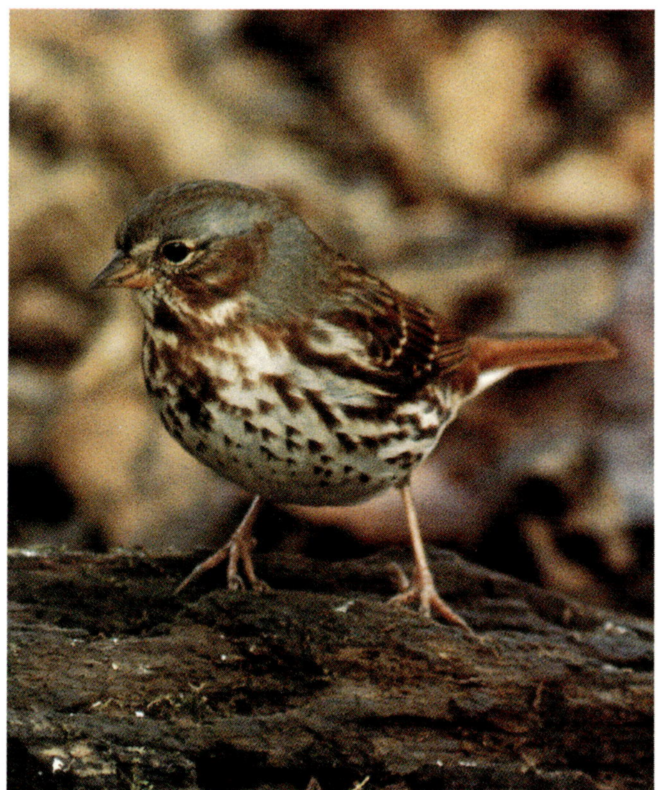

White-crowned Sparrow

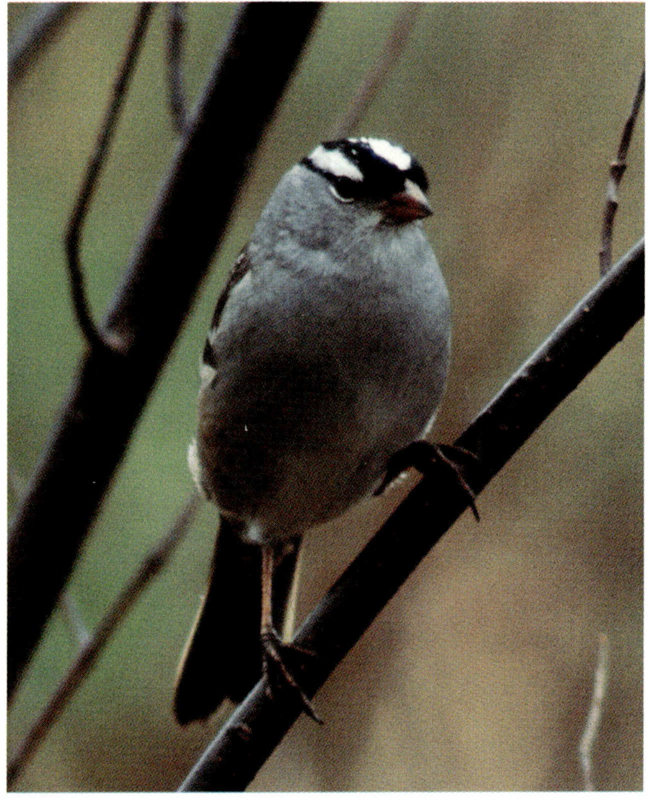

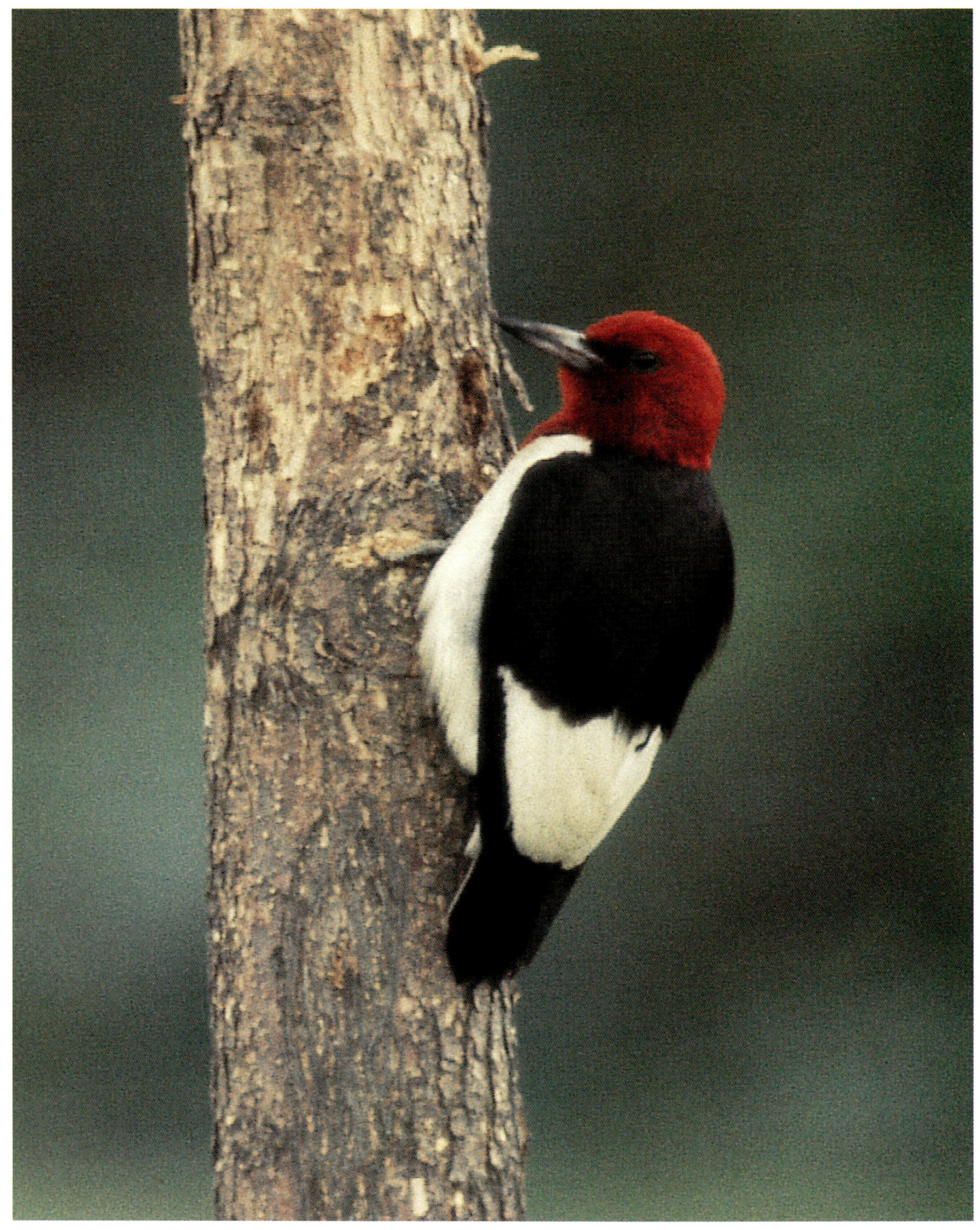

Red-headed Woodpecker

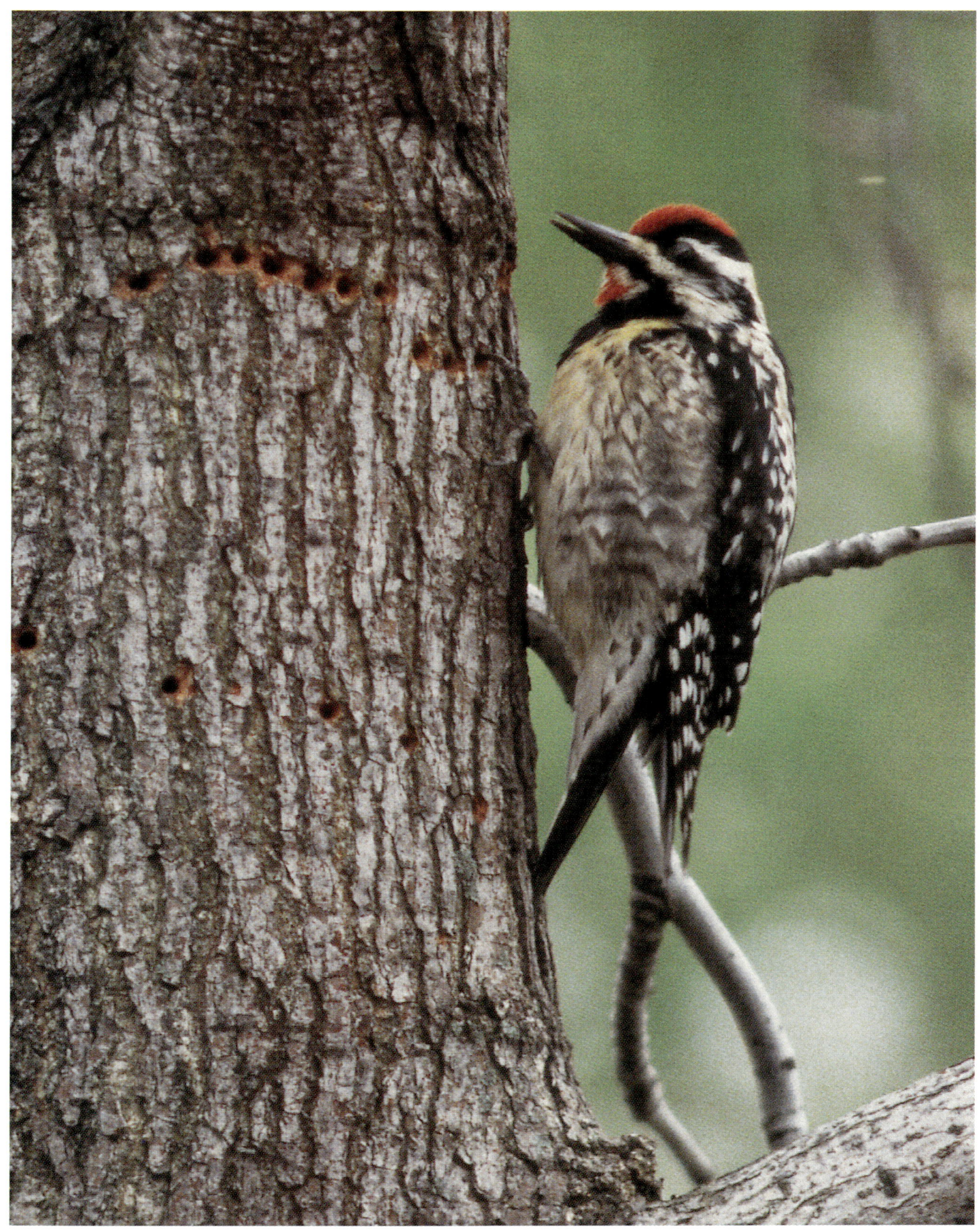

Yellow-bellied Sapsucker

There are several other excellent birding spots in the Toledo area.

Most of the birds seen at the Magee Marsh Bird Trail can also be seen in a number of these locations. Conversely, there are many birds, more commonly associated with other areas, that can also be seen on the Trail. The Oak Openings area, about twenty miles west of Toledo, is where you would expect to see the *Lark Sparrow* and *Grasshopper Sparrow* below.

The *Eastern Meadowlark* (opposite) and the *Eastern Bluebird* on the following page are also fairly common there.

The *Red-tailed Hawk* (*page 59*) can be seen almost anywhere in the open areas of the region.

Lark Sparrow

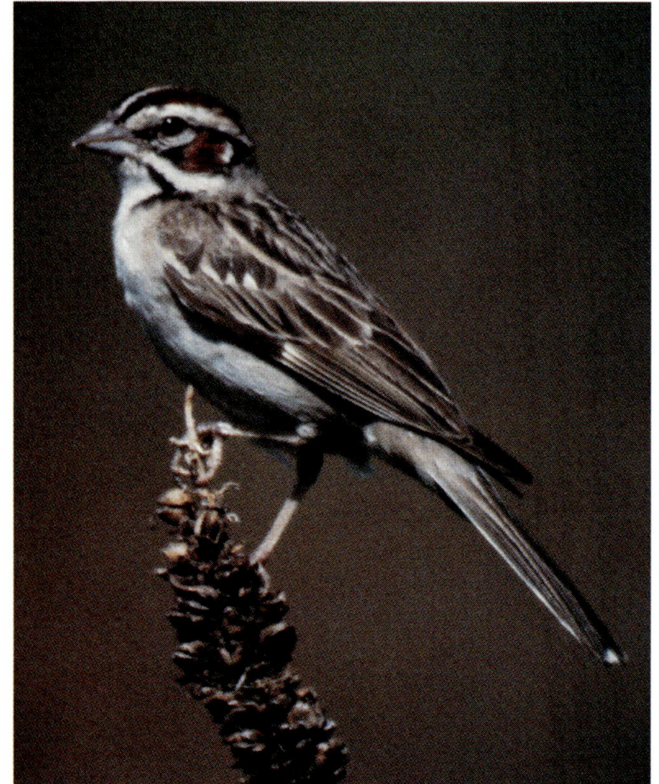

Grasshopper Sparrow

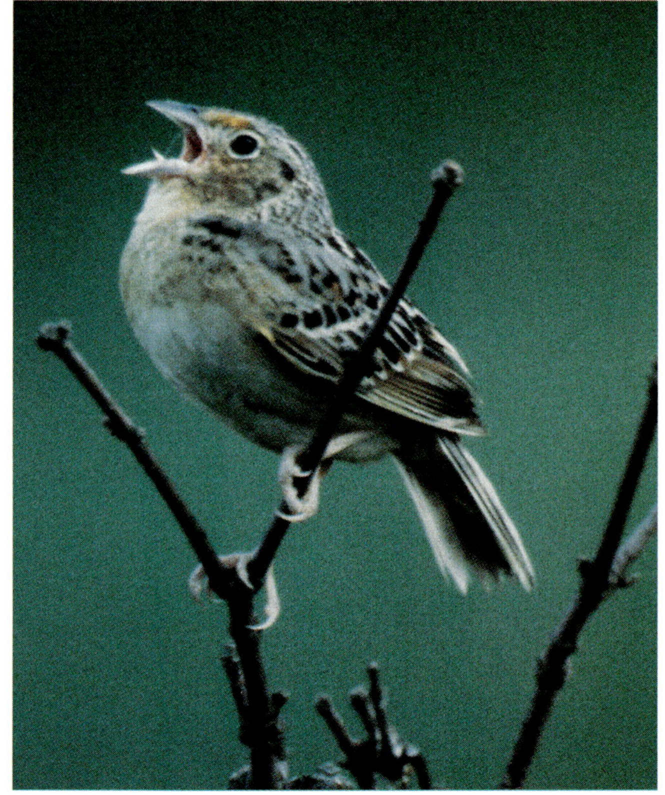

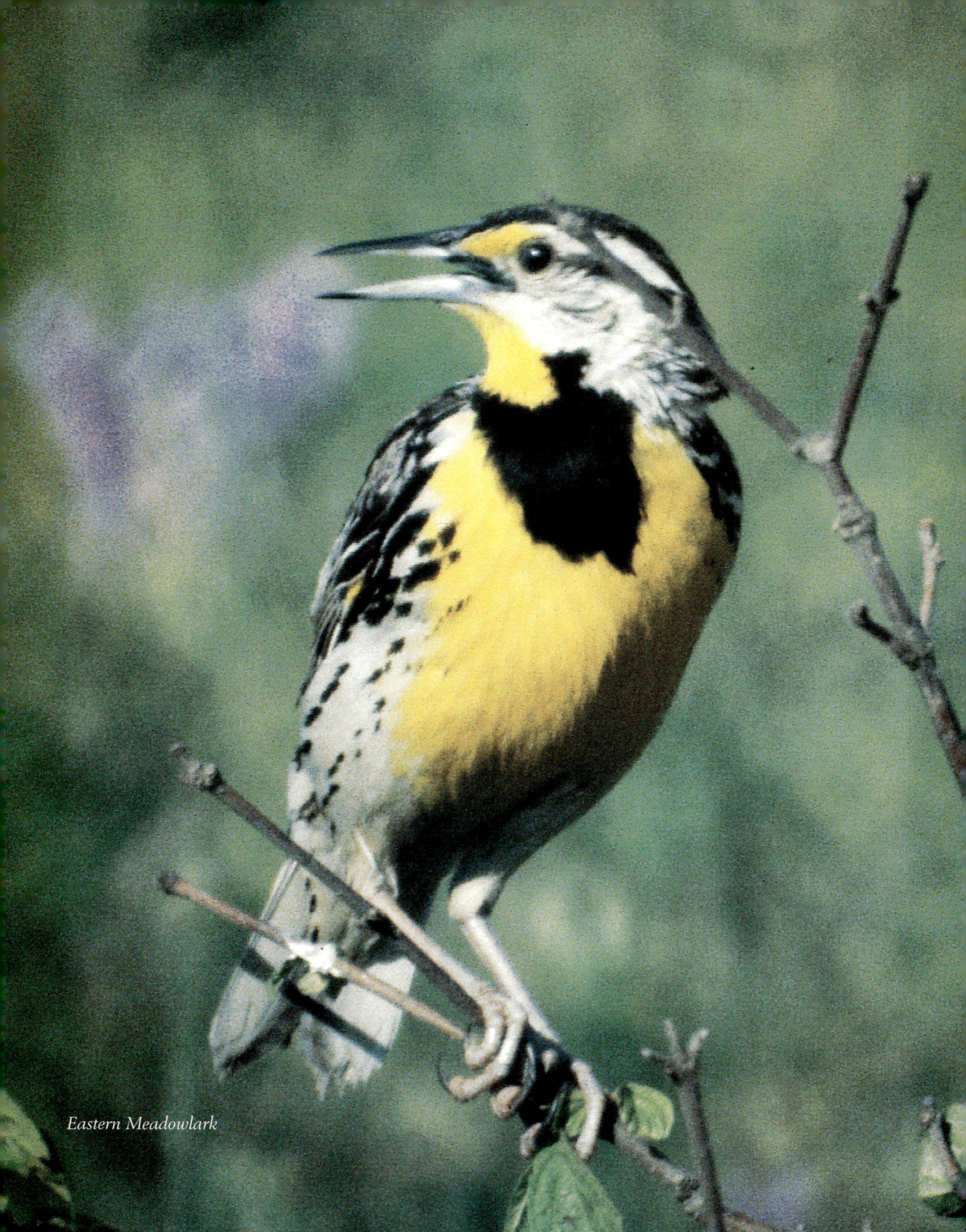

Eastern Meadowlark

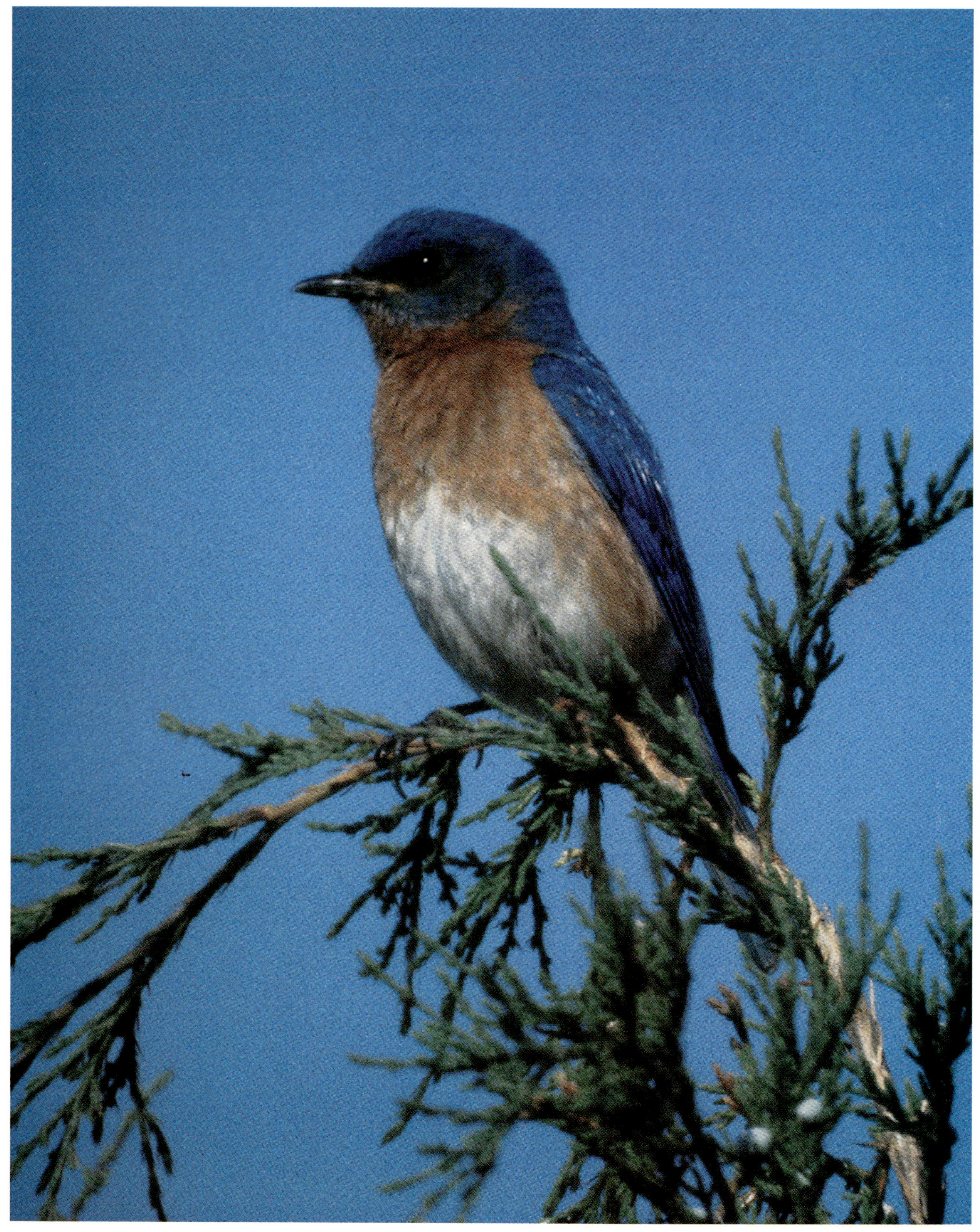

Eastern Bluebird

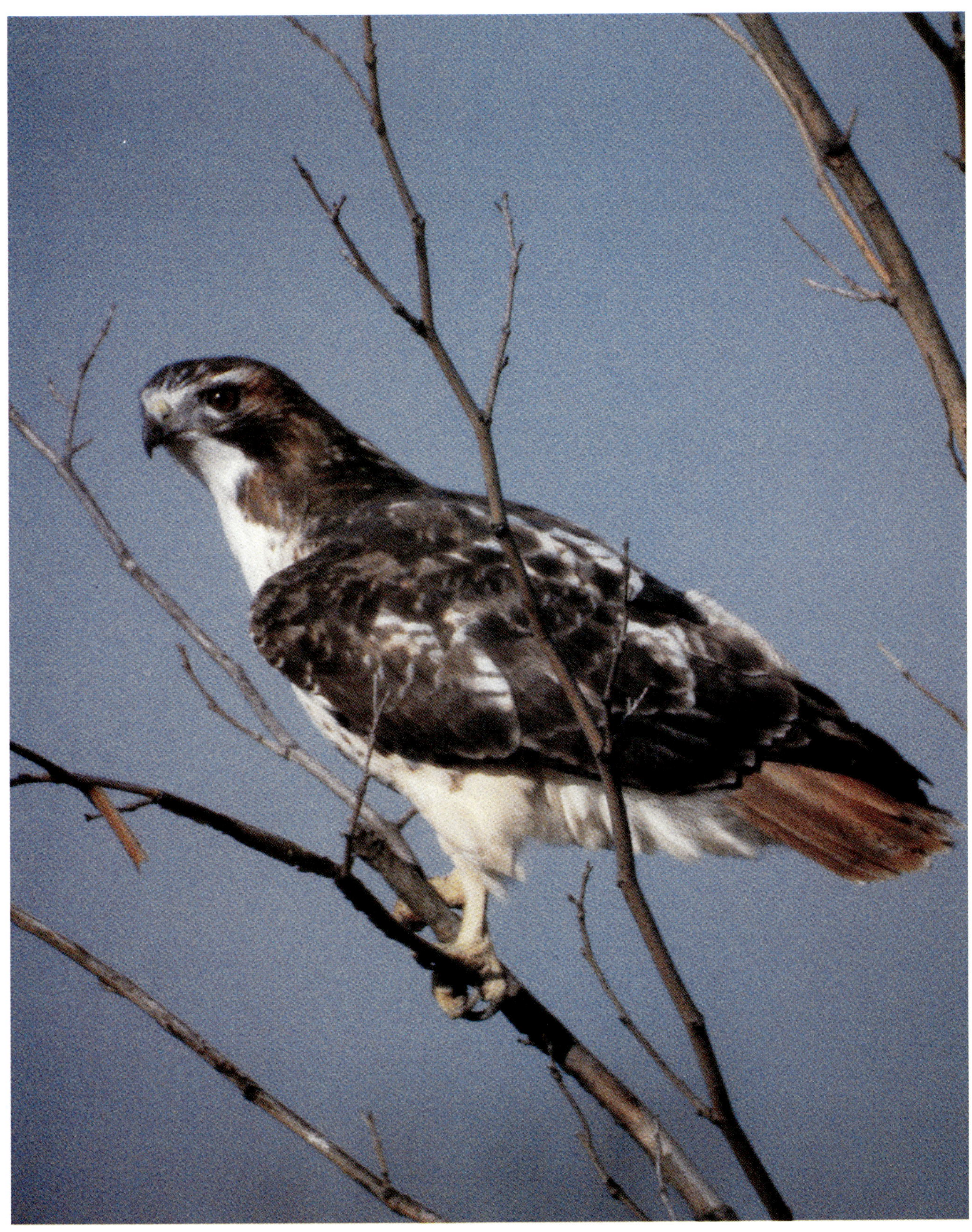

Red-tailed Hawk

Birds of Water, Marsh and Shore

Although a few of the pictures in this section were shot on or near Sanibel Island, they are all birds regularly seen in northwest Ohio. The open waters of Lake Erie, the marshes along its southwestern shore, and the rivers, streams and ponds in the area attract thousands of migrating waterfowl and shorebirds in the spring and fall. Northwest Ohio is also either the permanent or temporary residence of a large number of wading birds, rails, gulls, terns and other species that are attracted to water.

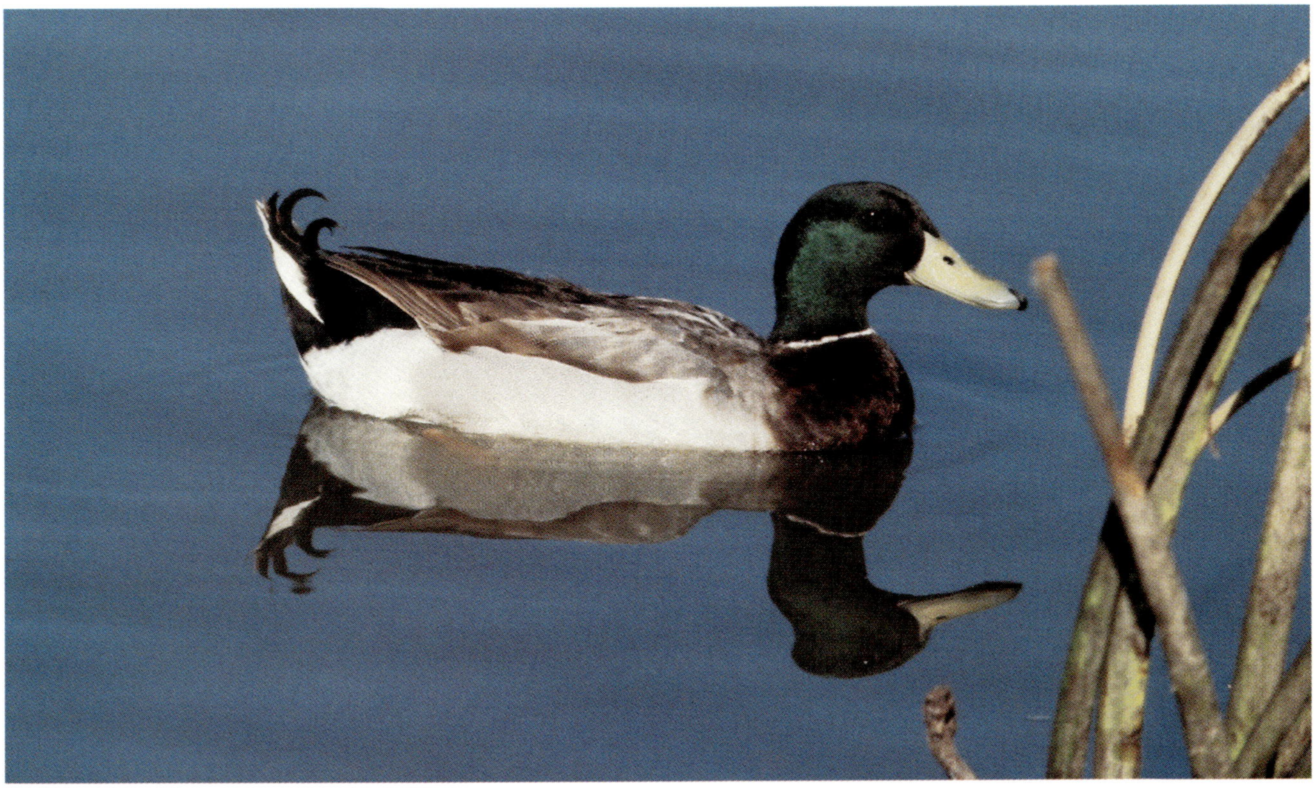

Mallard

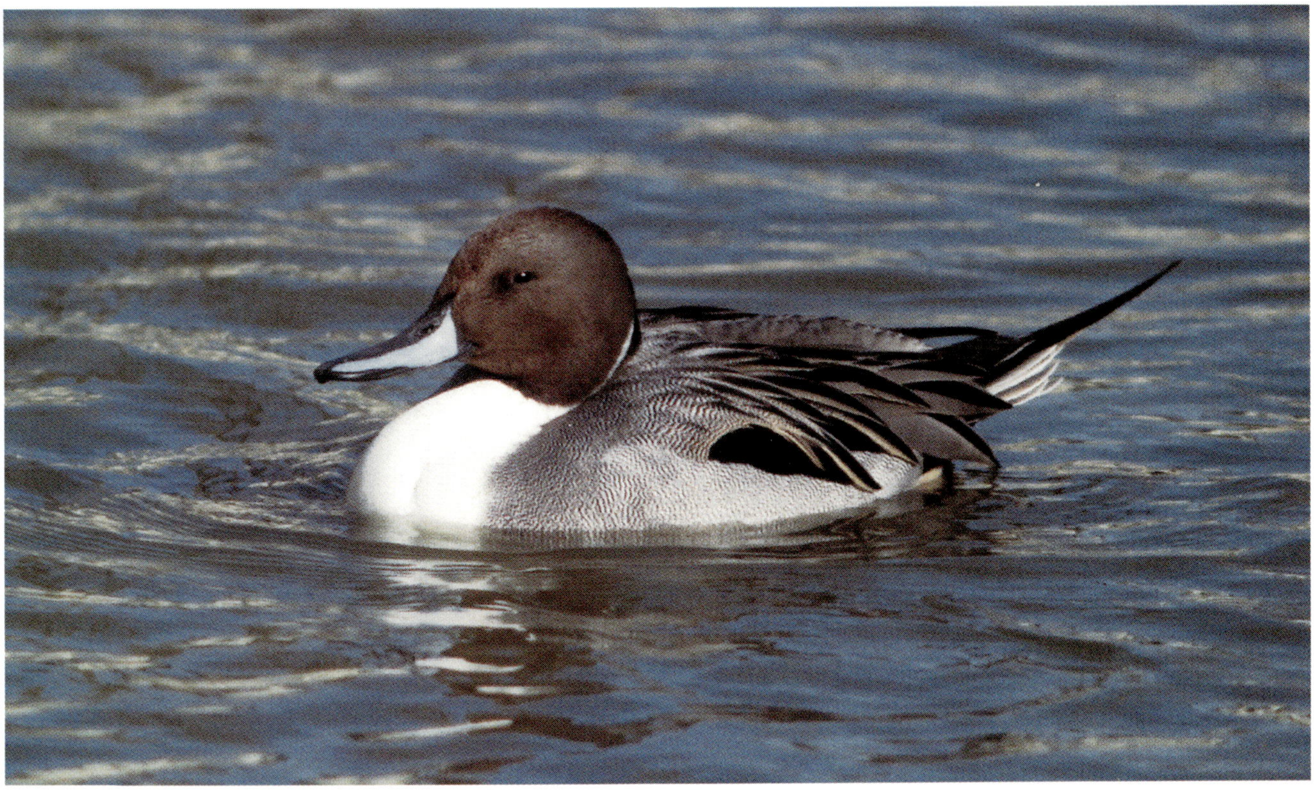

Northern Pintail

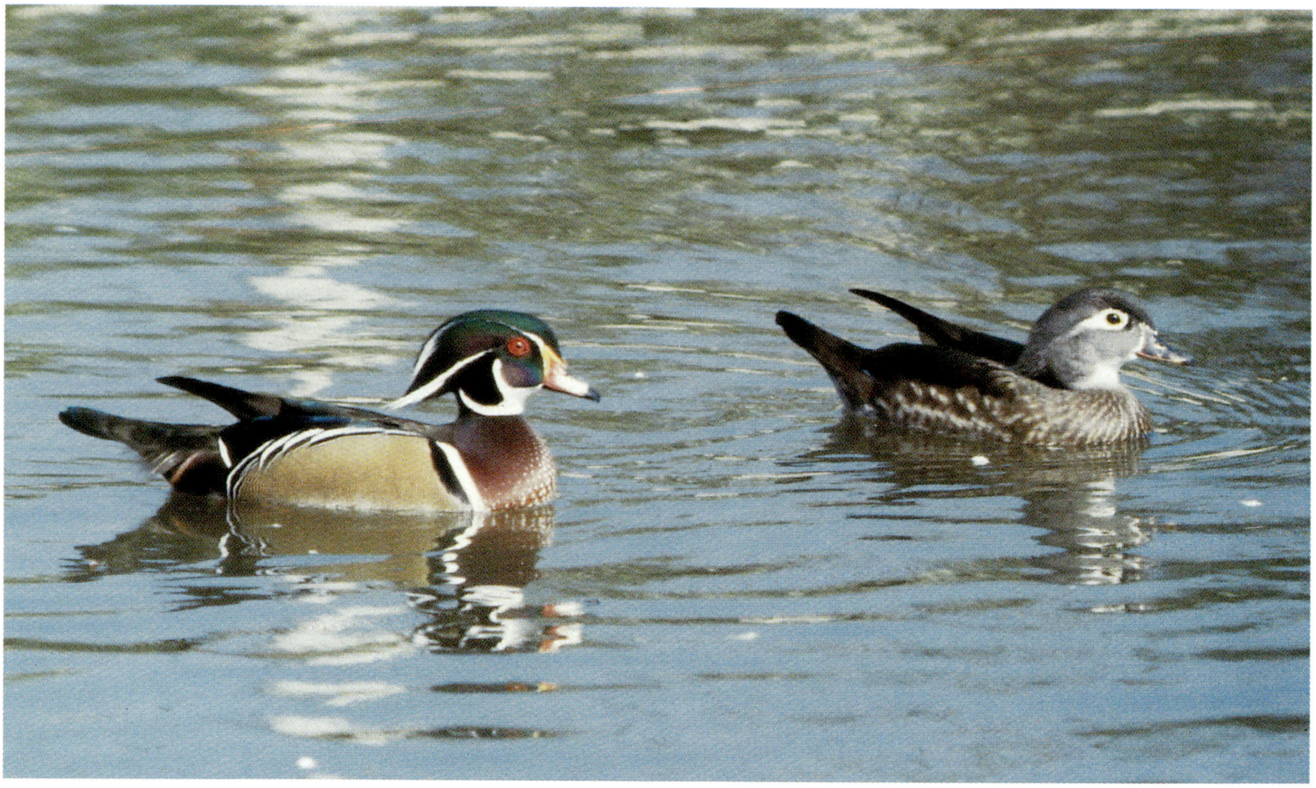

Wood Ducks

American Wigeon

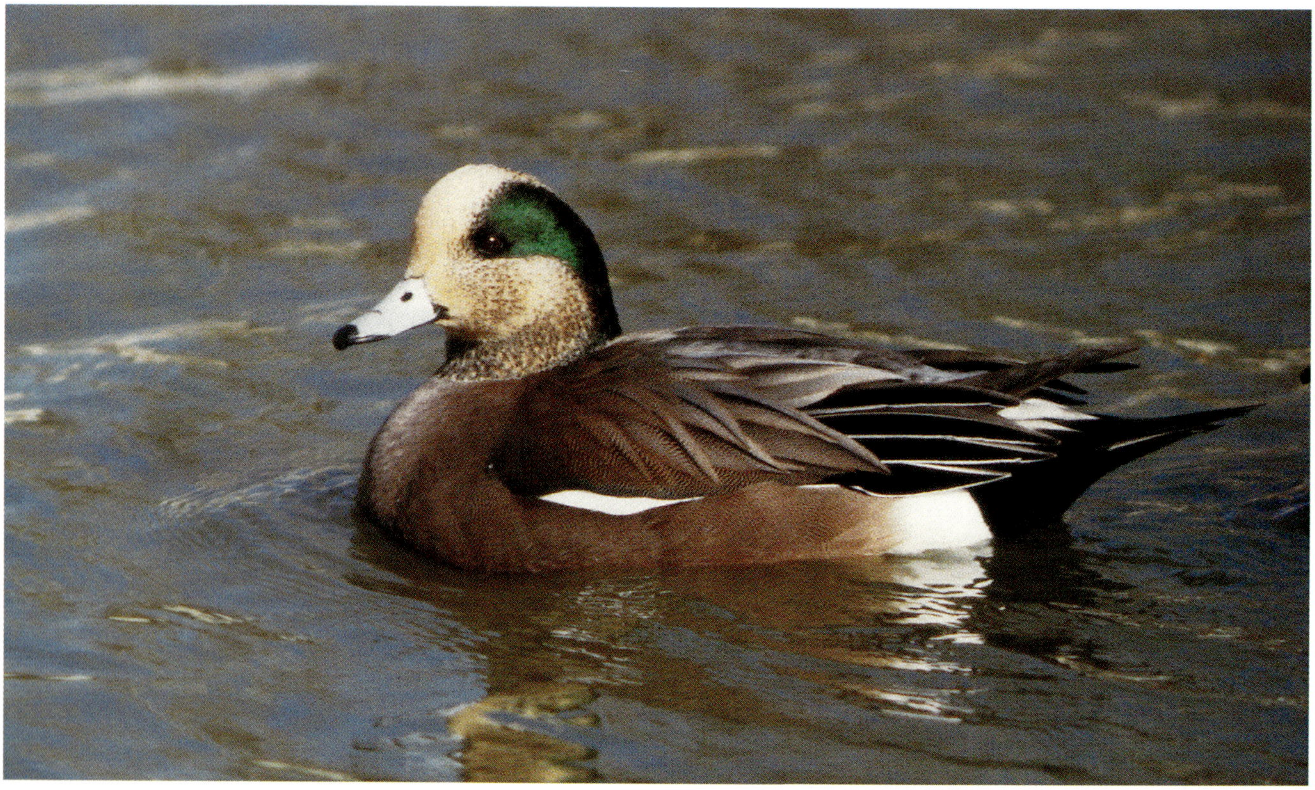

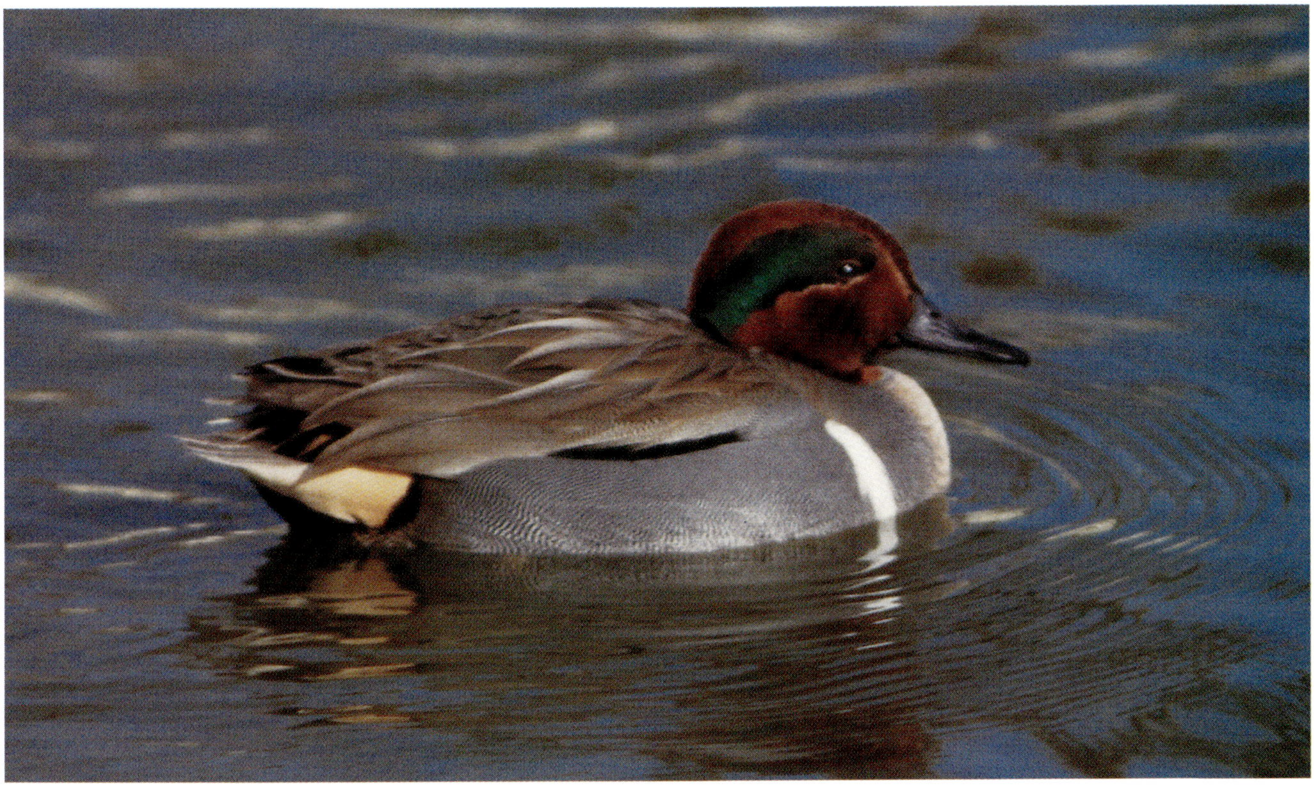

Green-winged Teal

Ring-necked Duck

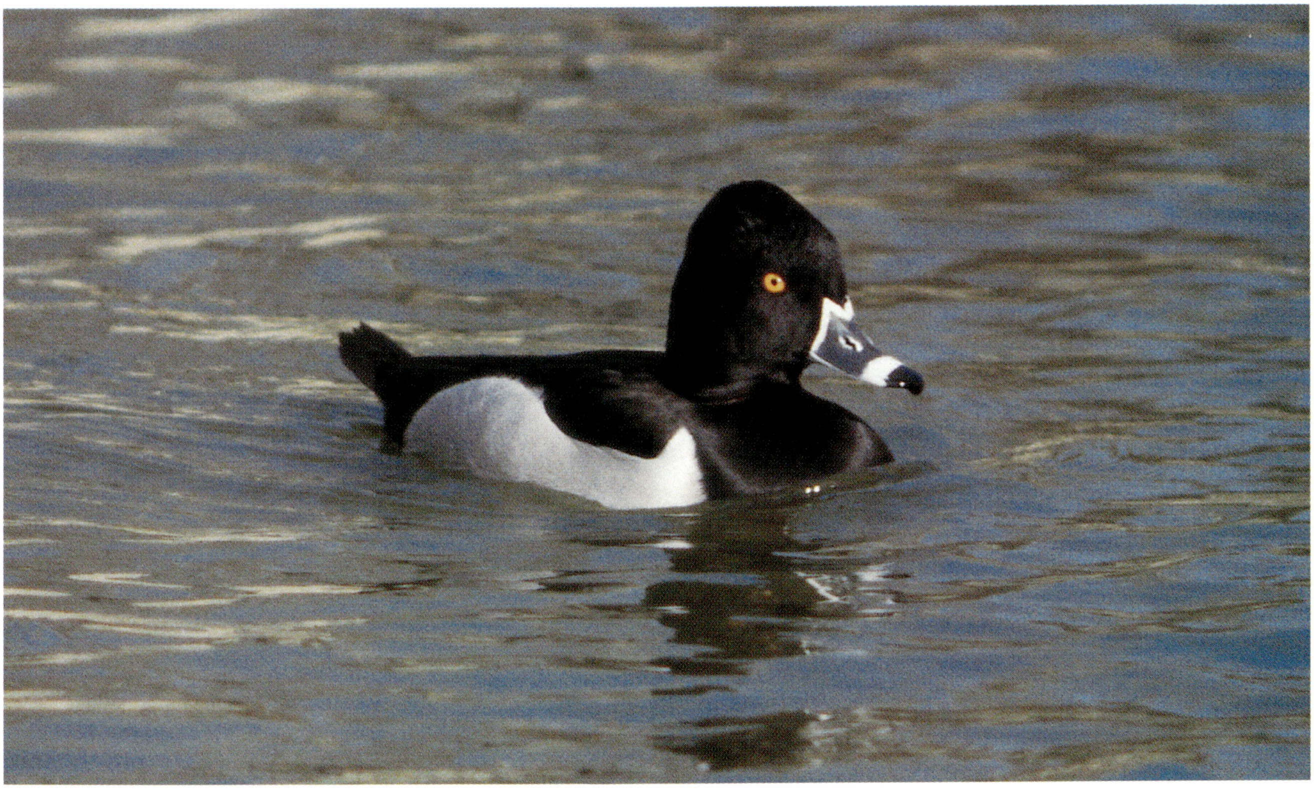

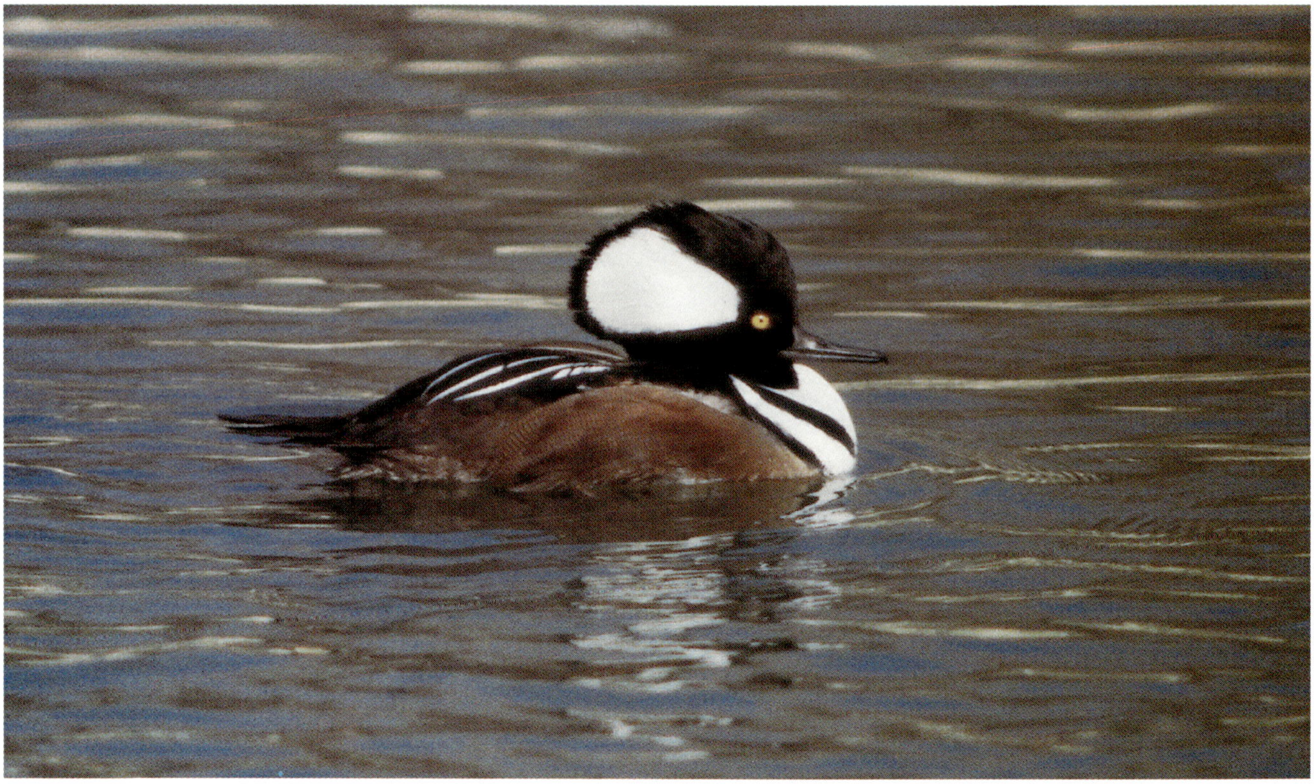

Hooded Merganser

Common Goldeneye

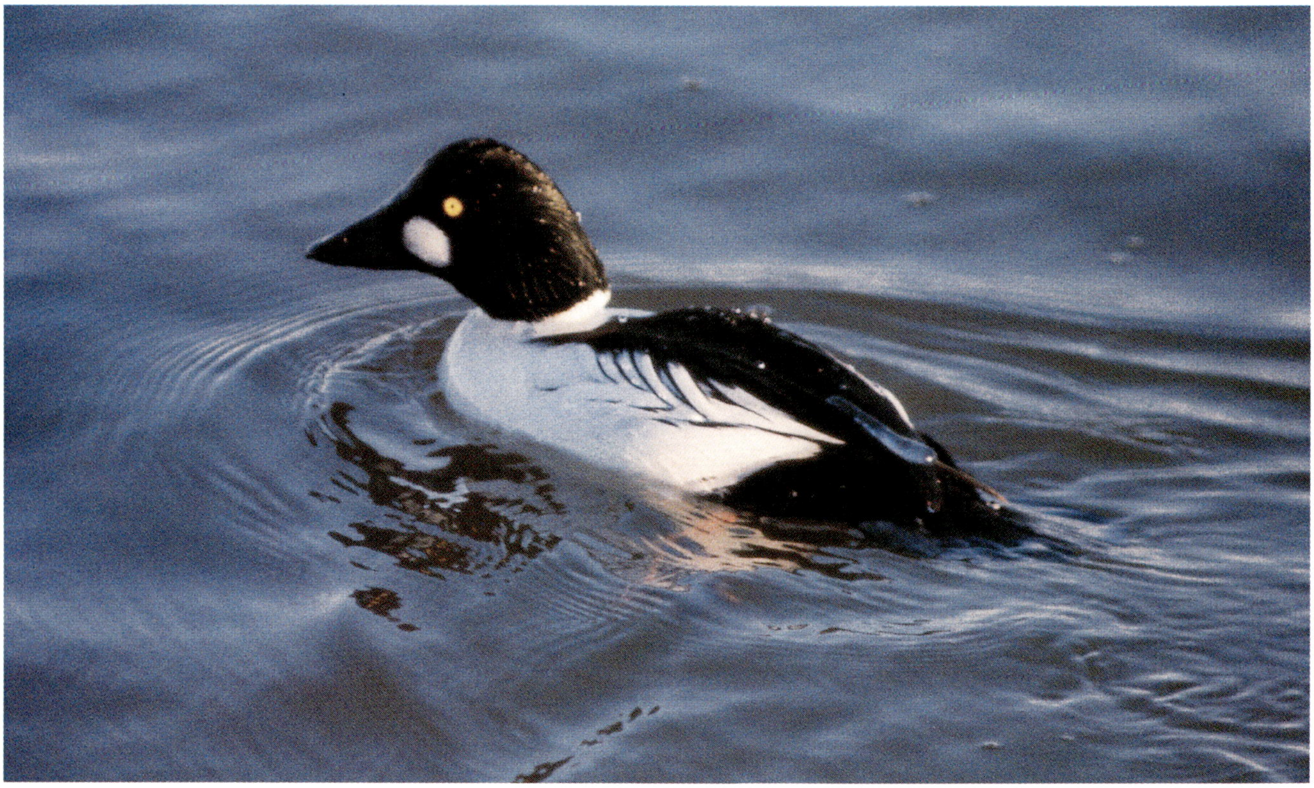

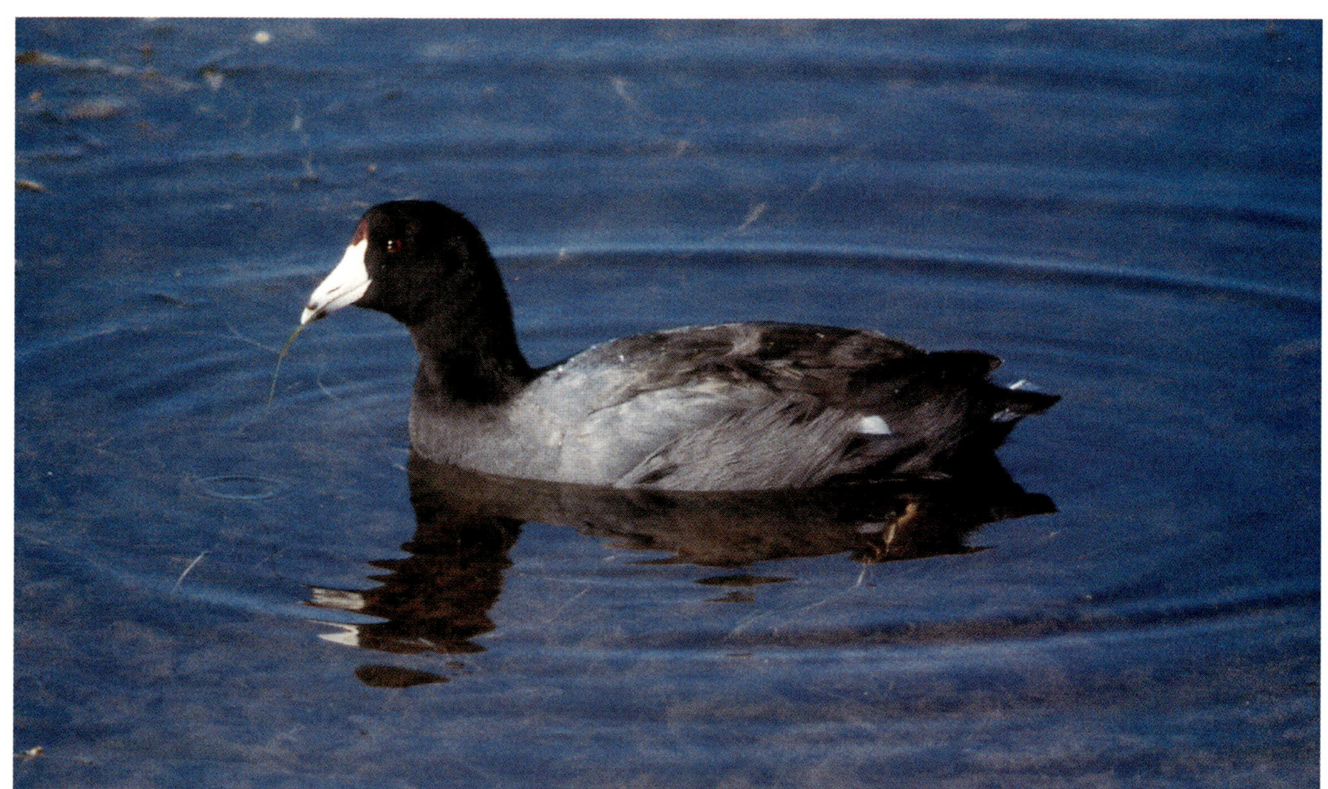

American Coot

The American Coot, also known as the Mud Hen, is an unglamorous bird

with equally unglamorous names. With all of the more appealing birds to choose from, The Mud Hens was the name chosen for Toledo's baseball team. Whether out of good luck or good sense, however, it may have been a stroke of genius. Without much doubt, it is one of the most recognized names in the minor leagues.

The Toledo Mud Hens, so it would seem
Is an unlikely name for a baseball team.
In my opinion, it hardly suits,
But at least it's better than The Toledo Coots.

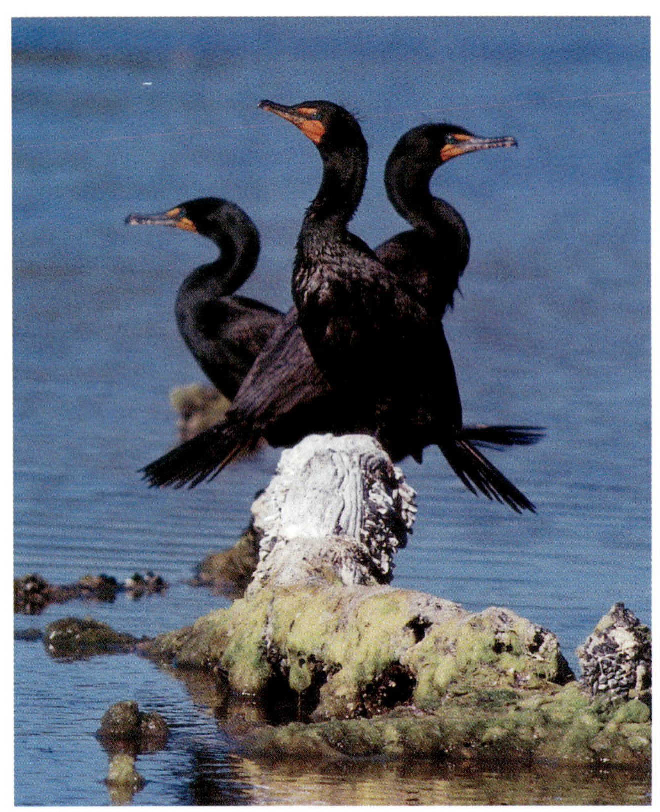

Double-crested Cormorant

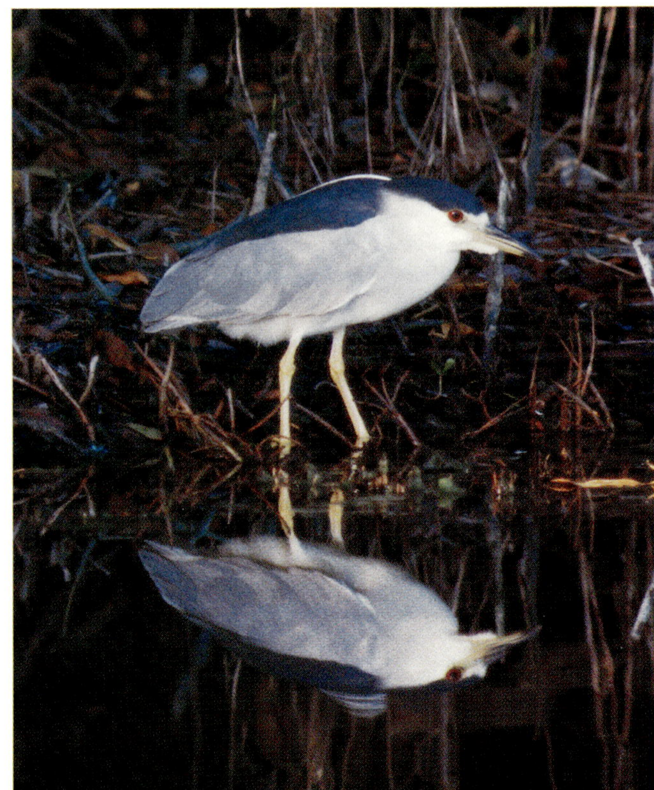

Black-crowned Night Heron

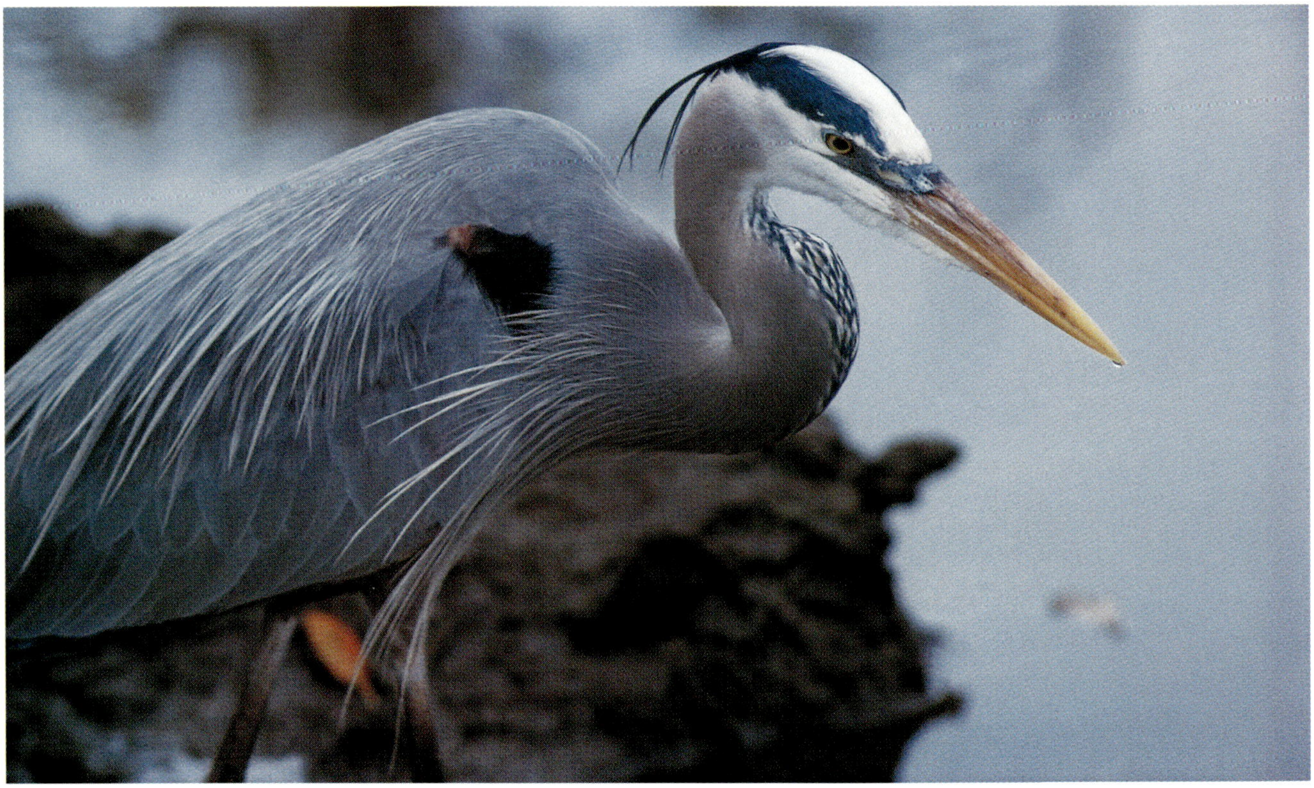

Great Blue Heron

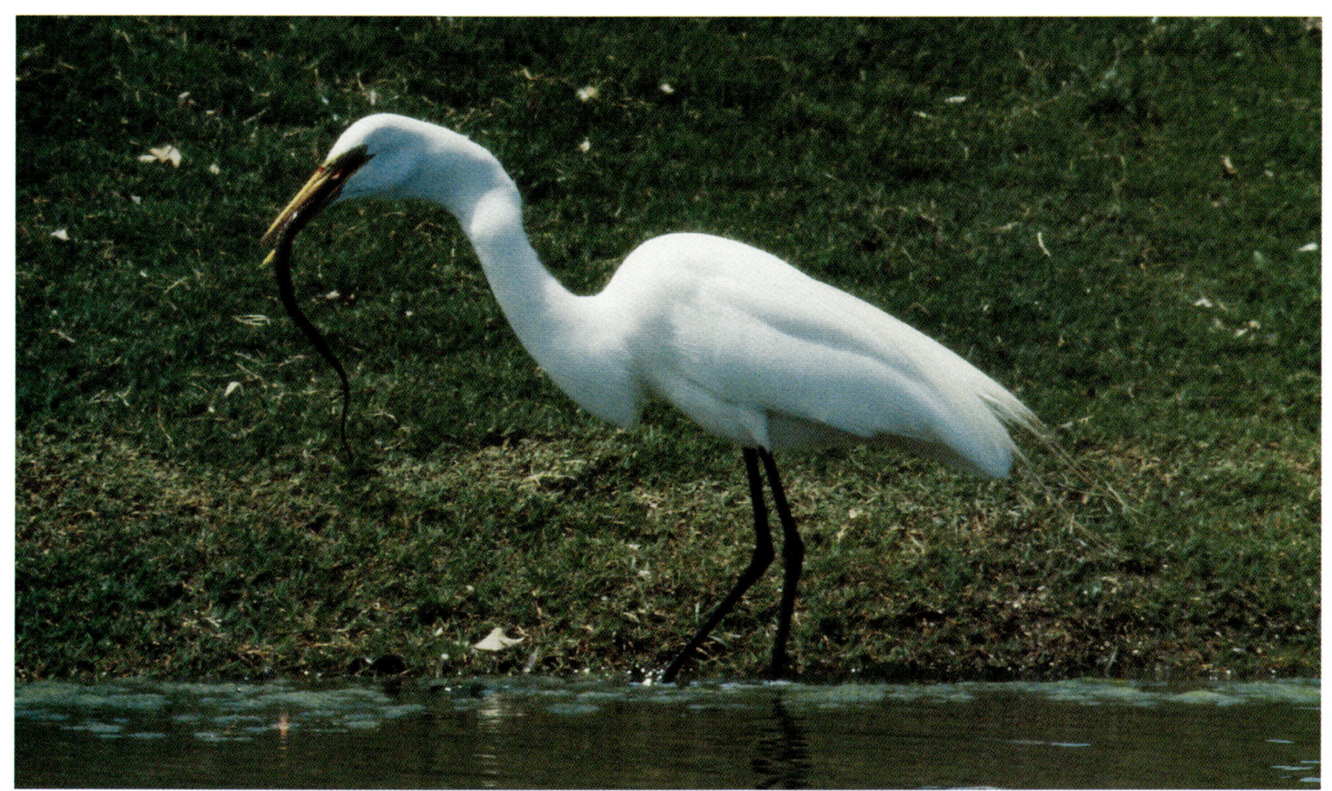

Great Egret

After a considerable struggle, the Great Egret pictured above managed to swallow a snake that was at least two feet long.

One day while Mary Pat and I were driving with our son Alex through the country near Fort Myers, Florida, we noted a *Great Blue Heron* out in the middle of a field. It had a fairly large snake (about 30 inches long) in its beak. The heron was trying to swallow it, but the snake was objecting. The heron finally got it headed down in the right direction until all but a few inches of its tail disappeared. Suddenly the tail curled around the heron's beak and that's as far as the snake went. The heron regurgitated it and beat its head savagely on the ground until it appeared to be stunned. A second attempt at swallowing was made, but once again the tail held on. The regurgitation and beating process was repeated, and on the third try the snake finally went all the way down. The whole episode must have lasted at least fifteen minutes.

If we gained nothing else from the experience, we certainly came away with a deeper appreciation of our position in the food chain.

Eating a snake must be quite an ordeal.
Bad enough for the diner, but even worse for the meal.

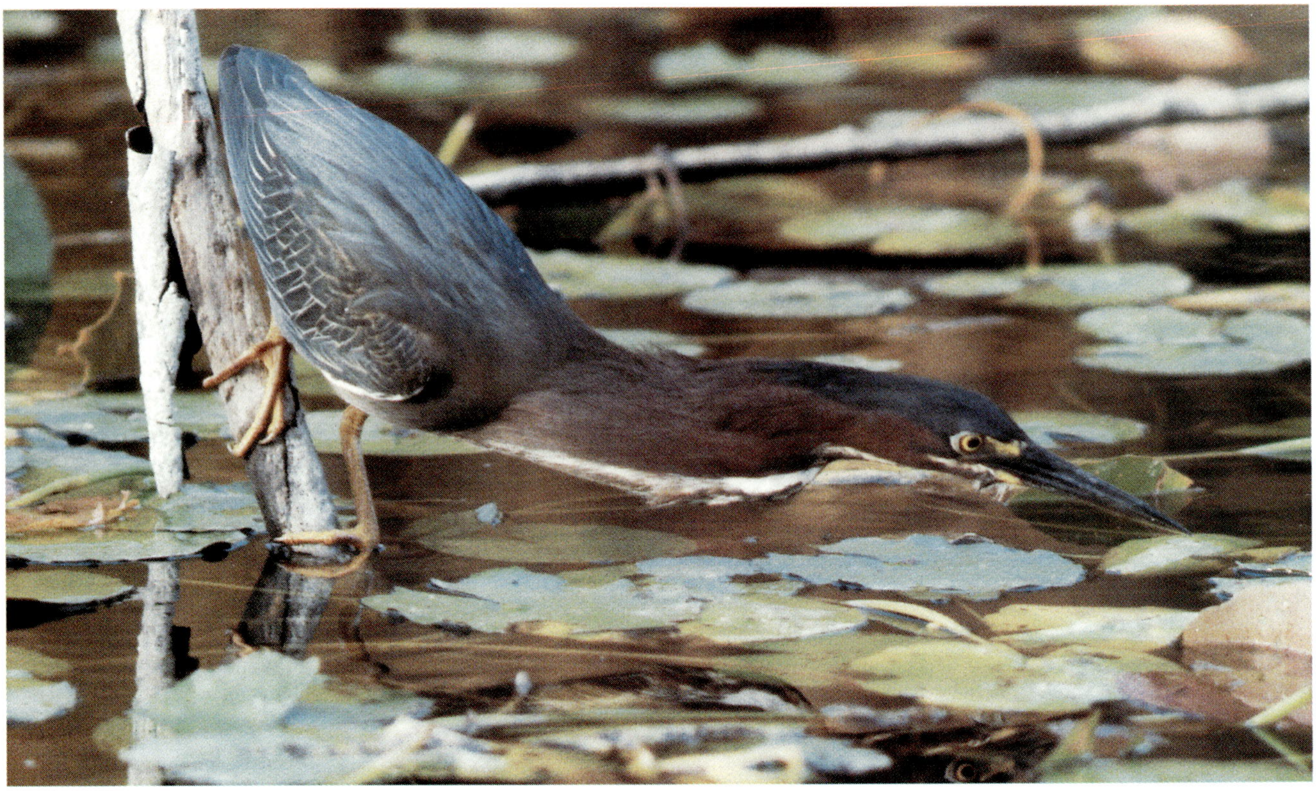

Green Heron

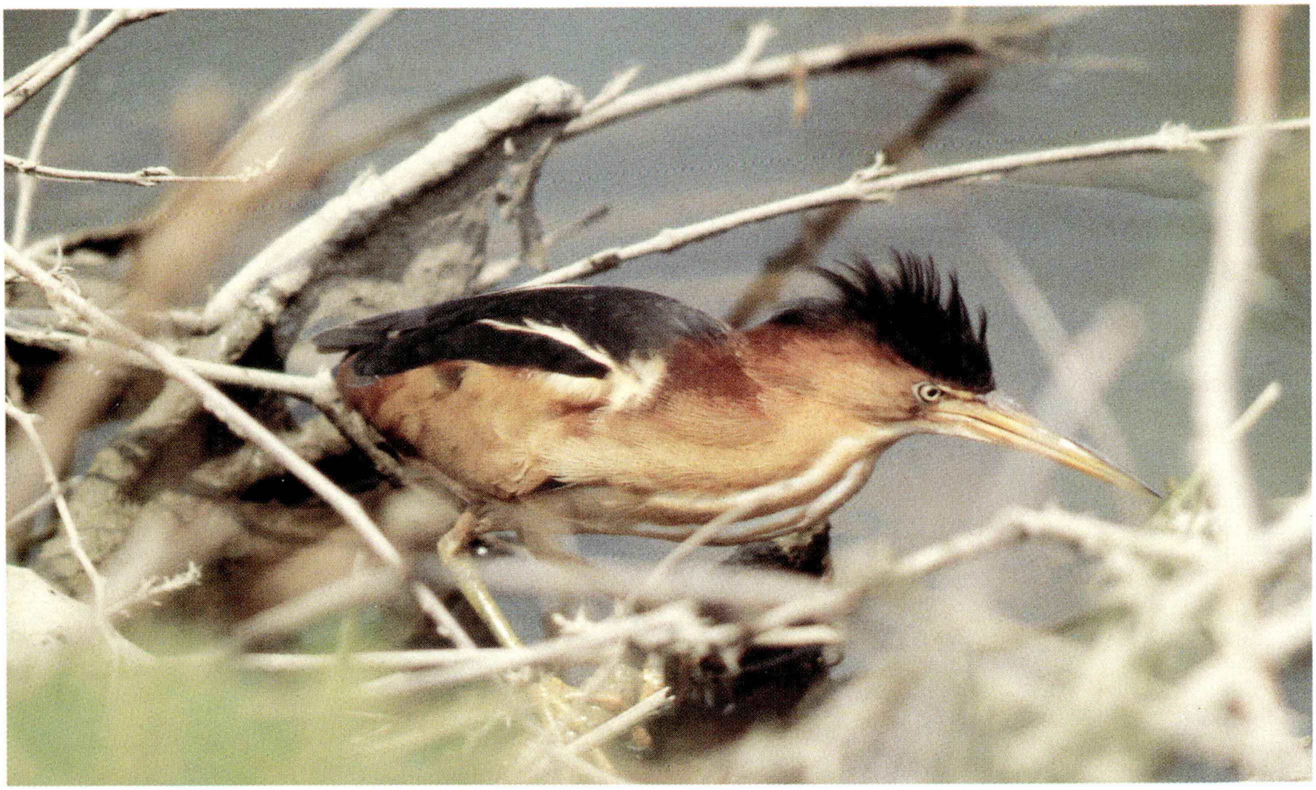

Least Bittern

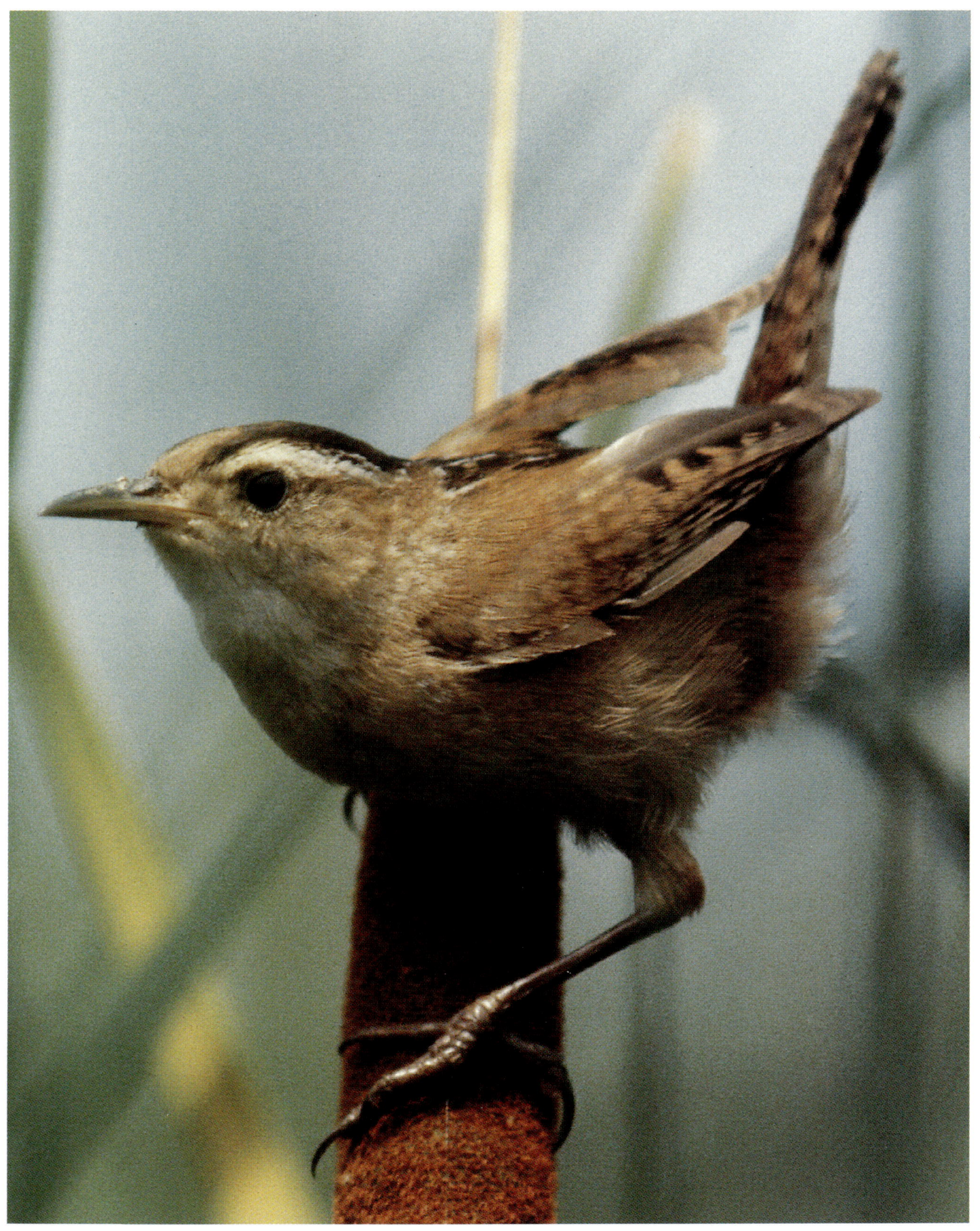

Marsh Wren

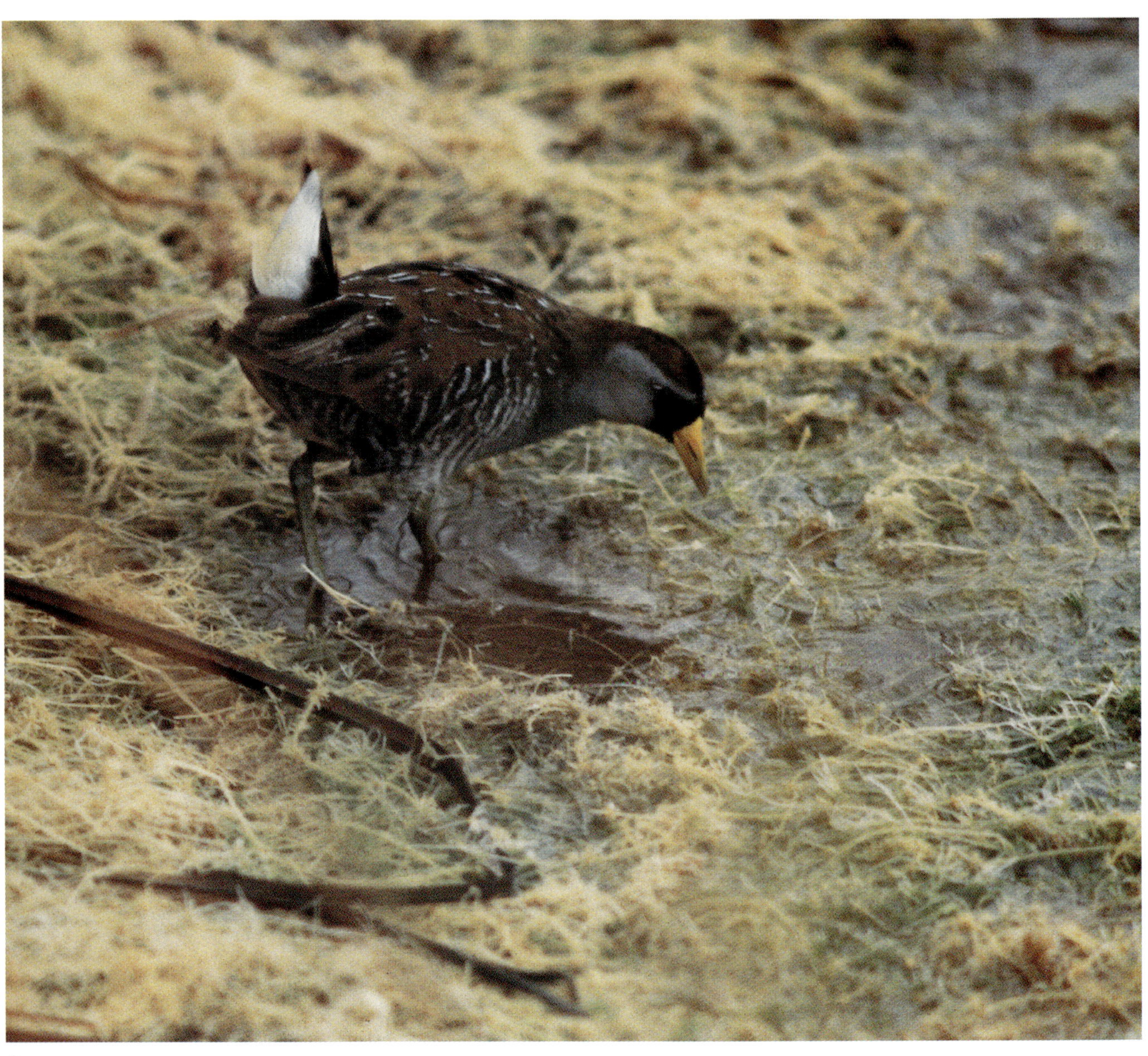

Sora

In the spring of 1980 a pair of Virginia Rails nested in a small marsh along the shore of the lake on our property. I was able to get a few pictures when one of the rails came briefly out into the open. I wasn't able to get very close, however, and I didn't want to tramp through the cattails for fear of disturbing the nest which had not been precisely located.

Knowing that rails will often respond to tapes of their calls, I located a tape with a brief segment of a *Virginia Rail* call on it. I hung a recorder/player on my belt and stepped into the edge of the marsh with my camera. After playing the rail's call only a few times, one of them appeared only a few feet away in the cattails. I continued to play the calls until it actually walked across my feet. Then my problem was that it stayed too close for me to get a picture. Finally, I managed to get the shot you see here.

Although tape recordings can sometimes be very effective in attracting birds into camera range, take care not to overdo it, especially in the vicinity of a nest.

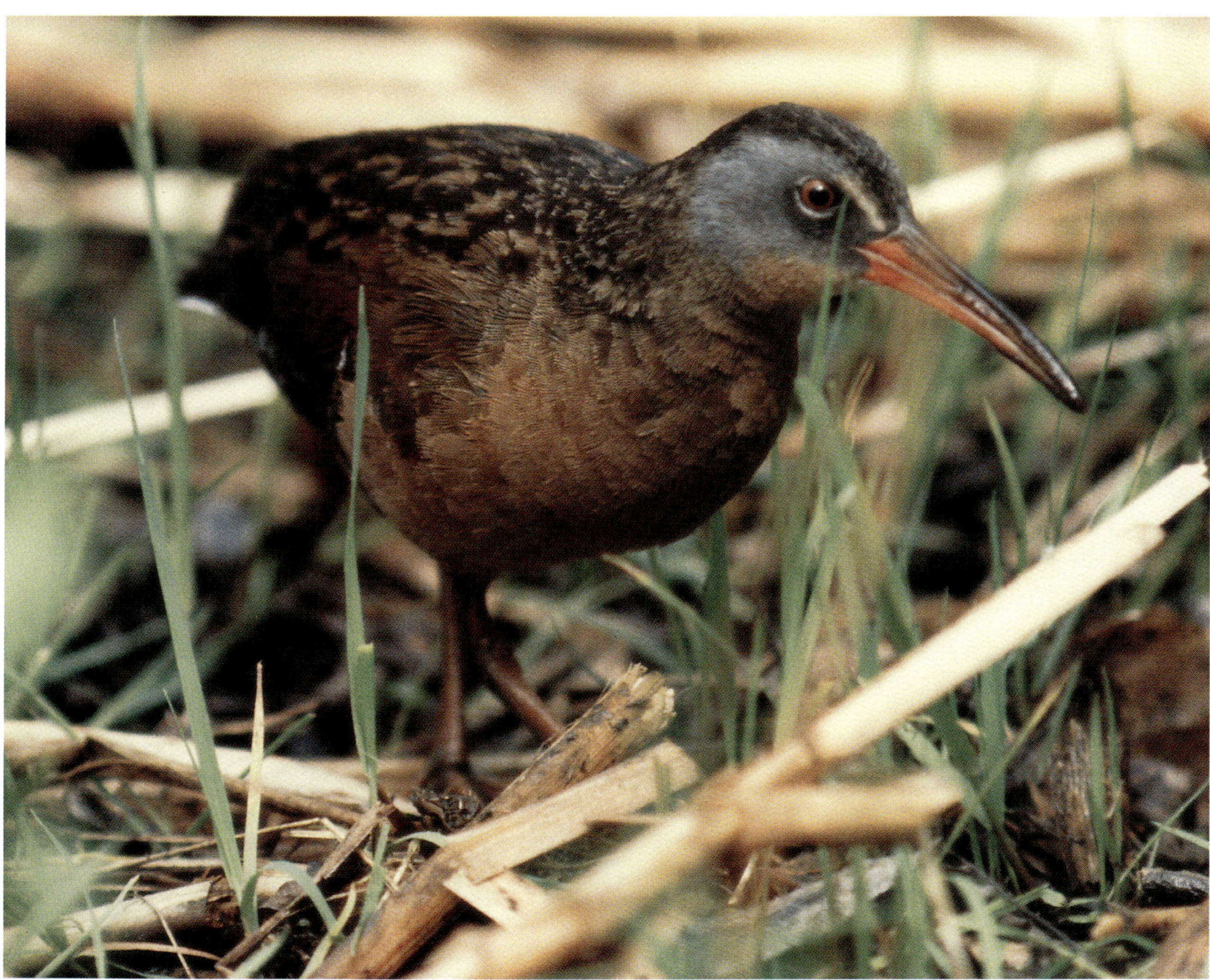

Virginia Rail

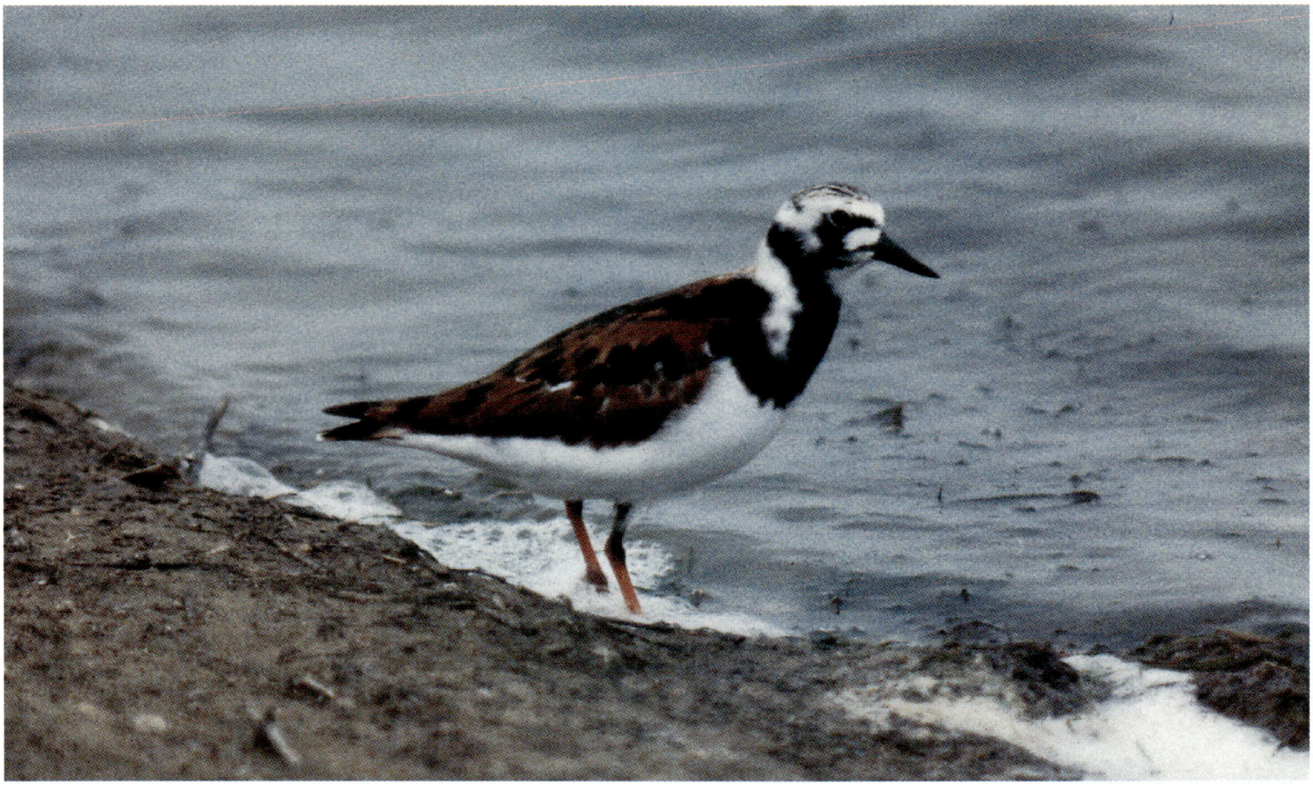

Ruddy Turnstone

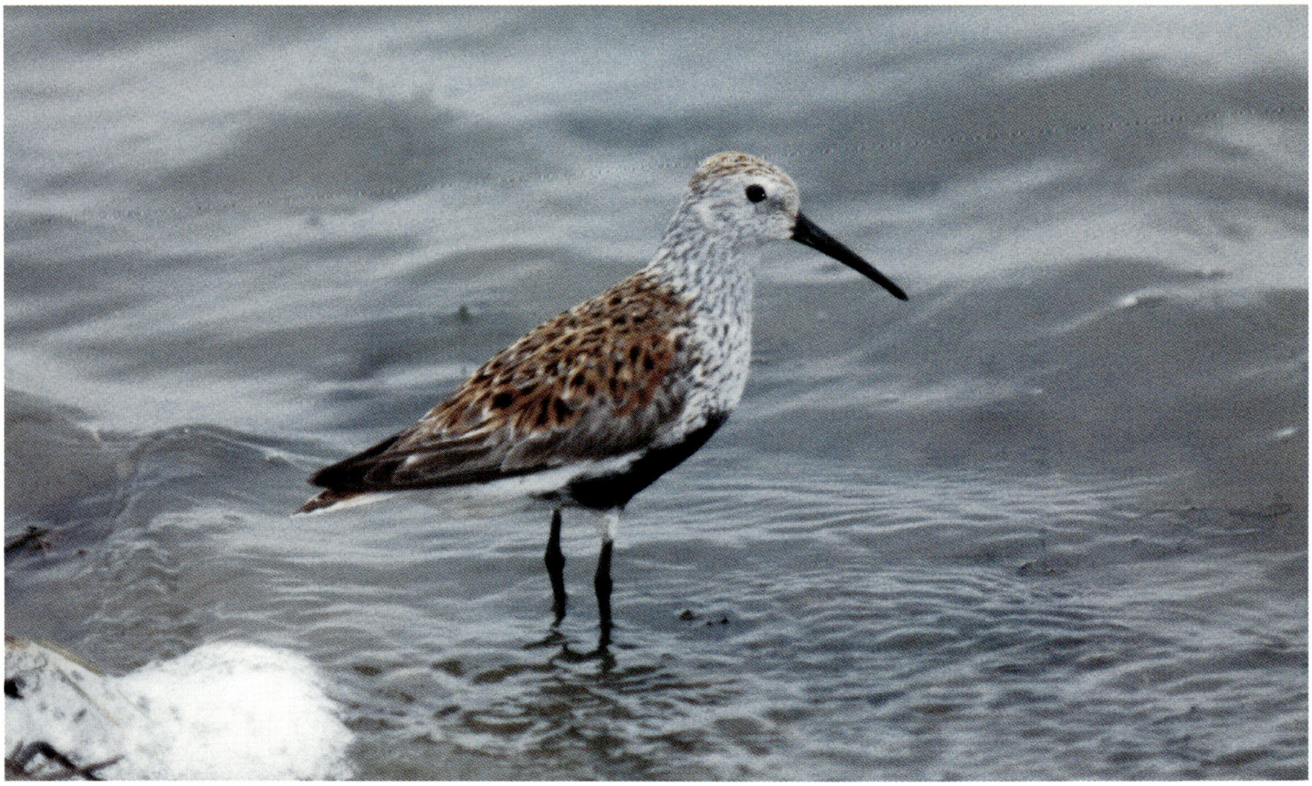

Dunlin

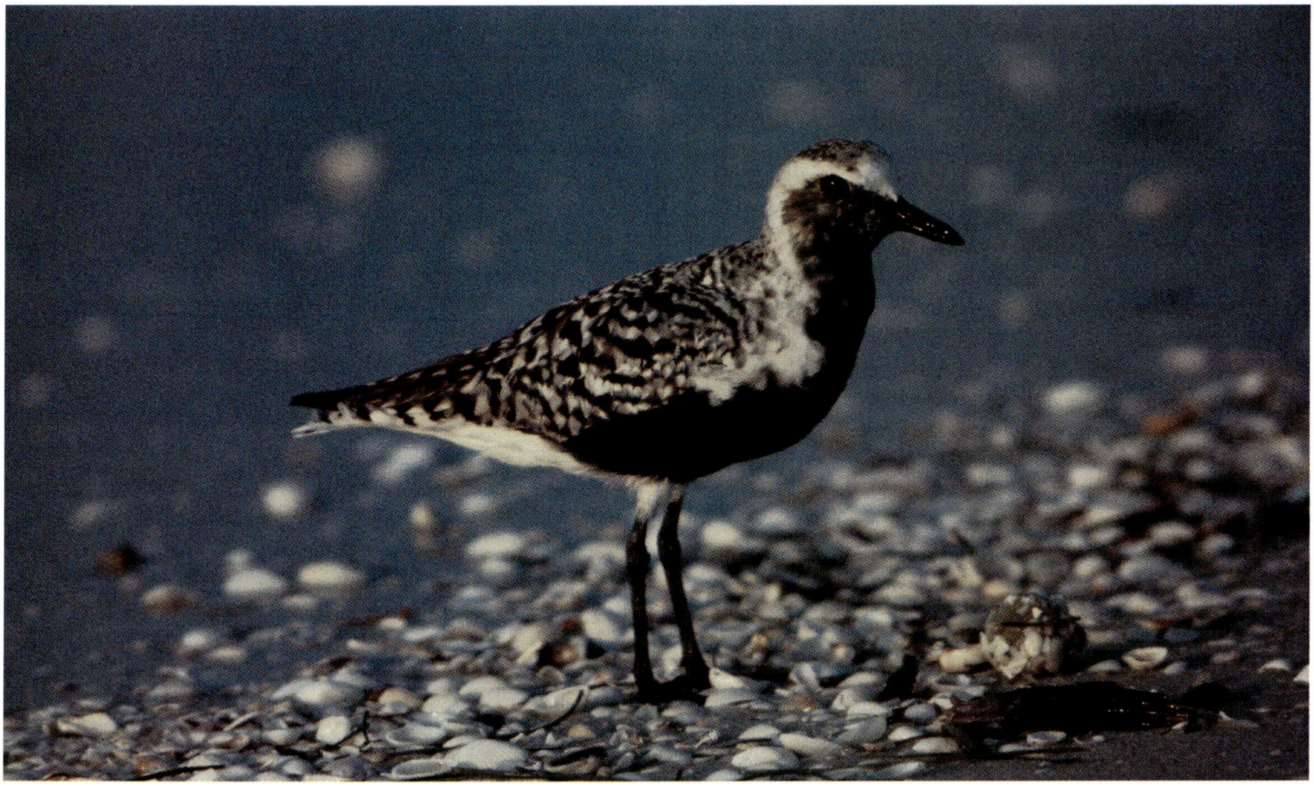

Black-bellied Plover

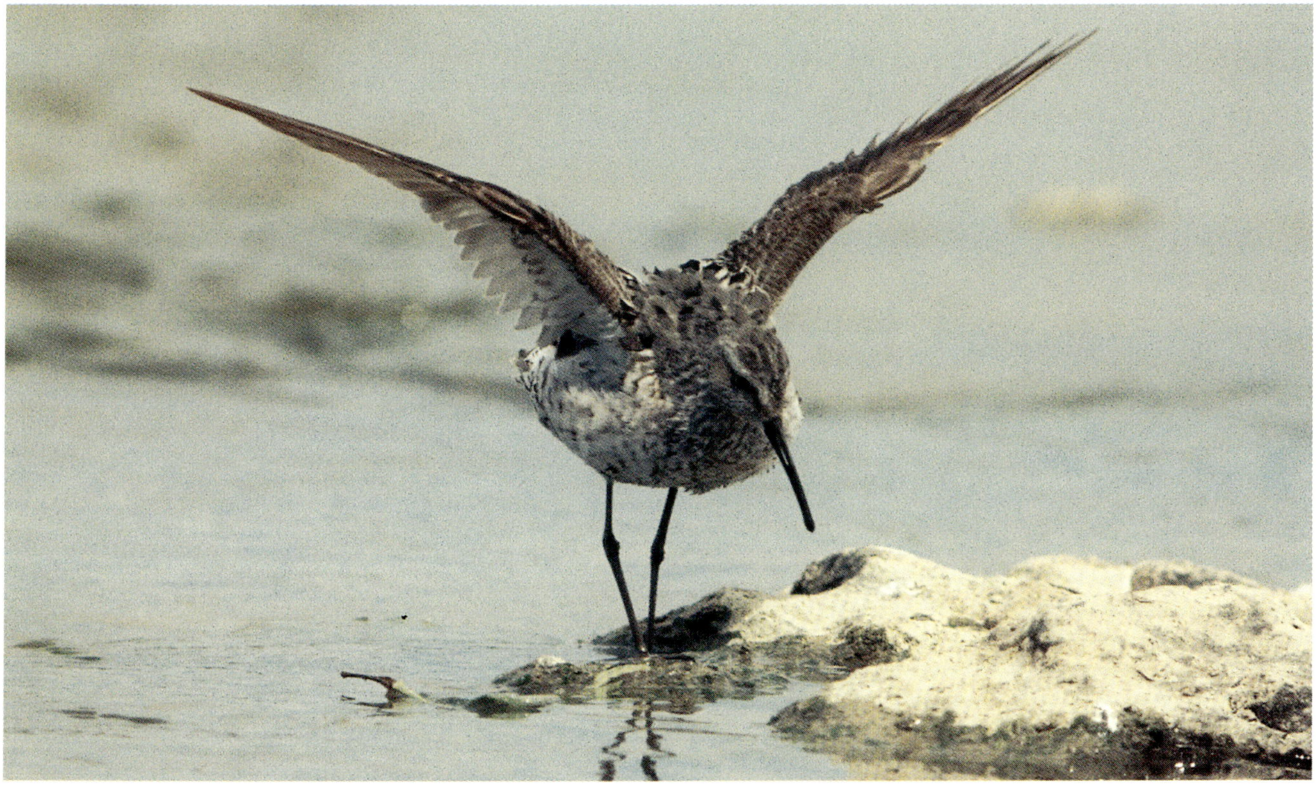

Stilt Sandpiper

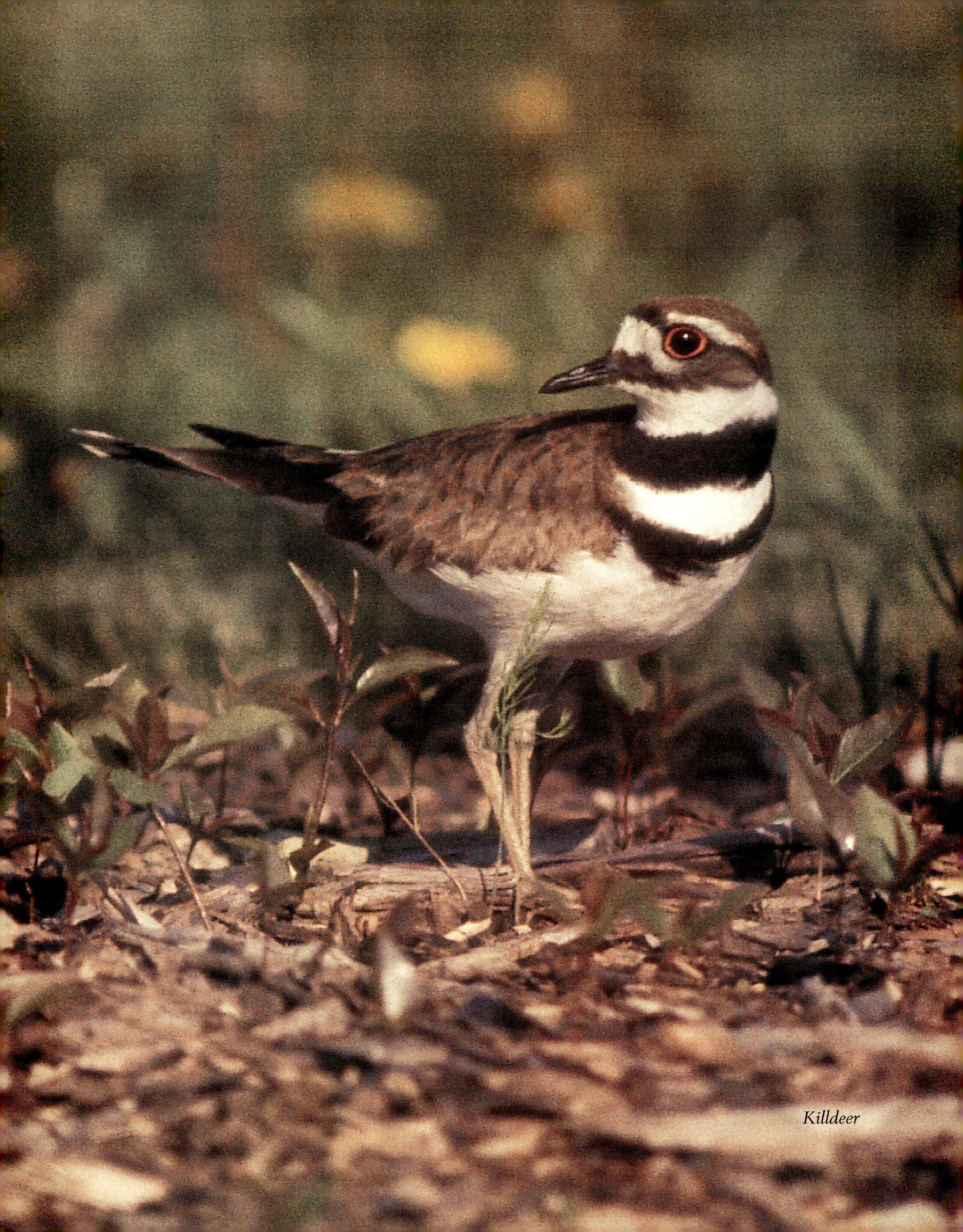

Killdeer

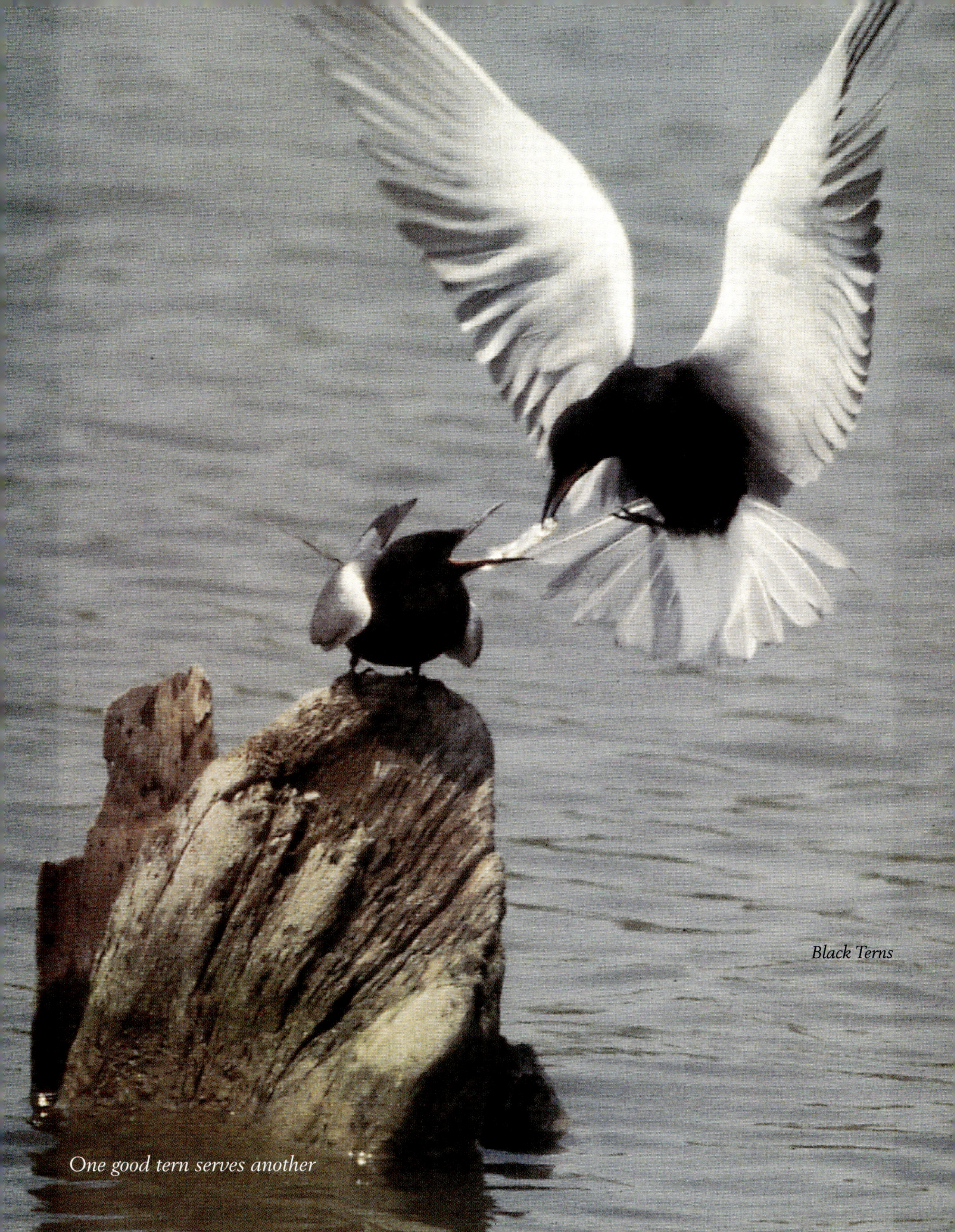
Black Terns

One good tern serves another

Sanibel Island

The birds in this section are some that can be seen in April either on Sanibel Island or within an hour's drive on Florida's mainland. A number of them can also be seen in the Toledo area. All of the pictures, however, were taken in Florida. Most were taken from Wildlife Drive at the "Ding" Darling Refuge.

The Limpkin (*page 88*), Painted Bunting (*page 89*), and the Barred Owl (*page 91*) were shot at Corkscrew Swamp Sanctuary near Immokalee, Florida. About an hour's drive from Sanibel, it's well worth the trip. The Sanctuary is operated by the Audubon Society and features about two miles of boardwalk through one of only a few remaining tracts of virgin cypress swamp. The flora and fauna of this unique location should prove fascinating to anyone who has any interest in nature.

The *Brown Pelican* and *Roseate Spoonbill* (opposite) and the *Osprey* (*page 82* and on the front of the book jacket) were taken in April 1998 with my new Nikon N70 camera and Nikkor AF 75-300 mm f 4.5 - 5.6 zoom lens (*page 6*). This was my first opportunity to get acquainted with this equipment. As you can see, it passed with flying colors!

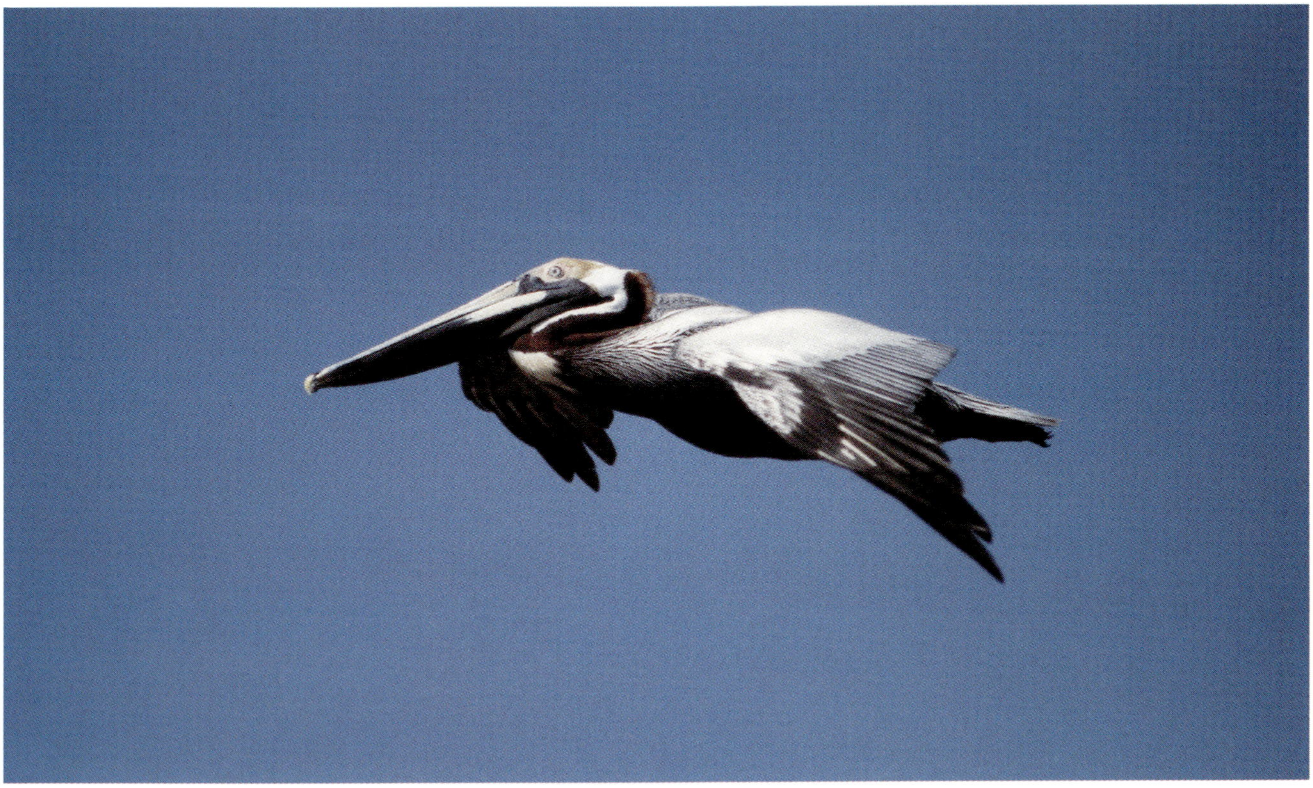

Brown Pelican

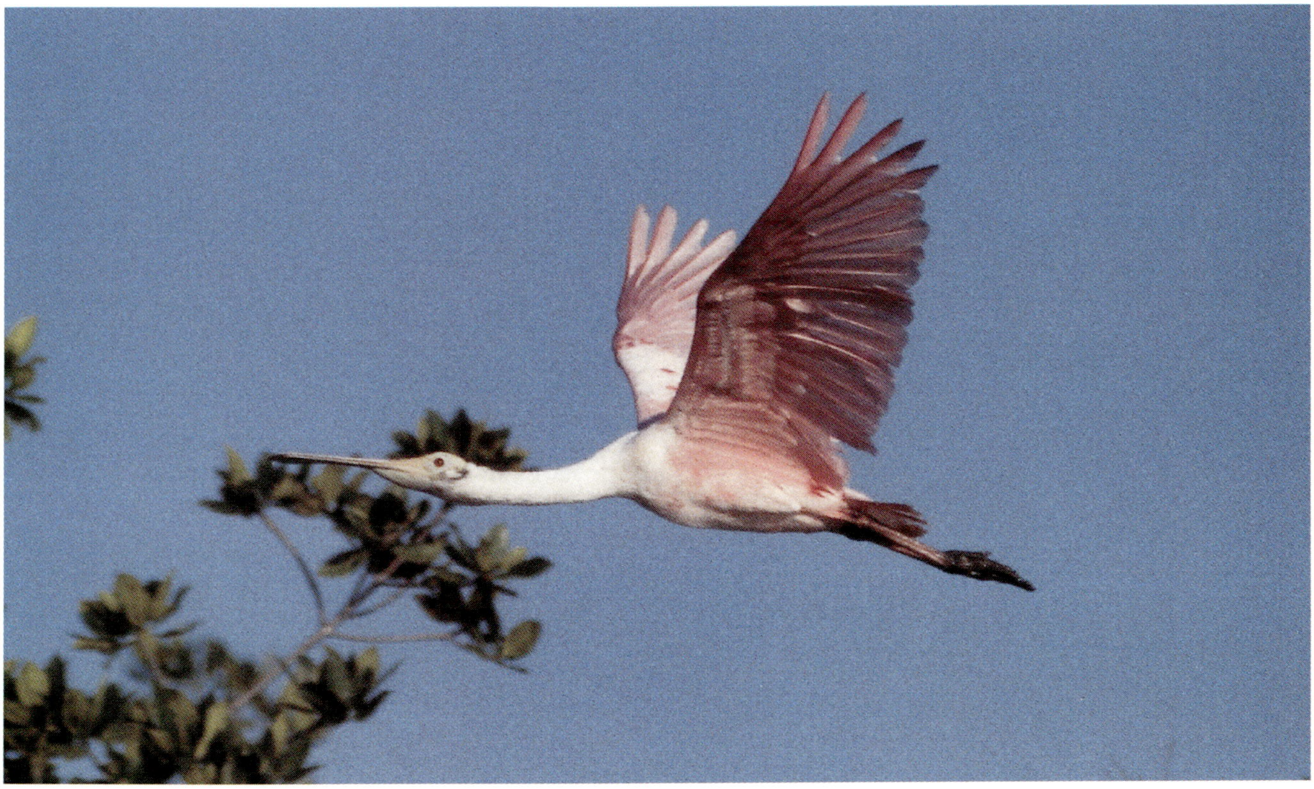

Roseate Spoonbill

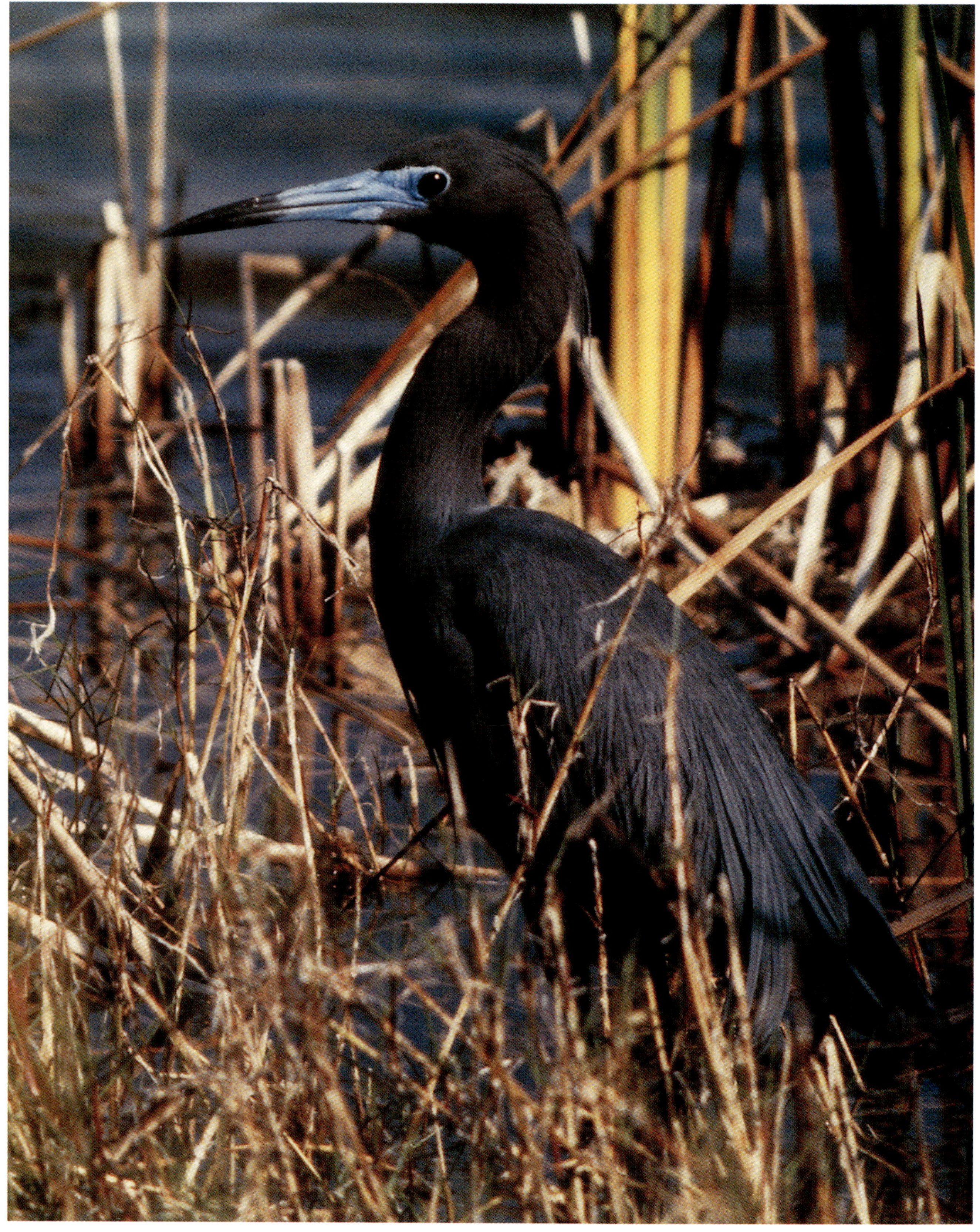

Little Blue Heron

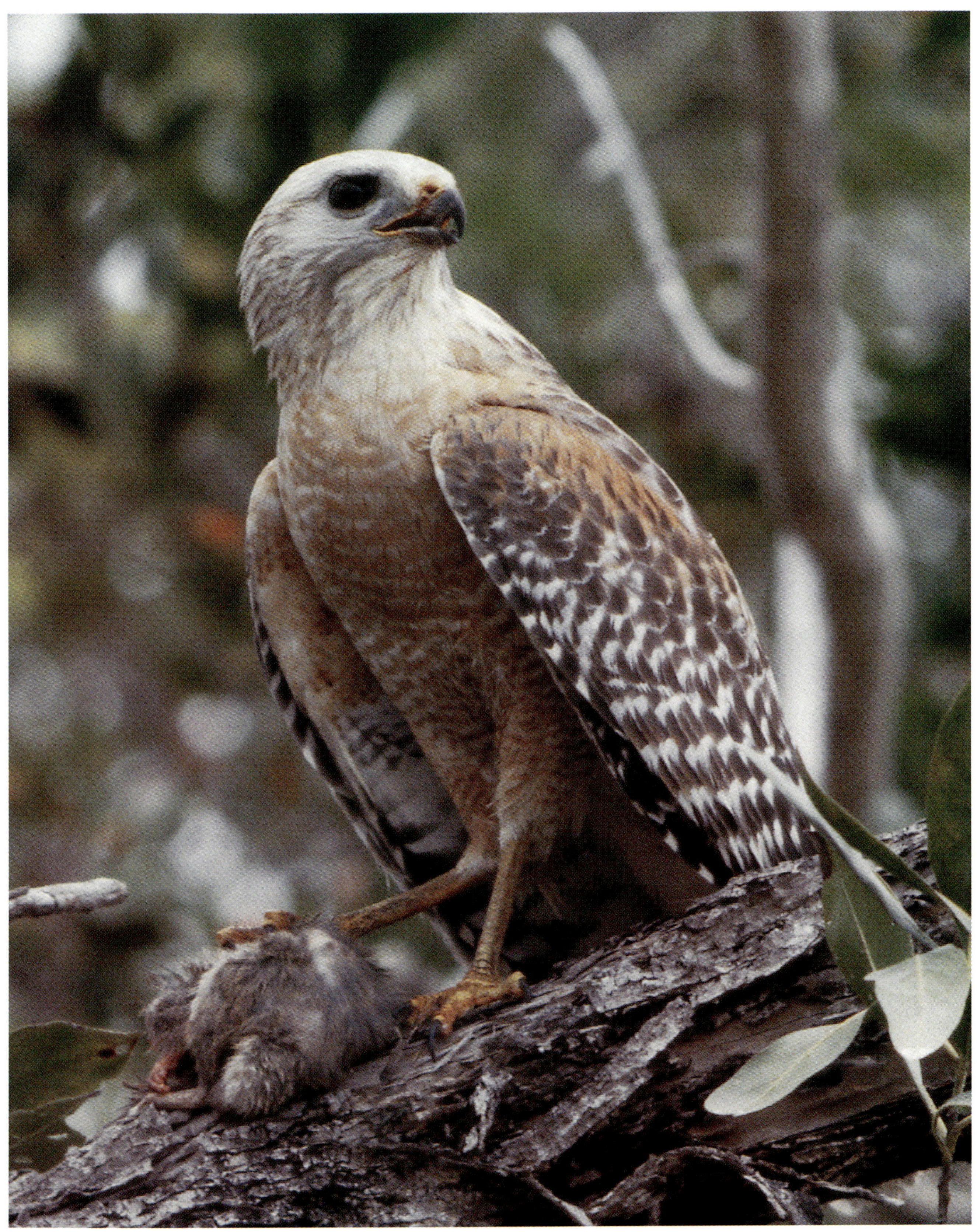

Red-shouldered Hawk

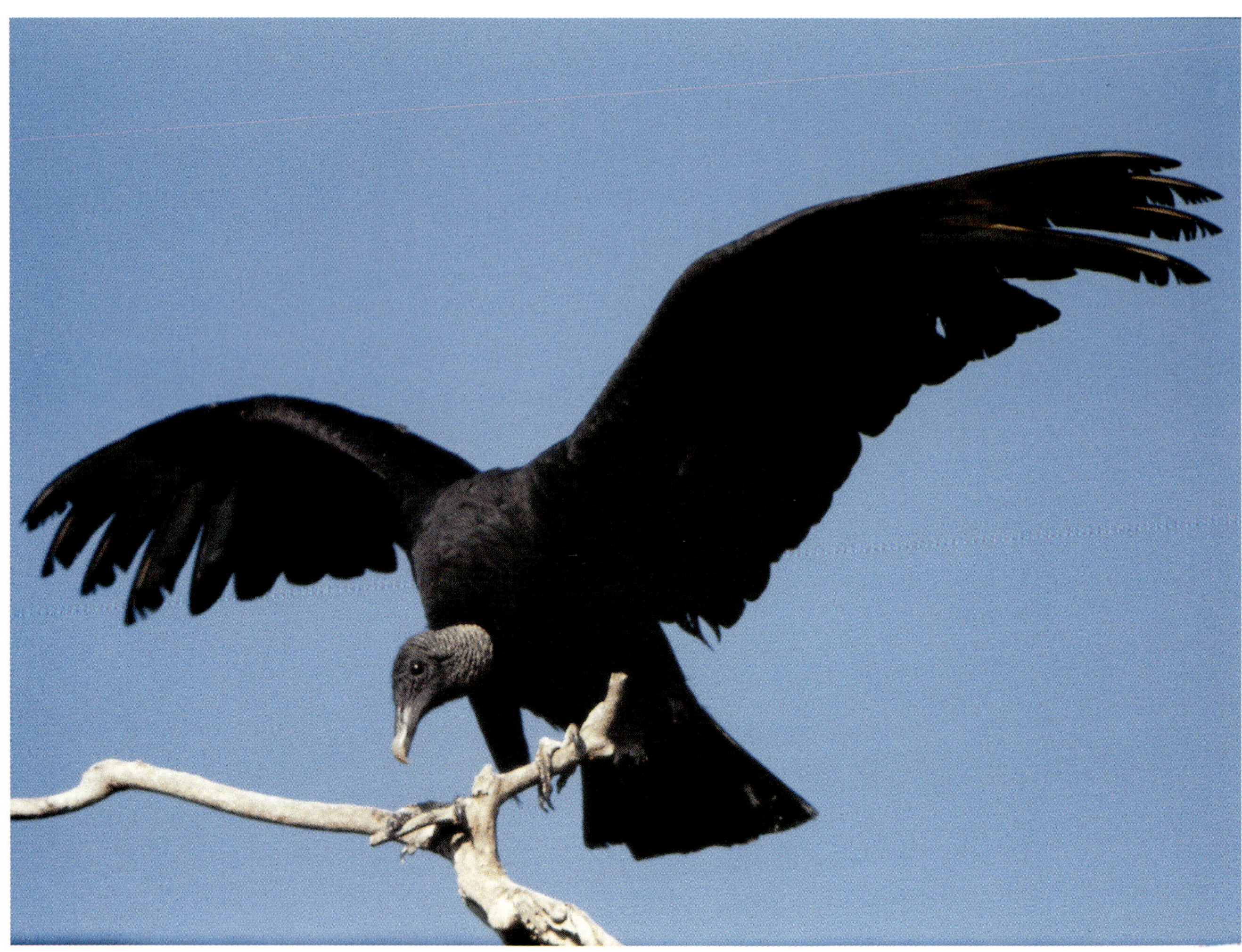

Black Vulture

There are only three species of vultures in the United States.

One, the *California Condor,* is almost extinct. The other two, the *Turkey Vulture* and the *Black Vulture,* are both common in the south, but the Black Vulture is only an accidental visitor to northwest Ohio. It is the Turkey Vulture, or "Buzzard" as it is known colloquially whose return each year in March is celebrated in Hinckley, a small town about fifteen miles south of Cleveland. Like other vultures, it feeds on carrion, which does not do much for its image.

Lacking in manners and devoid of culture,
Only its mother could love a vulture.

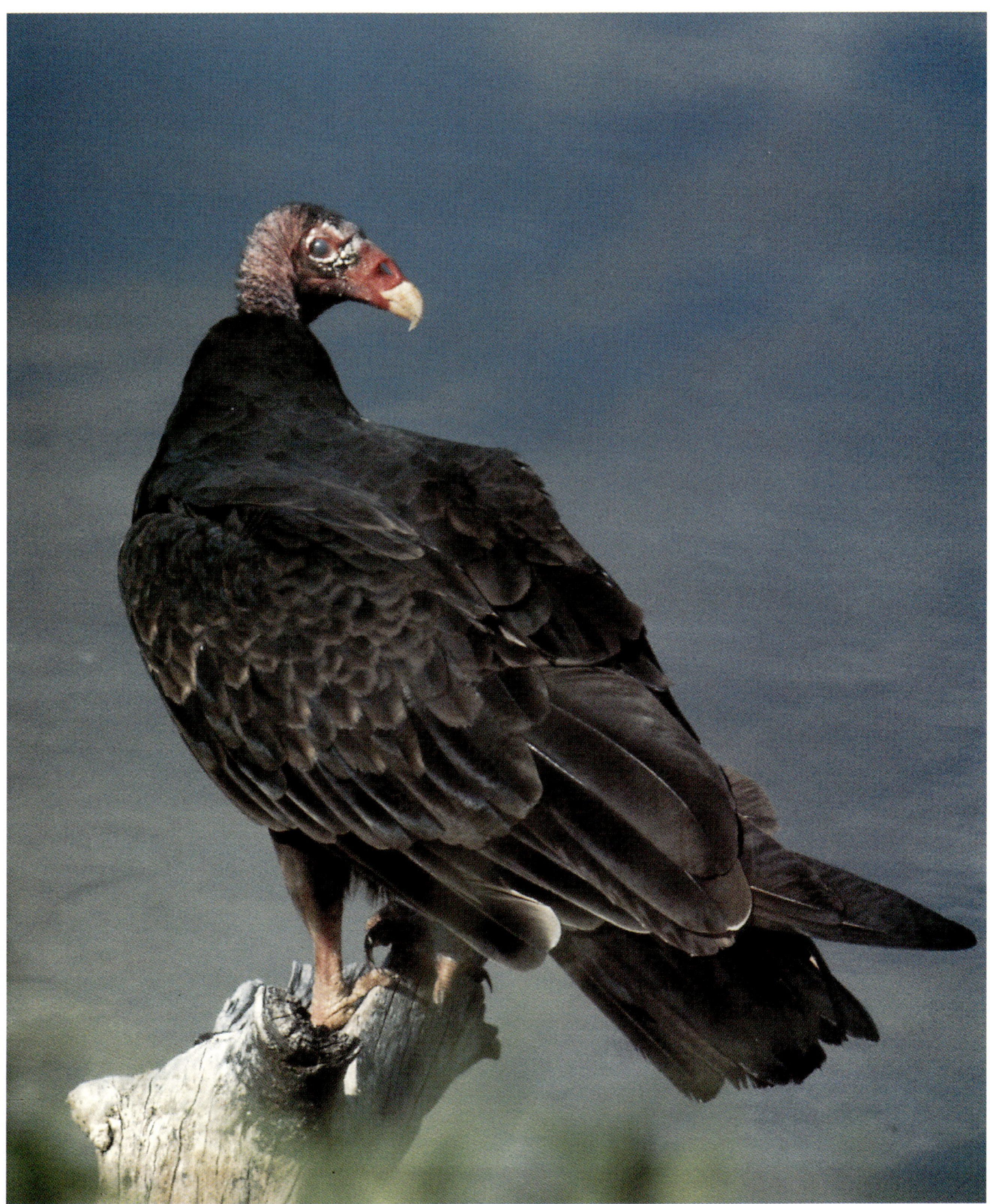

Turkey Vulture

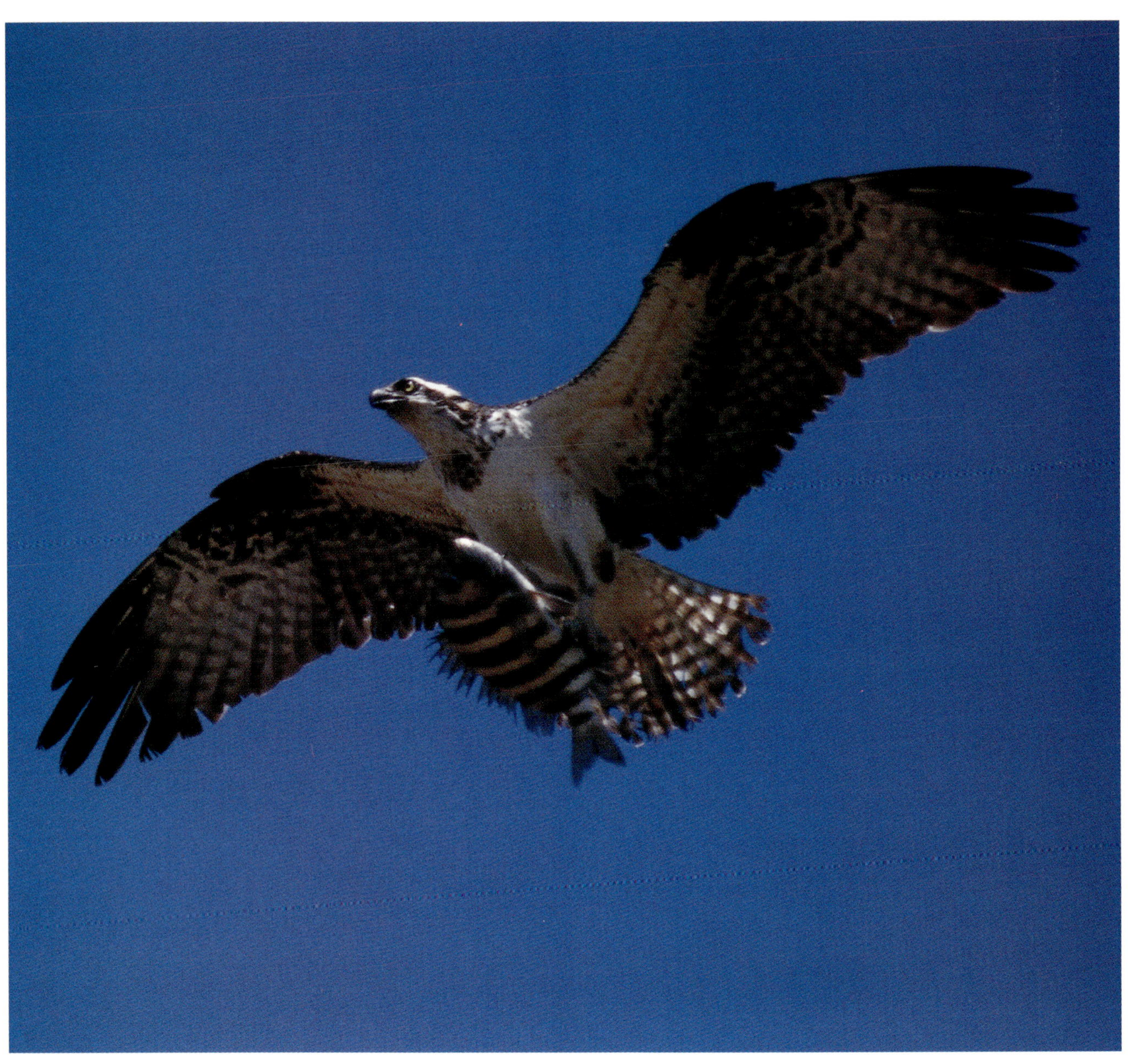

Osprey

The Snowy Egret on the opposite page is fishing on the wing. Dangling its feet in the water, the egret scatters the fish and as they dart about near the surface they are neatly picked off. This sequence of photographs was taken with the Novoflex. It would have been easier with the Nikon N70 and autofocus lens.

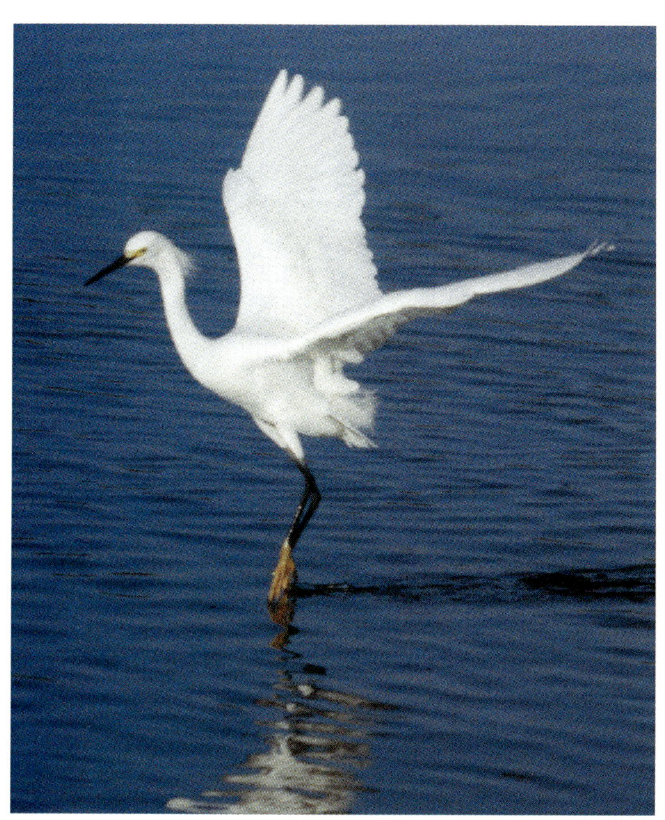

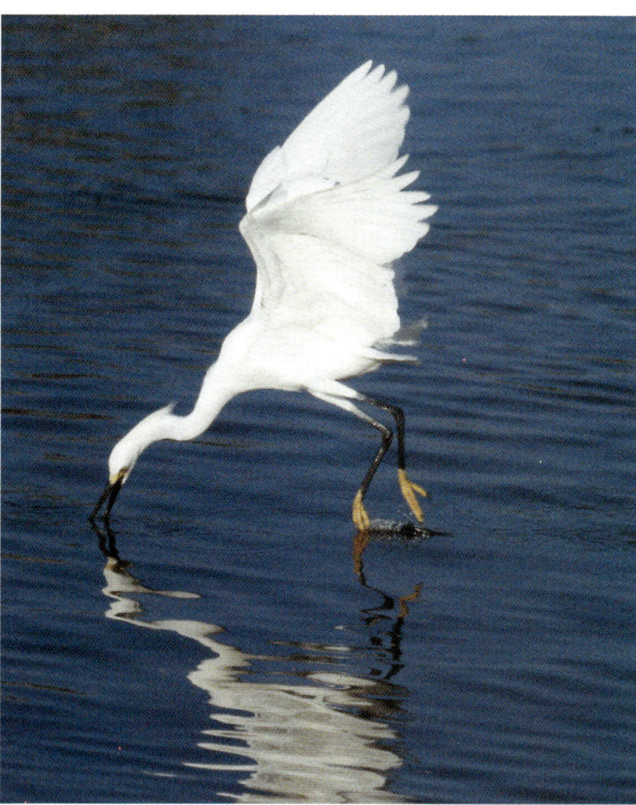

Snowy Egret

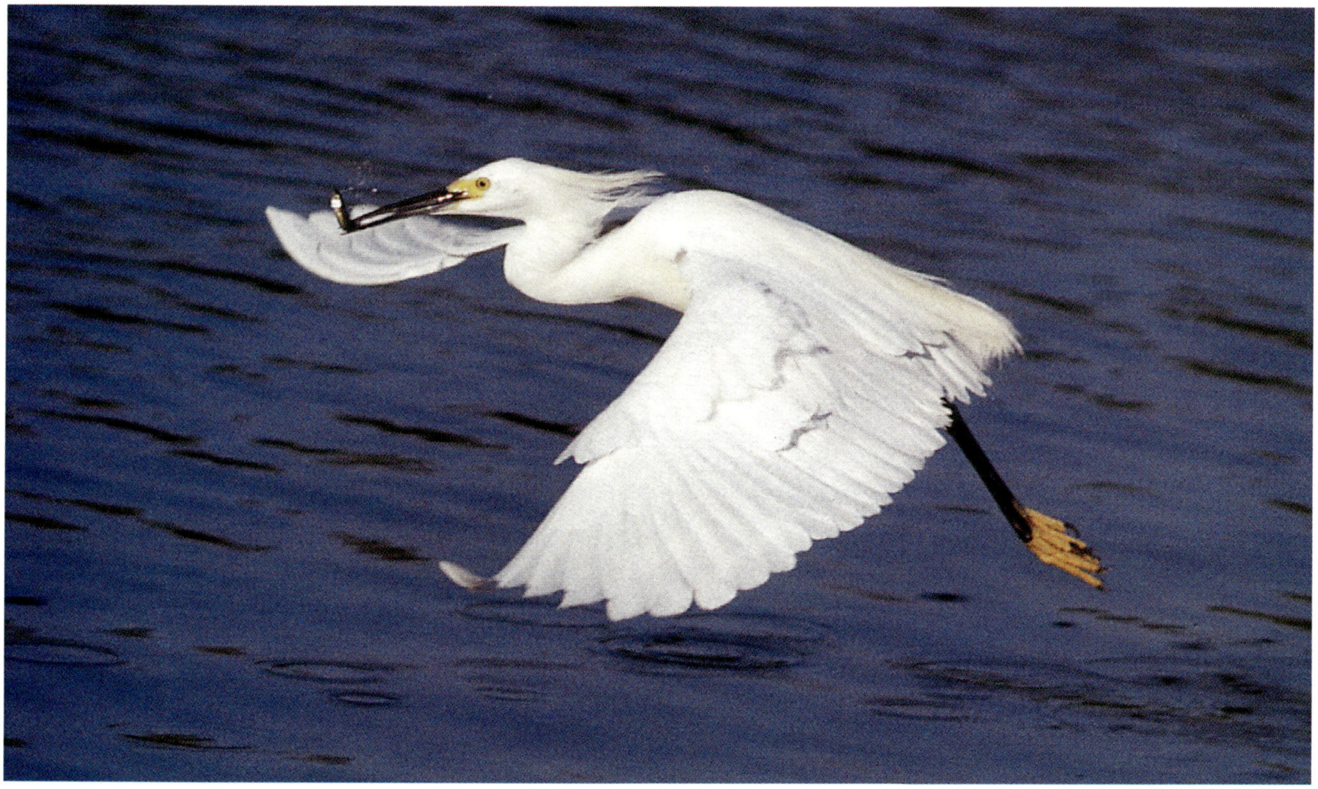

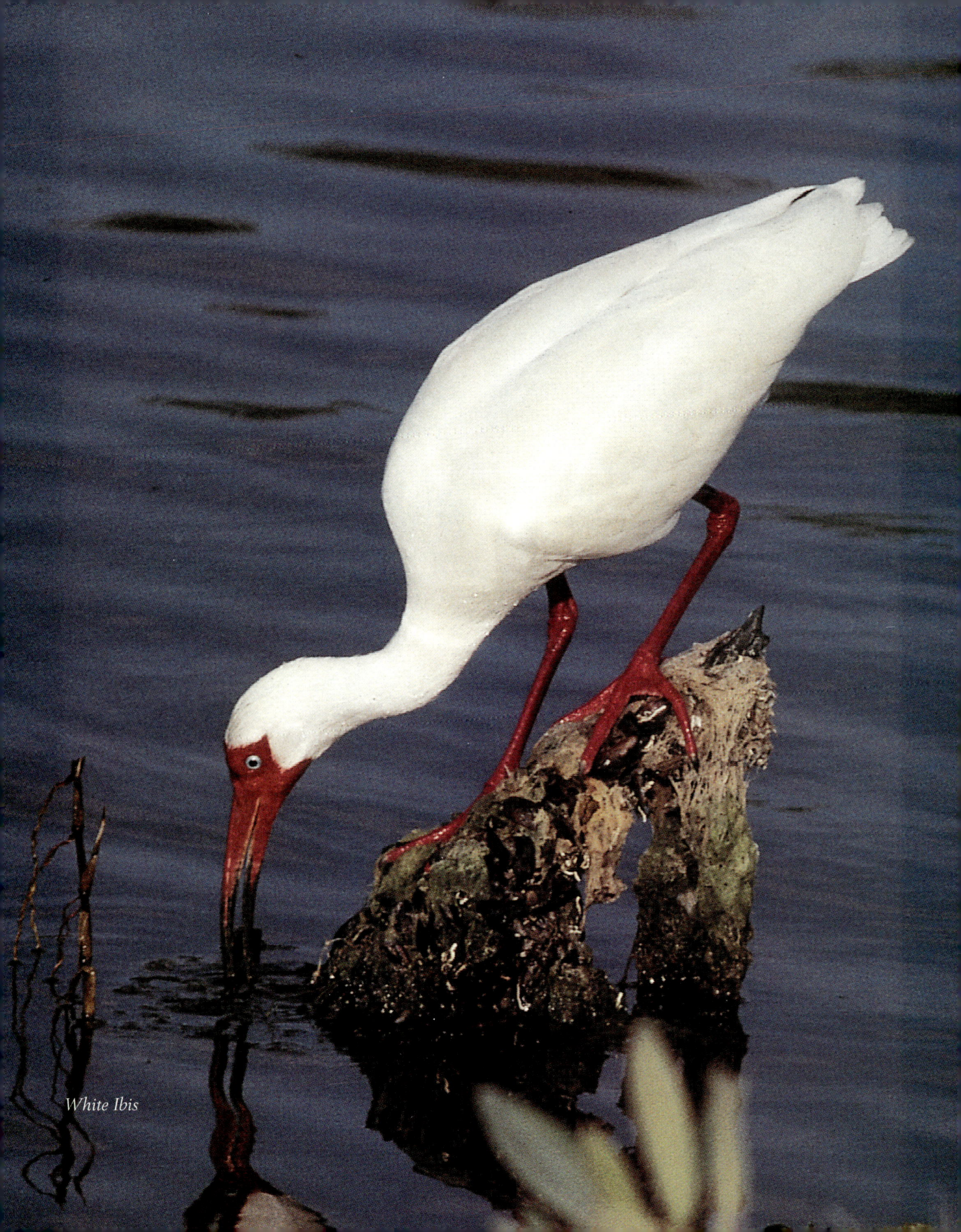

White Ibis

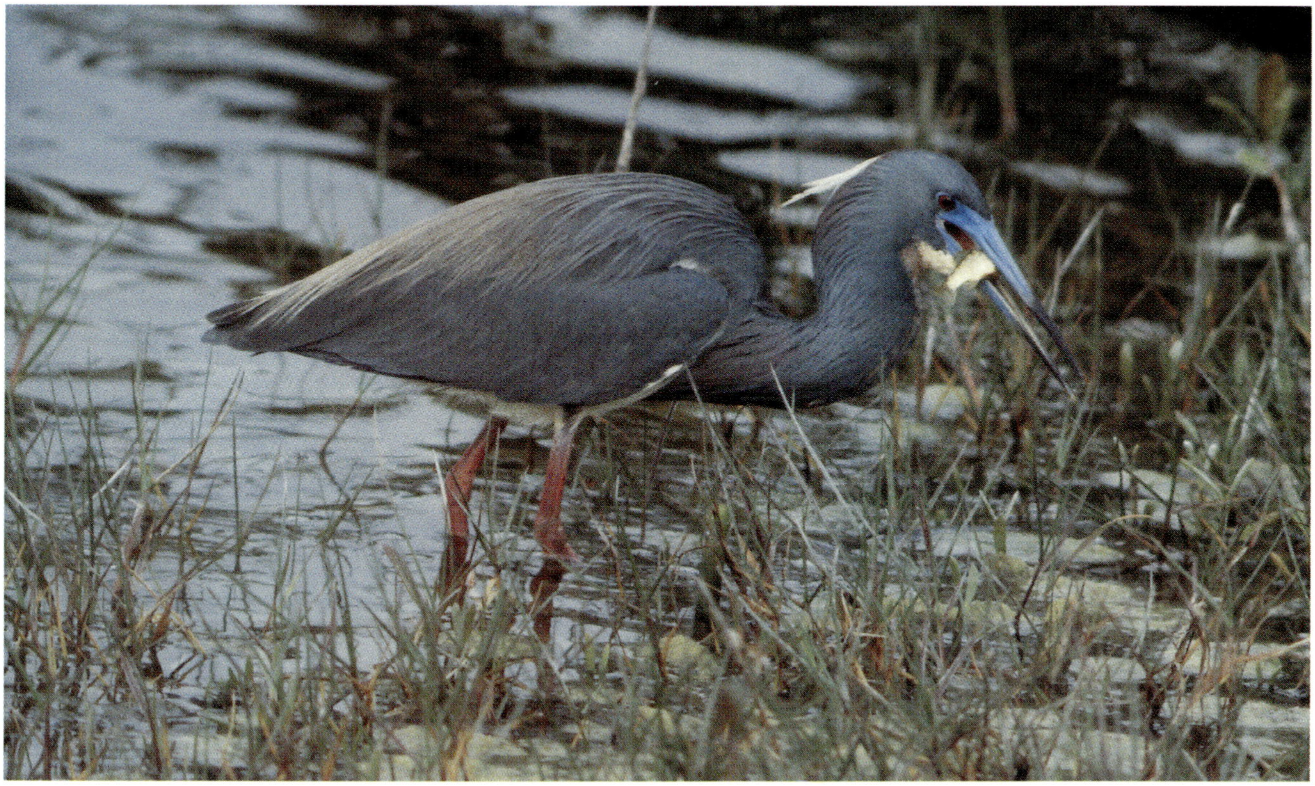

Tricolored Heron

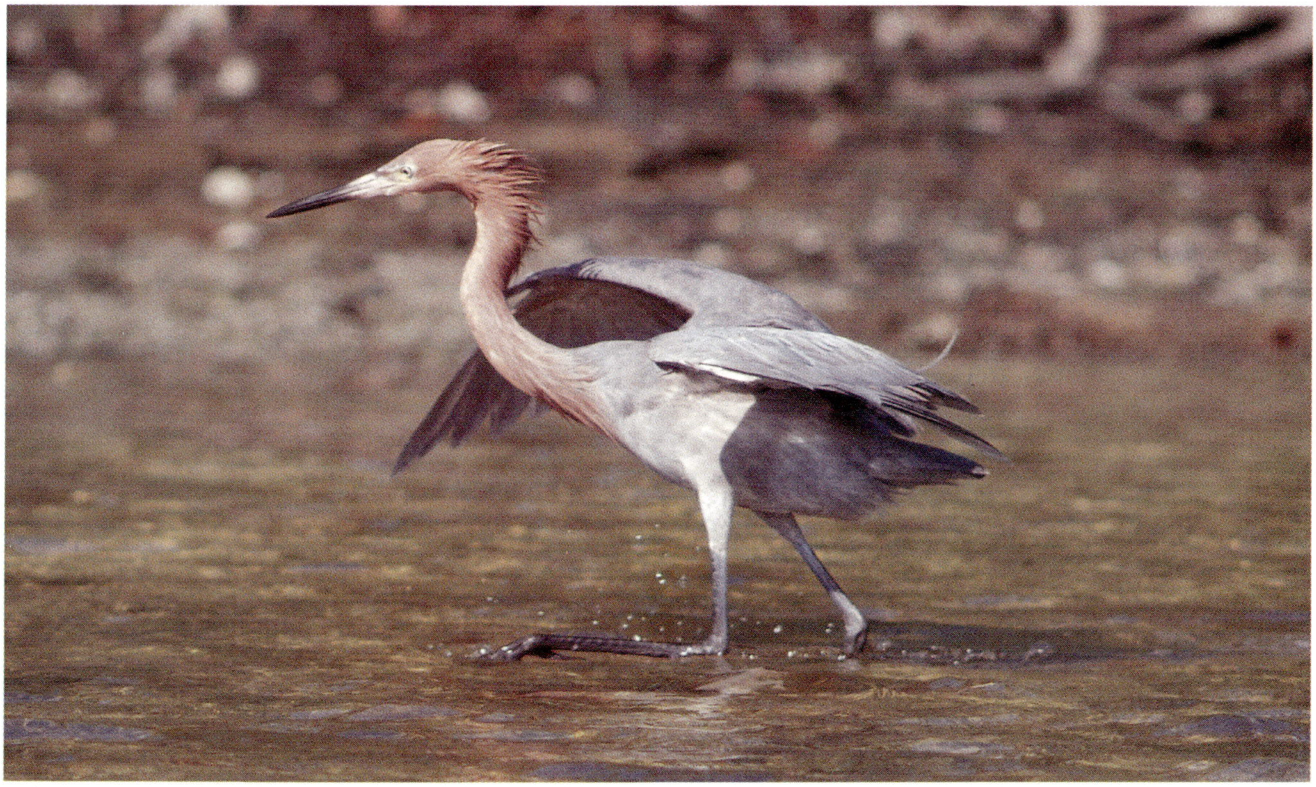

Reddish Egret

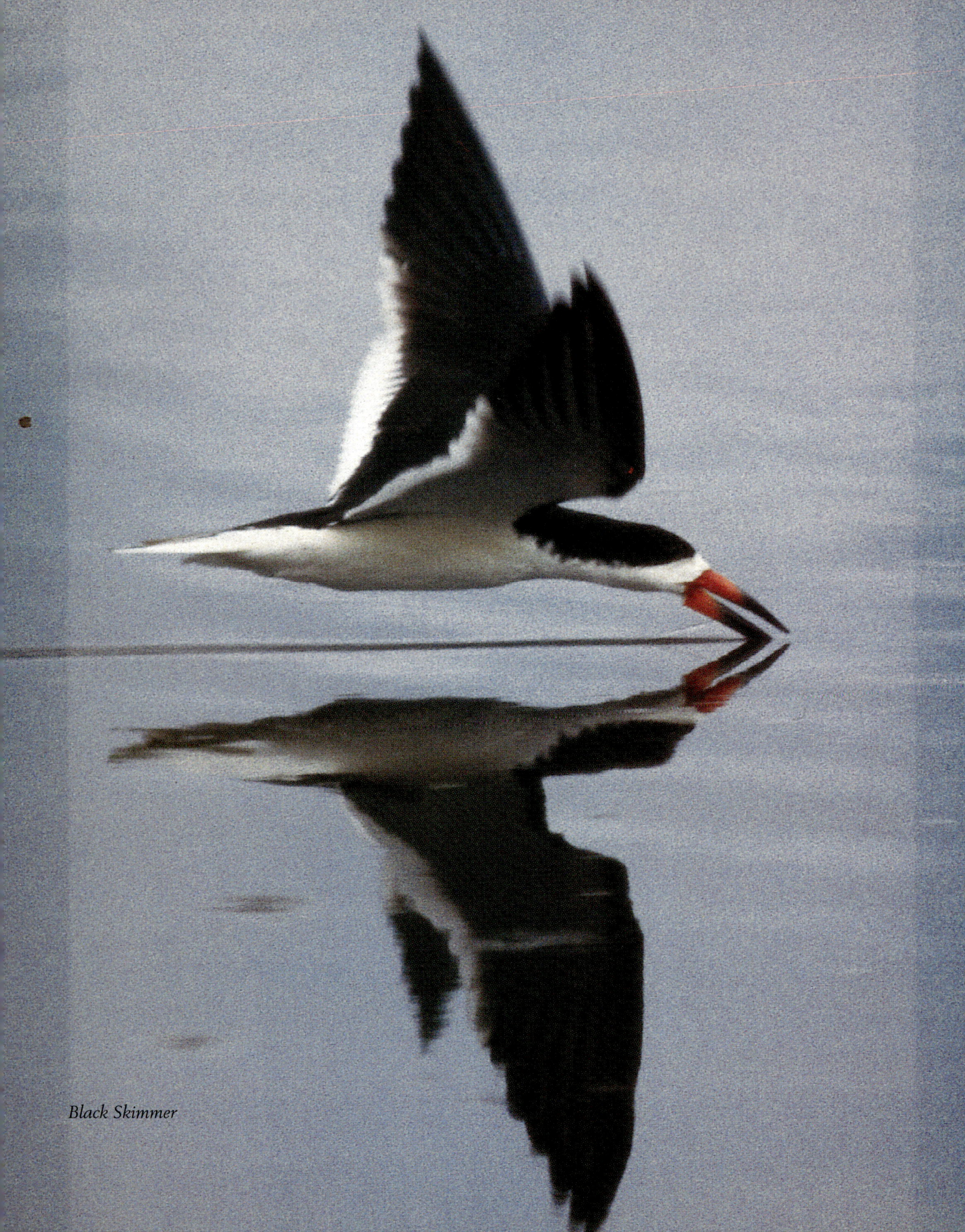

Black Skimmer

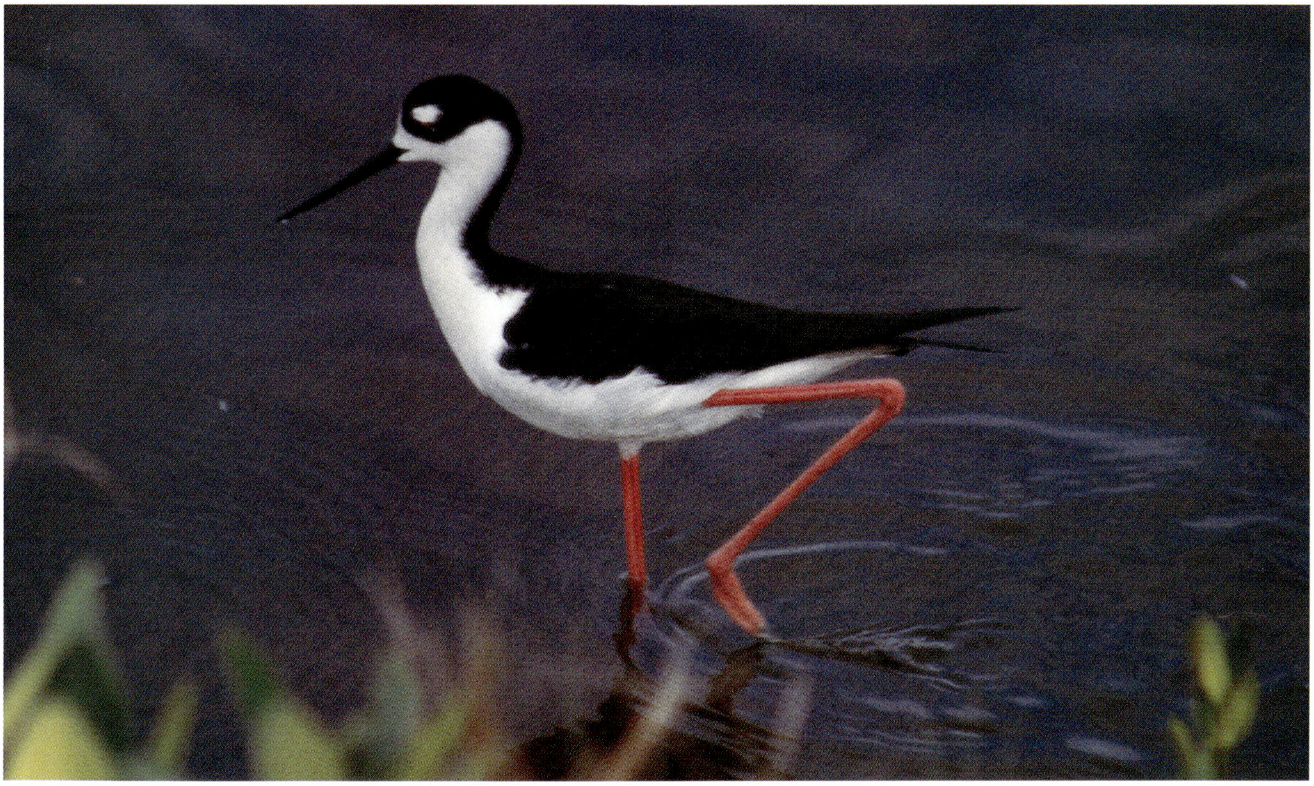

Black-necked Stilt

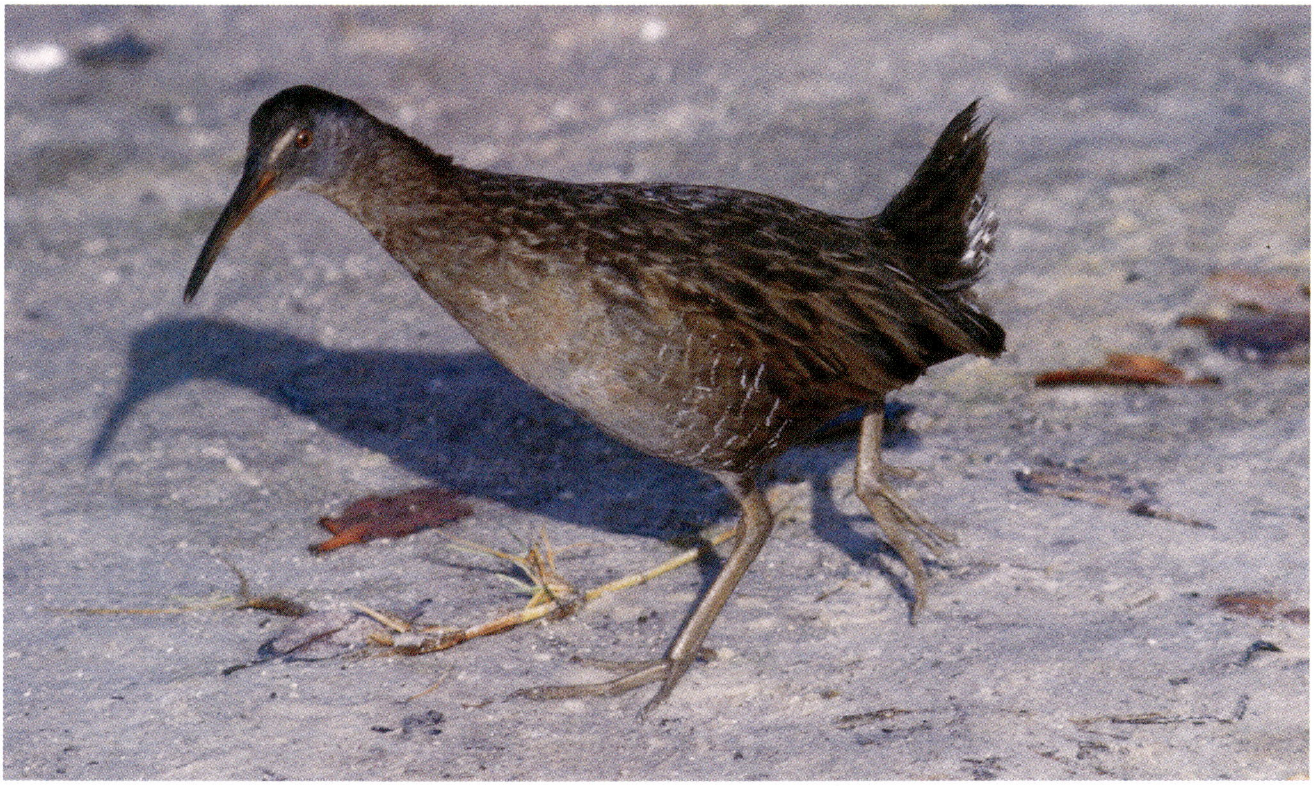

Clapper Rail

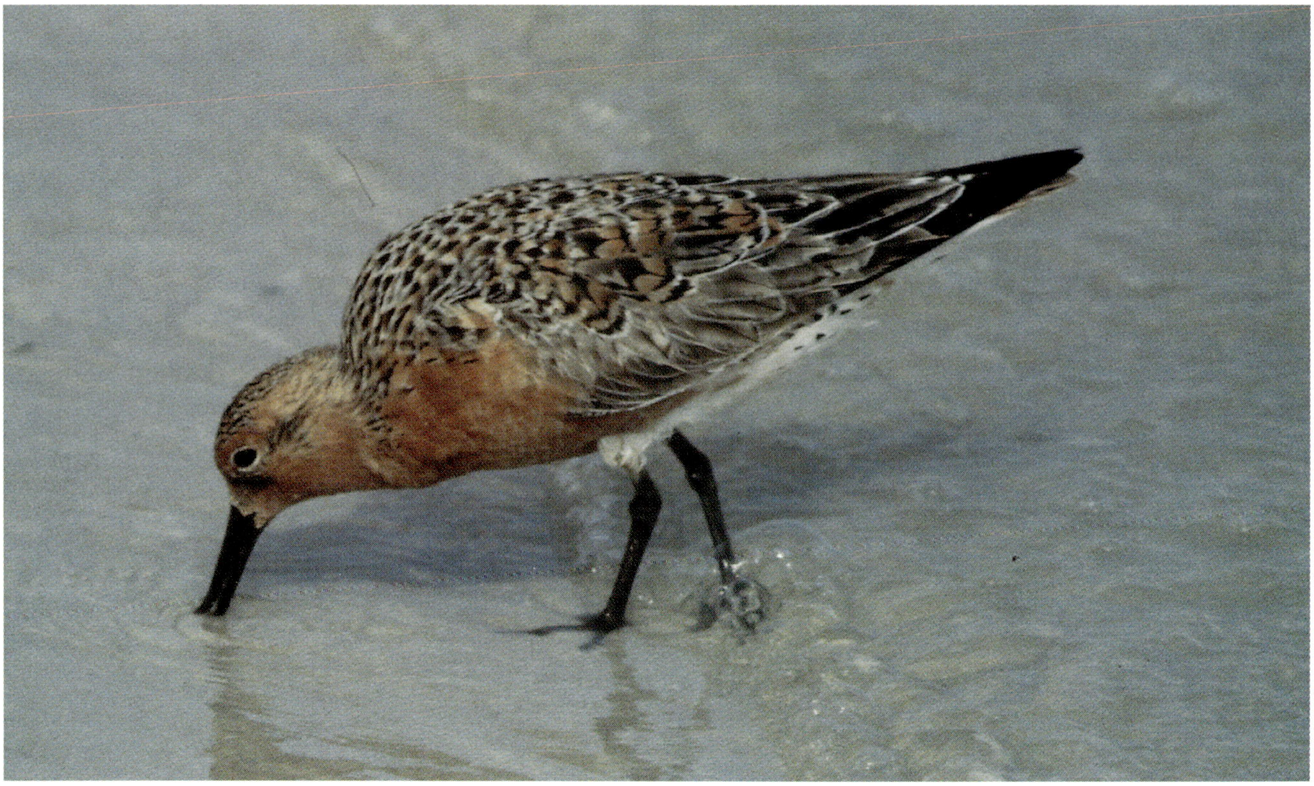

Red Knot

Limpkin

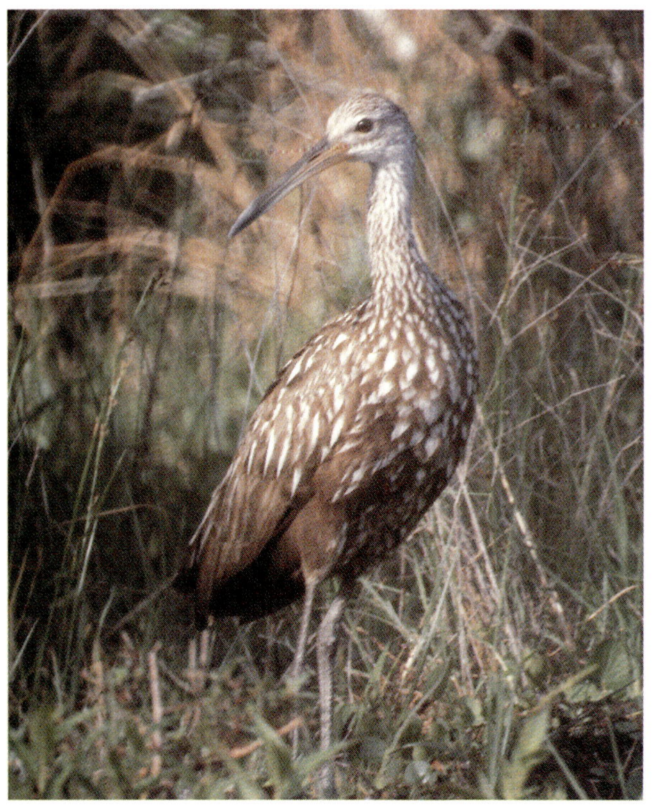

Pileated Woodpecker

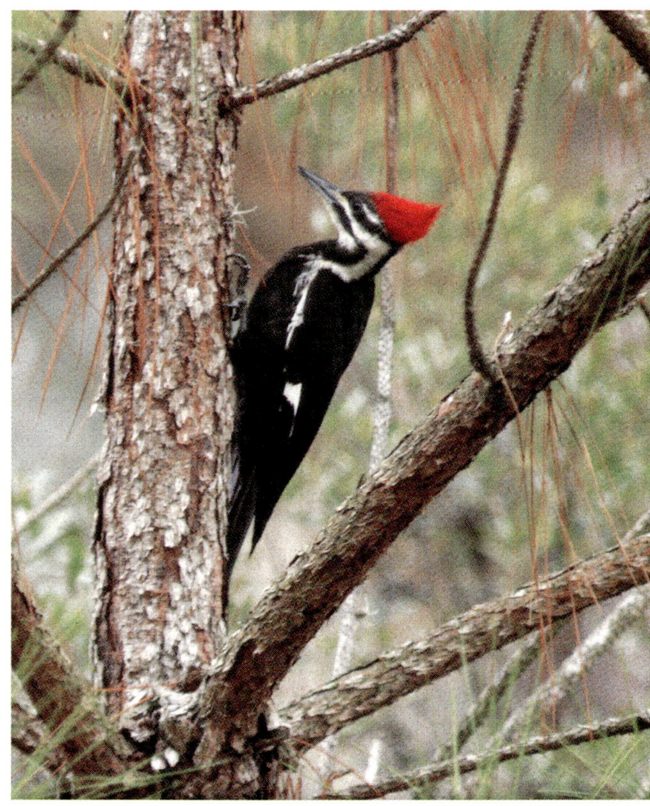

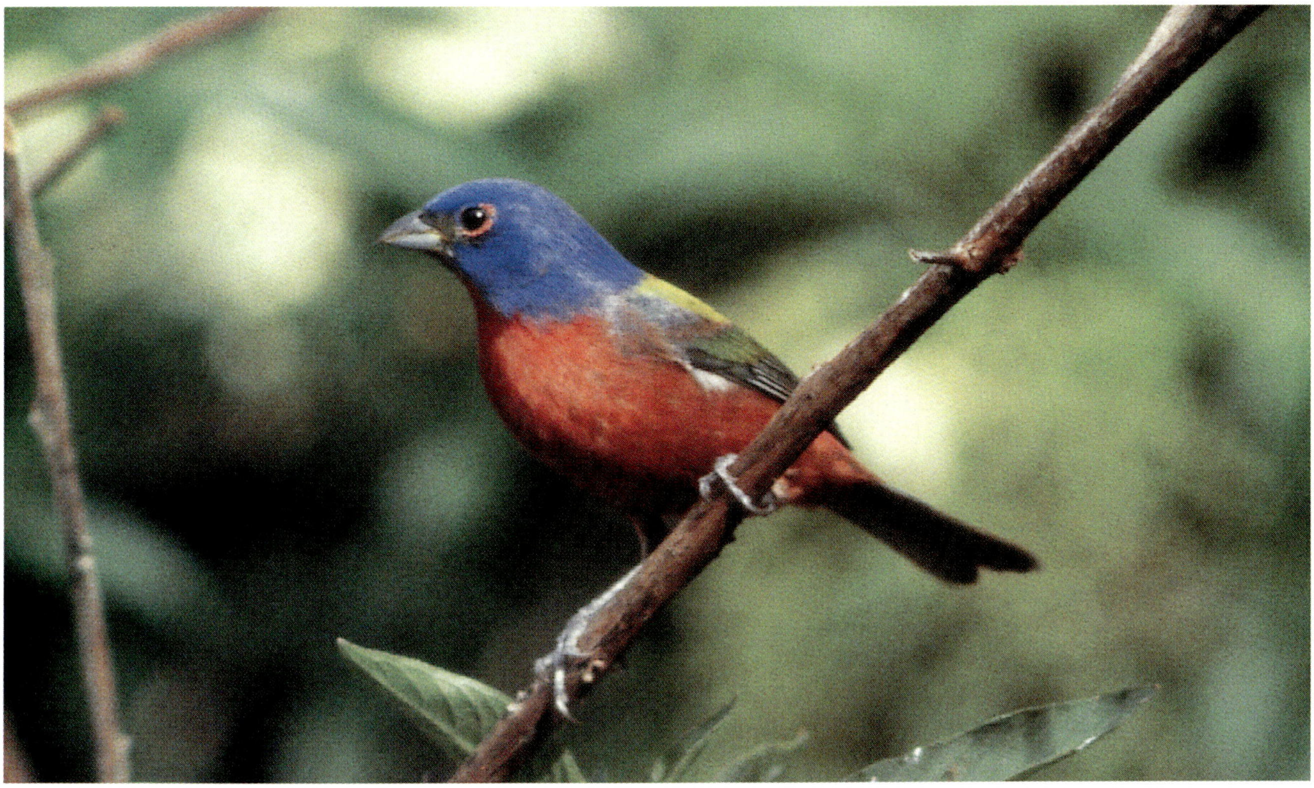

Painted Bunting

Yellow-throated Warbler

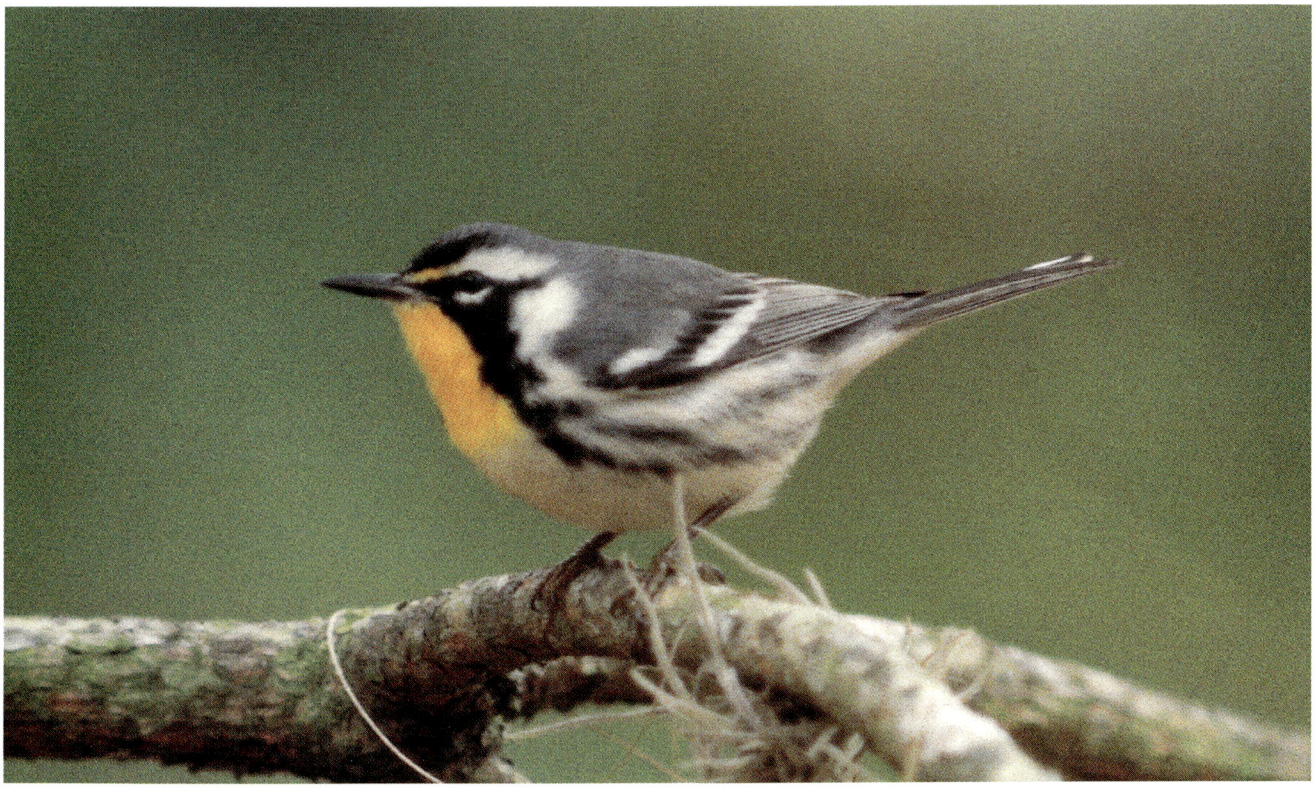

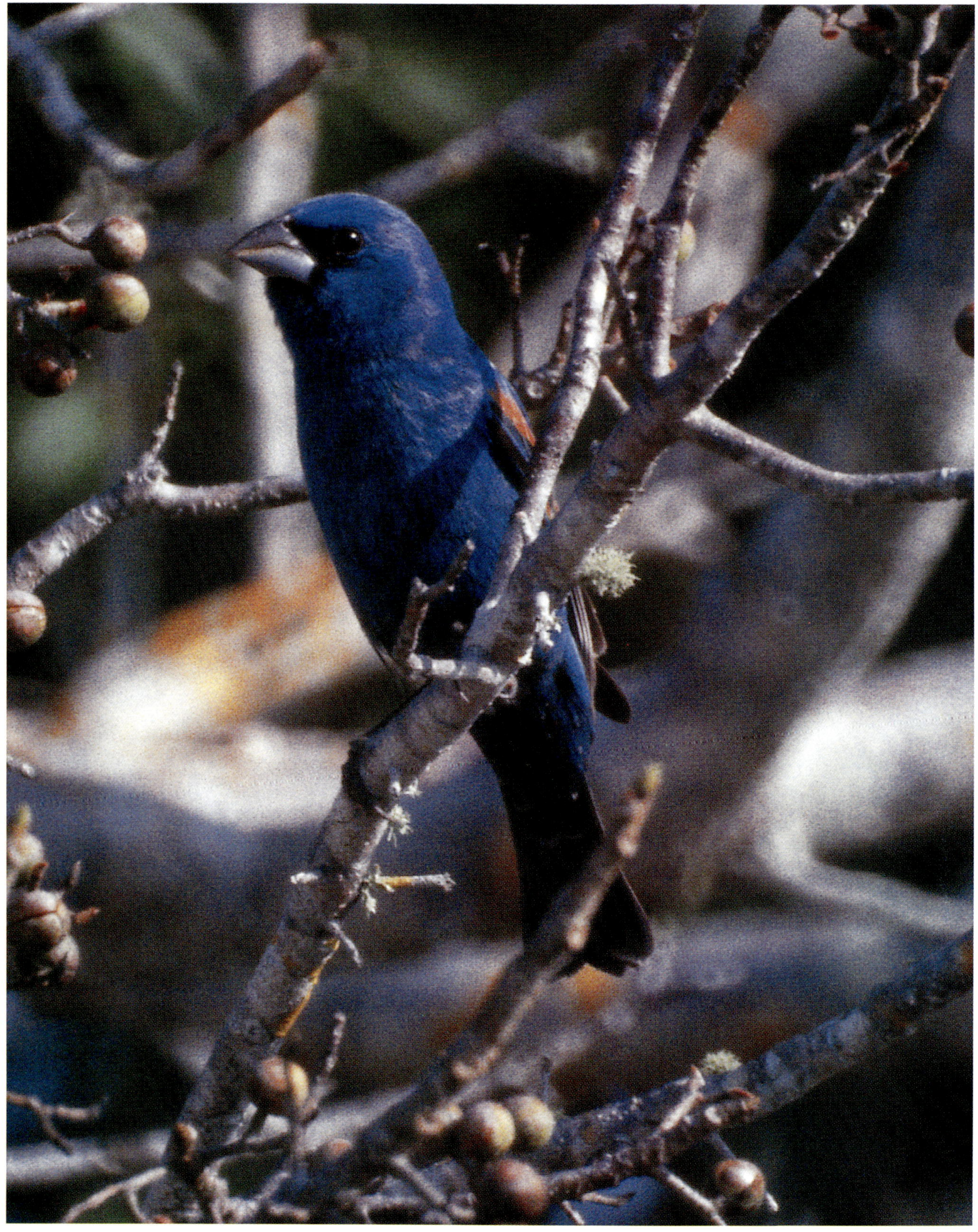

Blue Grosbeak

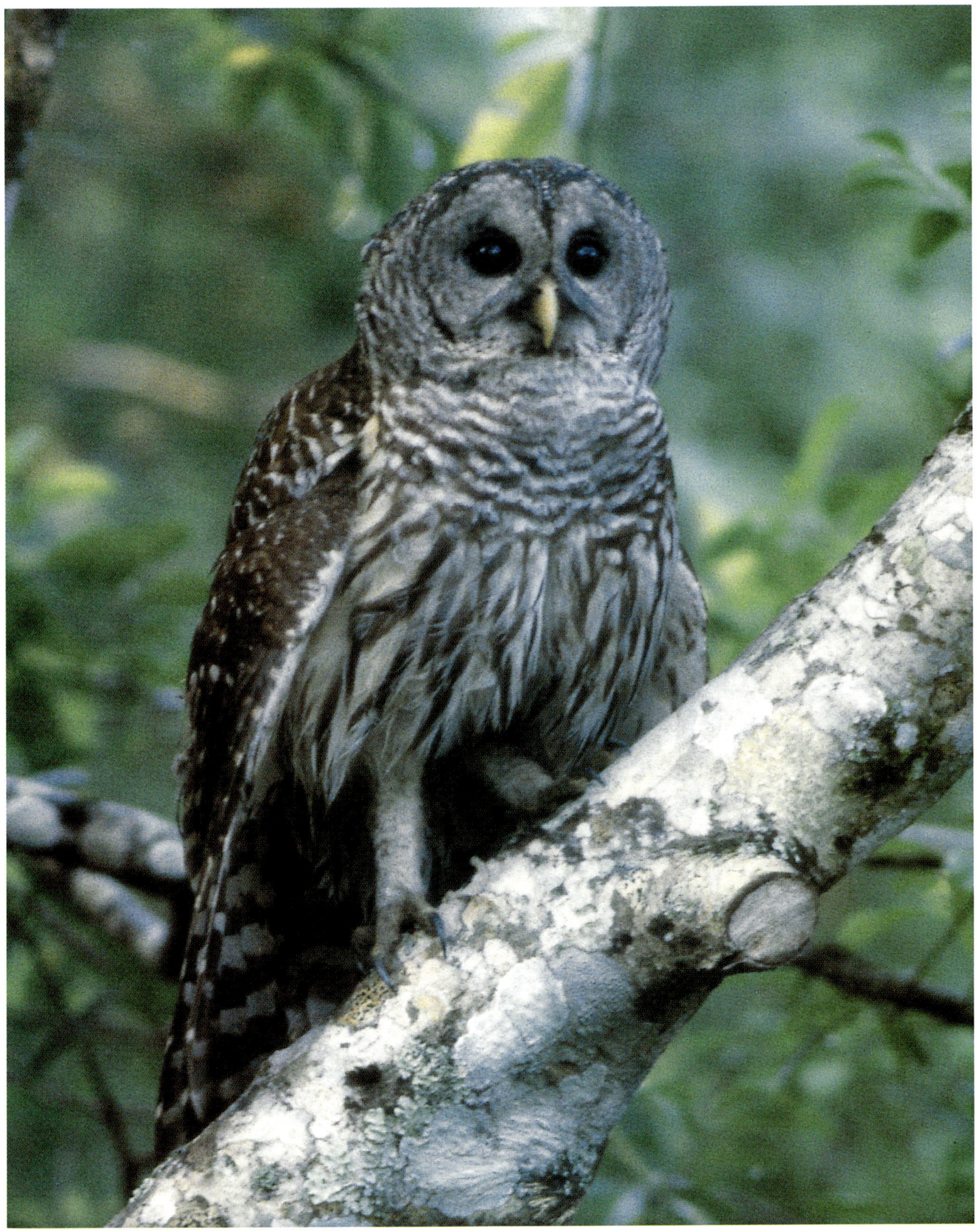

Barred Owl

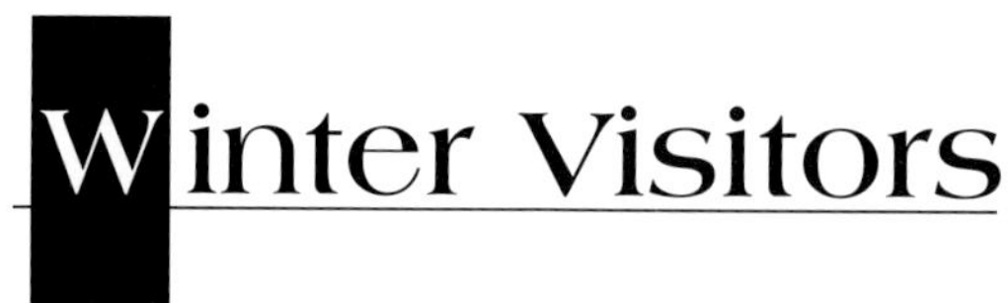

Winter Visitors

In northwest Ohio, when we talk about bird migration, we are generally speaking of birds that come from the south, many from South and Central America, in the spring and return after nesting in the fall. This movement occurs like clockwork with arrival and departure dates predictable within a few days. There is, however, another kind of movement which is far more irregular.

During the fall and winter, we sometimes have visitors from Canada and the far north. Some species will show up quite regularly while others might only be seen every few years. This kind of migration probably has more to do with their local food supply than anything else.

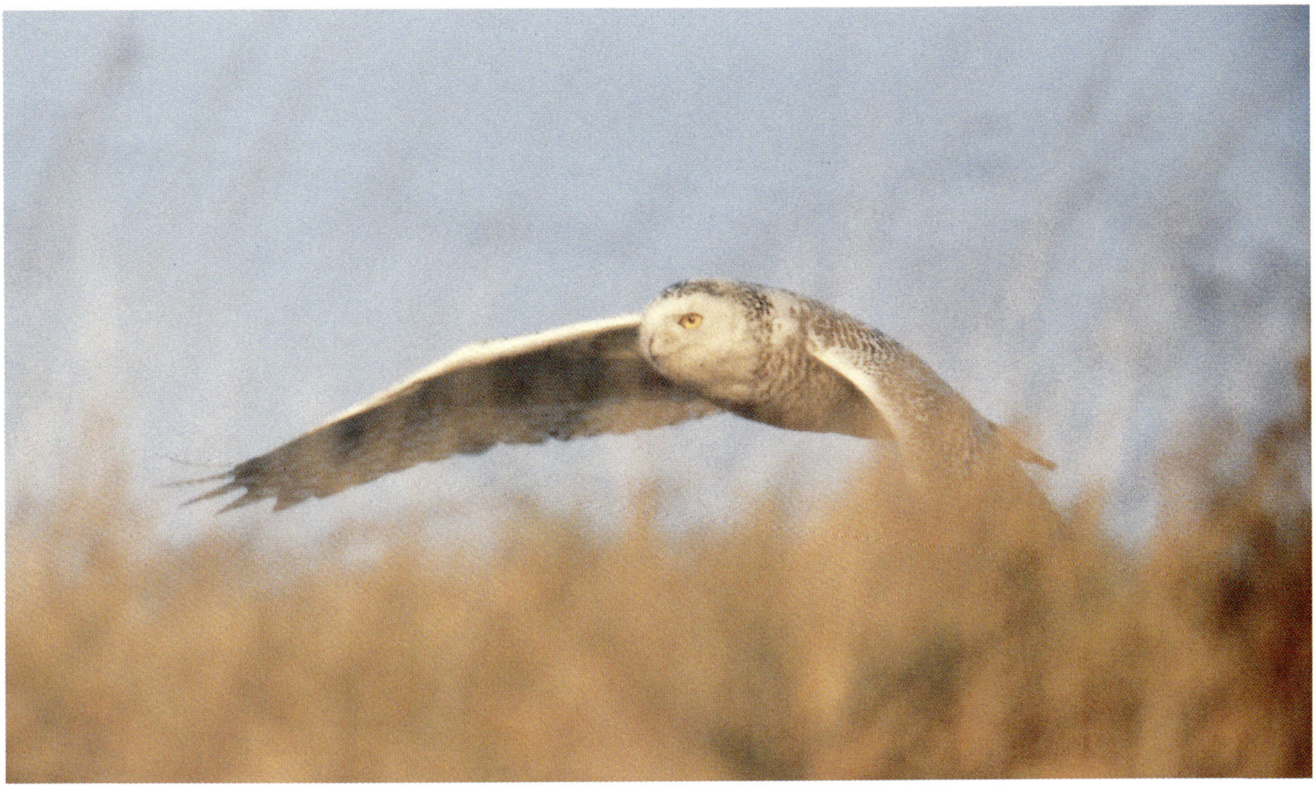

Snowy Owl

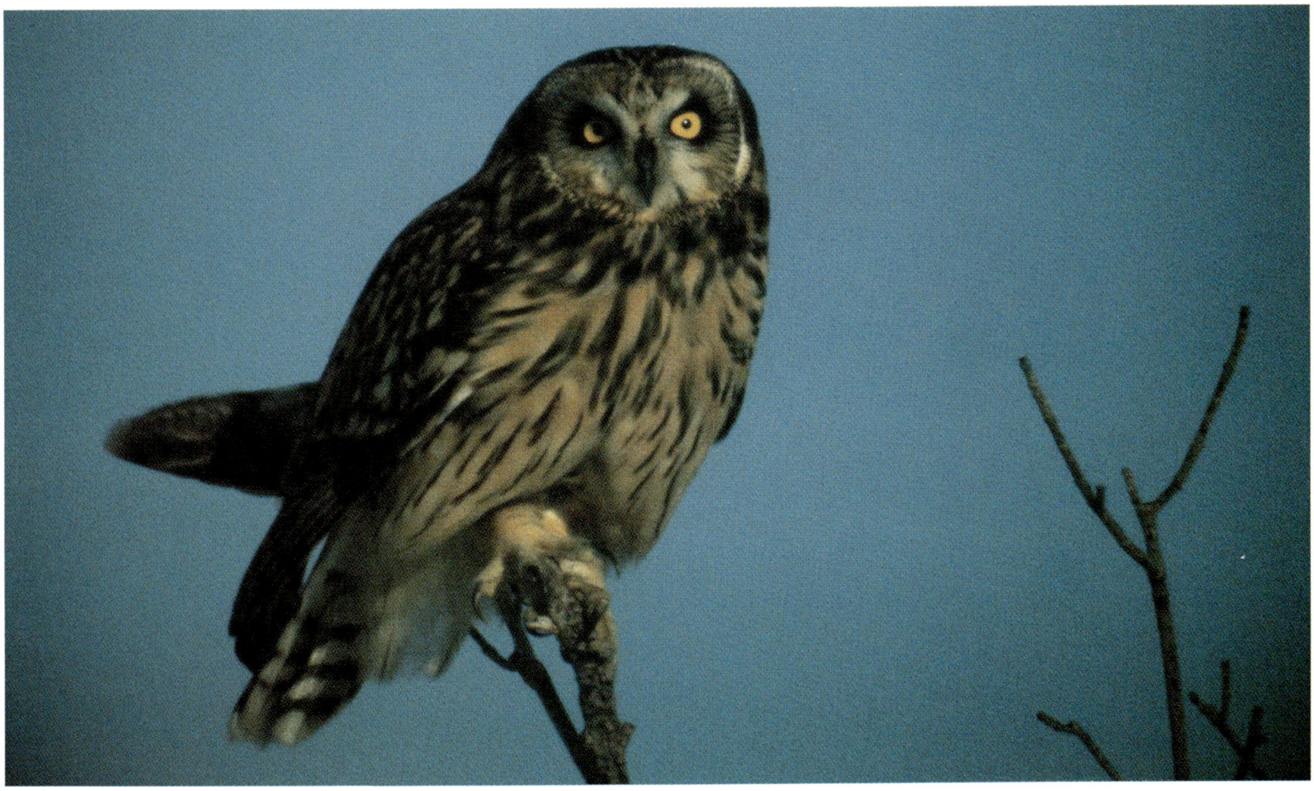

Short-eared Owl

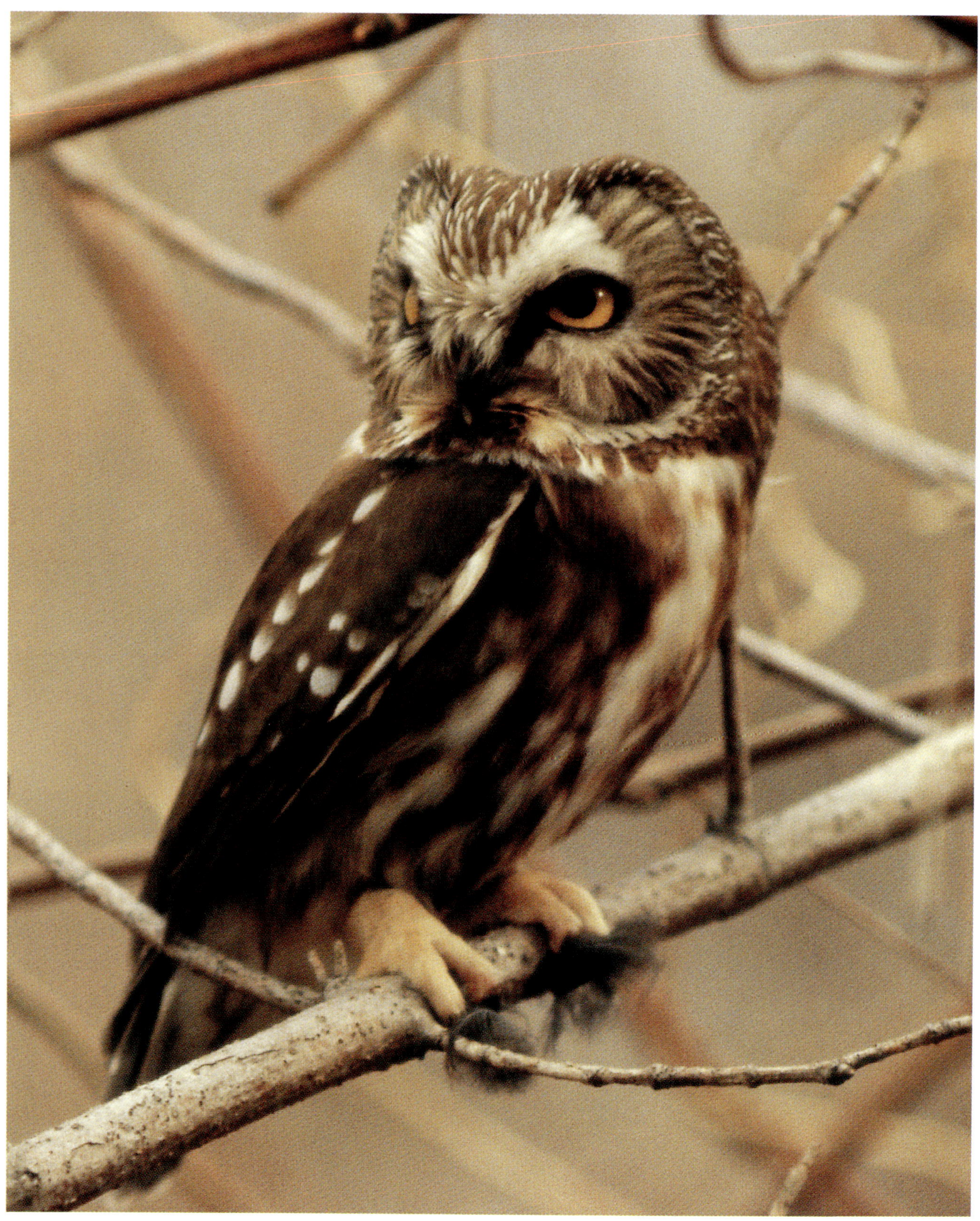

Northern Saw-whet Owl

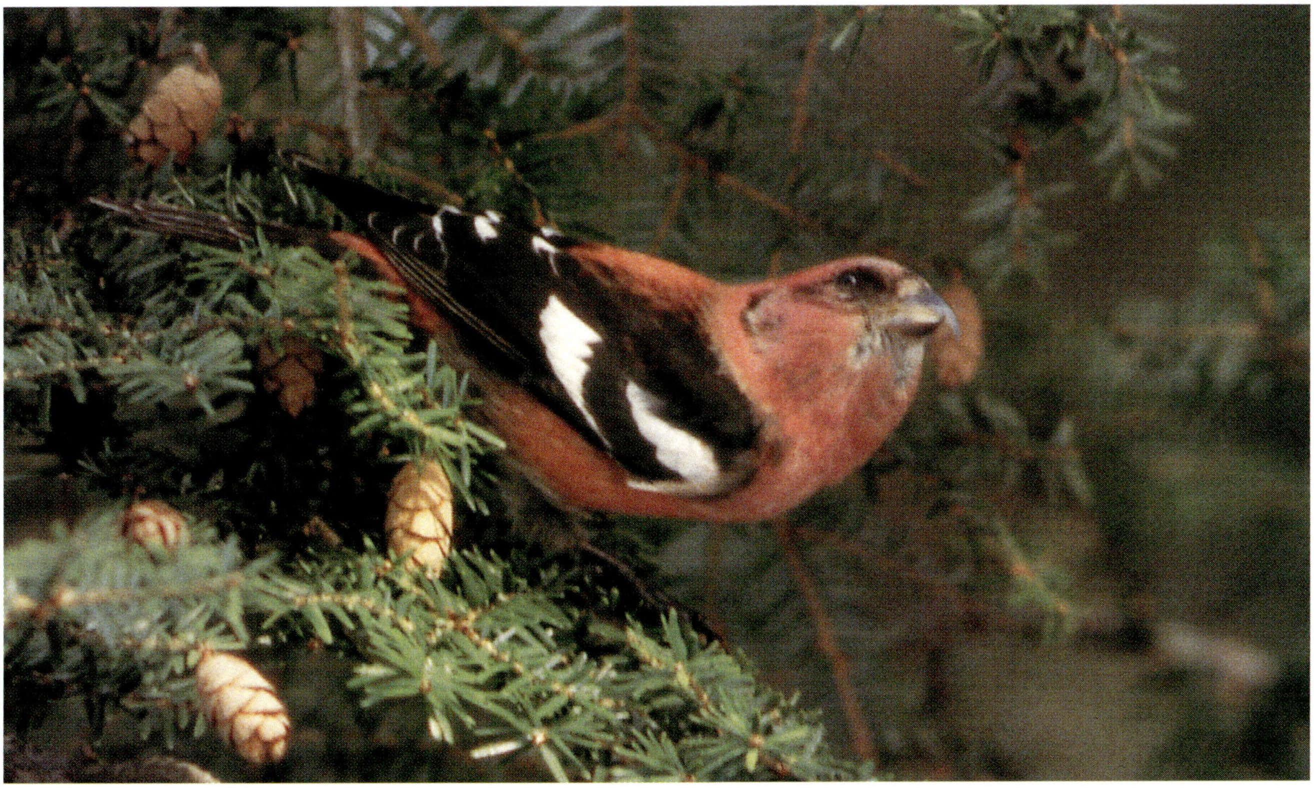

White-winged Crossbill

Evening Grosbeak

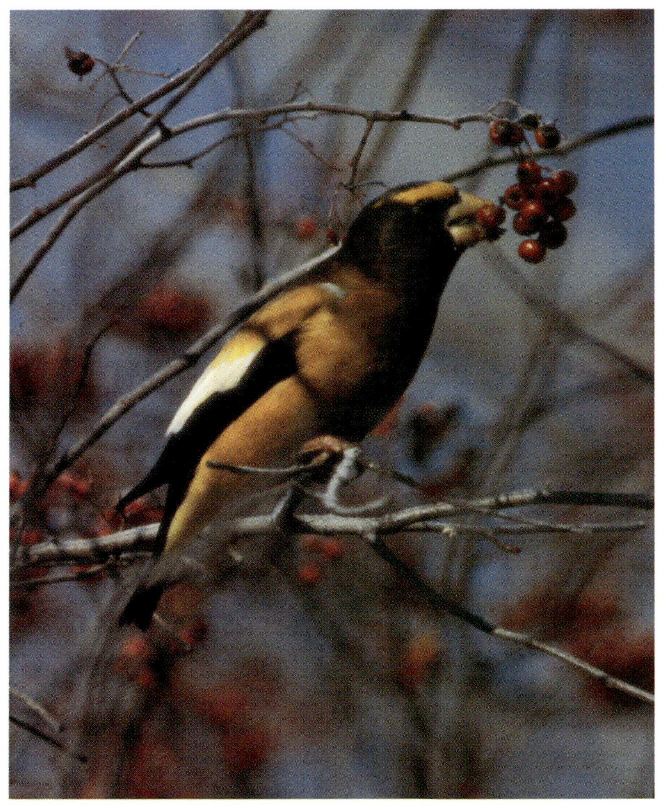

Common Redpoll

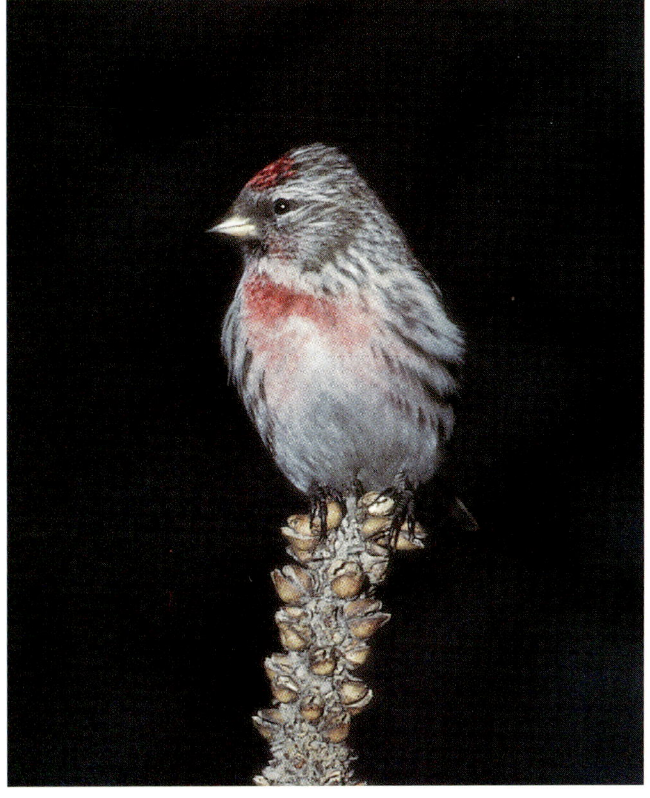

Screech-Owl Encounter

Cardinal rule number 1 (*page 9*) is Keep it simple. But what good is a rule if it can't be broken once in awhile?

In June of 1980, I discovered an Eastern Screech-Owl nest about twenty feet off the ground in a hollow oak tree. After observing it for a couple of hours one night, I decided to try to get some shots of the owls in flight as they approached the nest. I located a piece of equipment that was designed to count items passing by on a conveyor. It projected a black light beam to a reflector, and whenever the beam was interrupted it tripped a switch which activated a counter.

I recognized that with a few modifications, I could get the device to trigger my camera and flash, so I bought it. I installed it on a bracket a few feet below the nest hole and about 18 inches from the tree, with the light beam aimed vertically at the reflector which was positioned above the nest entrance. The circuitry was equipped with a time delay switch which would allow the device to be triggered only at intervals longer than a preset time span. This would prevent triggering the camera if the owl left the nest before the set time limit.

I had completed installation and testing of the apparatus (with considerable difficulty, I might add). I was standing near the top of a twenty-foot ladder trying to install the camera and flash in a tree, about ten feet from the nest tree. Suddenly I got a sharp blow on the head.

A screech-owl bounced off my head and landed on a nearby branch where it sat glowering at me. I managed to get a picture (*page 98*) before it took off and gave me another good rap. Fortunately, it had its talons closed both times. I decided it was time to get to the ground as quickly as I could before the owl got even more serious.

After giving the situation some thought, I went home and got my hard hat—resolved to give it another try. I went back up on the ladder and finished installing the camera and flash. The entire time I was up there, I was bombarded by the owl. It must have ricocheted off my hat at least a half dozen times. When everything was completed and tested, I stowed the ladder and returned at about dusk to turn on the power and wait to see what happened.

Soon one of the owls flew up and perched at the nest-hole, giving me an opportunity to trigger a couple of shots by hand. (*page 99*) It was a moonless night, and in the deep woods it soon became so dark I could barely see anything except the occasional flash of my equipment as an owl passed through the light beam. With everything apparently working as planned, I went home and went to bed.

Early the next morning I returned to find the entire 36 exposure roll had been taken. I could hardly wait to get it developed. As soon as I got the slides back I could see that, even though I had some great shots, the light beam was too close to the tree. I found there was a delay of about one tenth of a second between the moment the owl broke the beam and the exposure was made. By that time, the owl's head was often already in the nest hole!

I repositioned the light beam to about three feet from the nest entrance to catch the owl a little sooner and set things up for another night of picture taking. Once again, when I returned the next morning, the entire roll was exposed. This time, almost every shot was good. The pictures on page 102 are from the first roll and those on pages 100 and 101 are from the second.

These shots were obtained with a little more effort than was my custom, but I'm glad I broke my rule (Keep it simple.) at least this one time. The whole experience is one I'll never forget, and it only increases my awe of the amazing things that go on all around us in nature; things that we seldom have a chance to see, or that we see and don't notice.

The owls were hunting in what to us would have been considered almost complete darkness, yet every few minutes they would return to the nest with a wide variety of prey. On each trip, the owl flew through a dark dense woods, missing all the trees and branches and approached the nest hole with such speed and accuracy that it often covered the last 18 inches and had its head in the hole in the one tenth of a second between the time the light beam was broken and the exposure was made. They brought birds, small mammals, what appeared to be a crayfish, and several kinds of insects. Note the bottom picture on page 102. It looks like the owl has a tomato worm. If you have ever tried to find a green tomato worm on a tomato plant in broad daylight, you should begin to appreciate what amazing night vision these creatures possess.

In addition to acute night vision, owls rely on stealth in capturing prey. Their flight feathers have very soft edges which enable them to fly in almost total silence. When the owl attacked me on the ladder, I was taken by complete surprise. I heard absolutely nothing before it hit me the first time. Subsequently, even when I could see it coming I could barely hear a sound.

Nature is awesome!

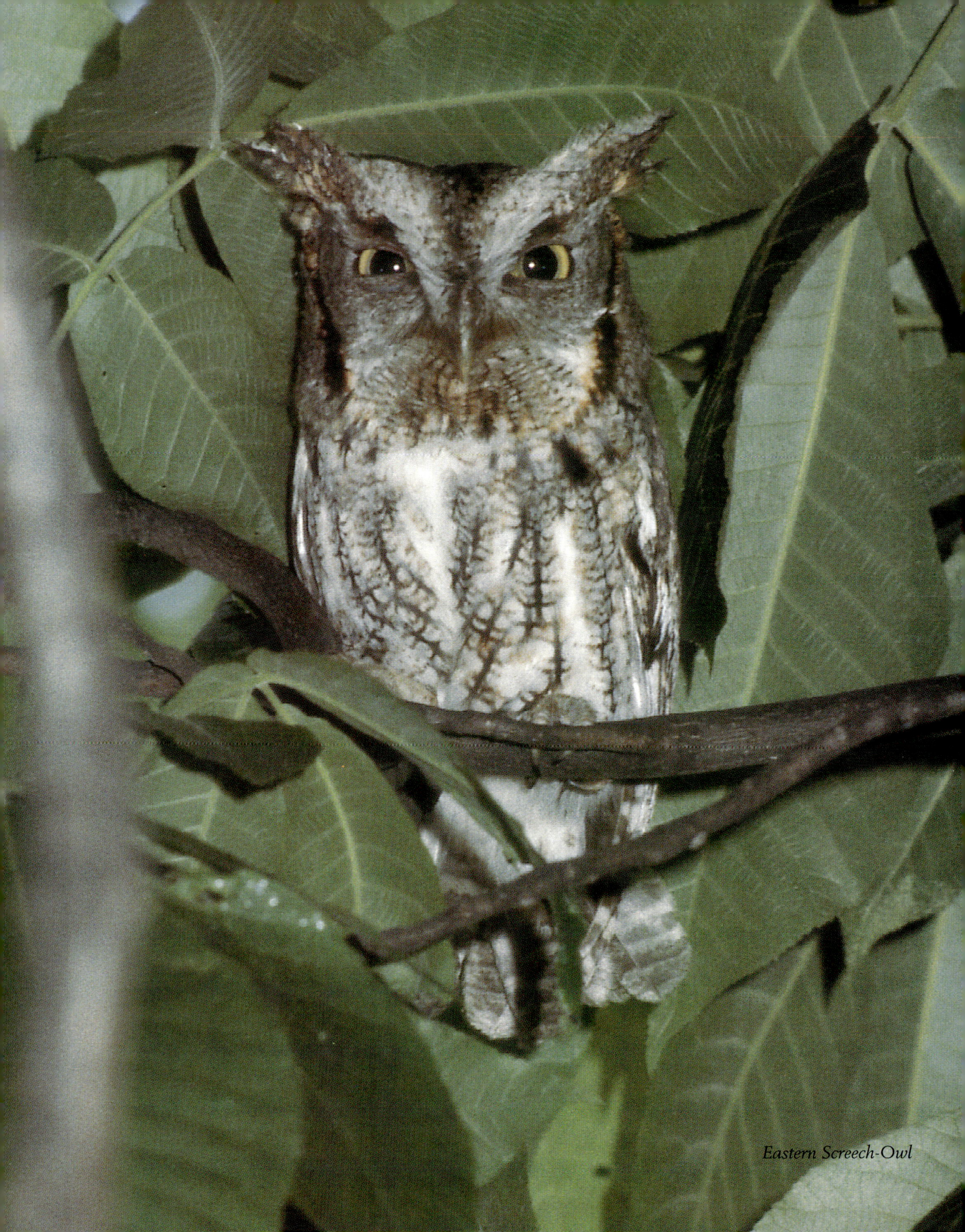

Eastern Screech-Owl

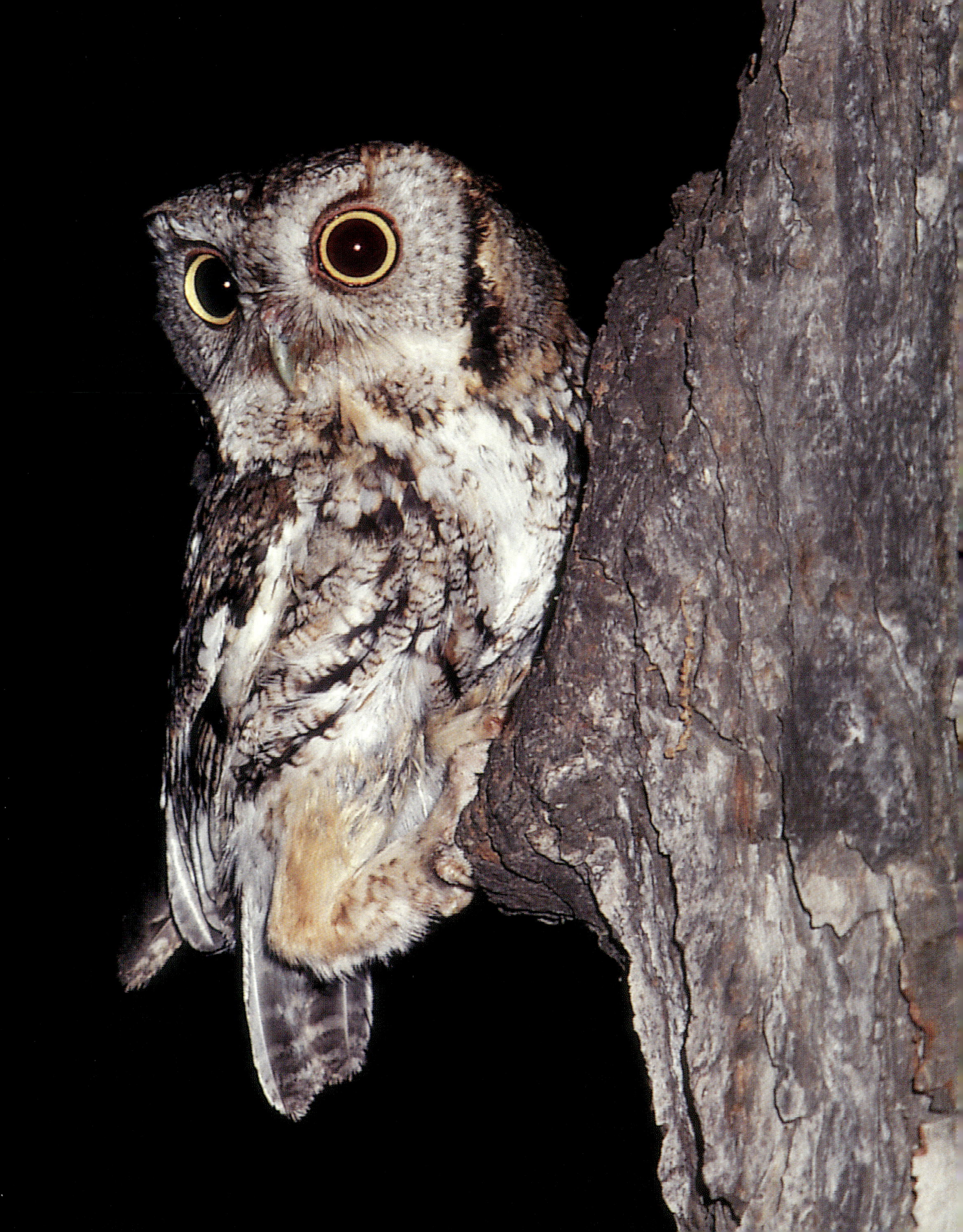

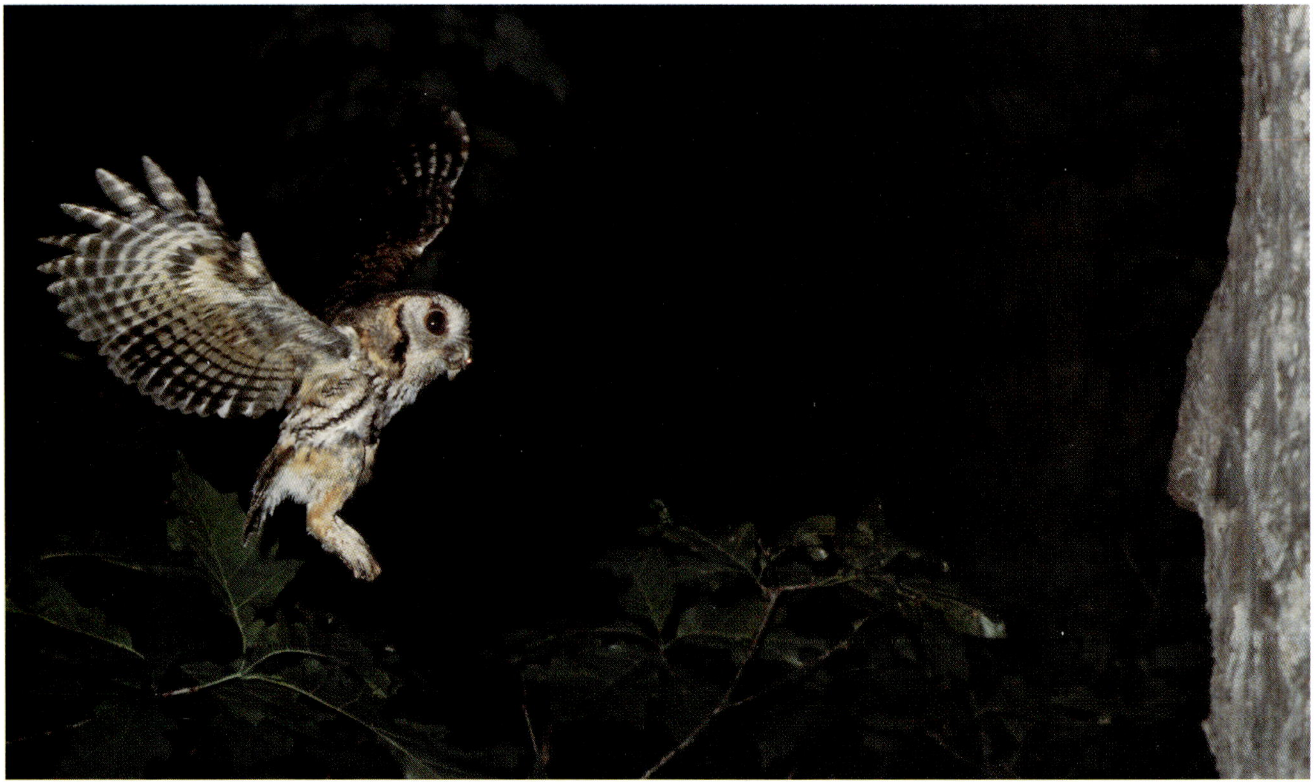

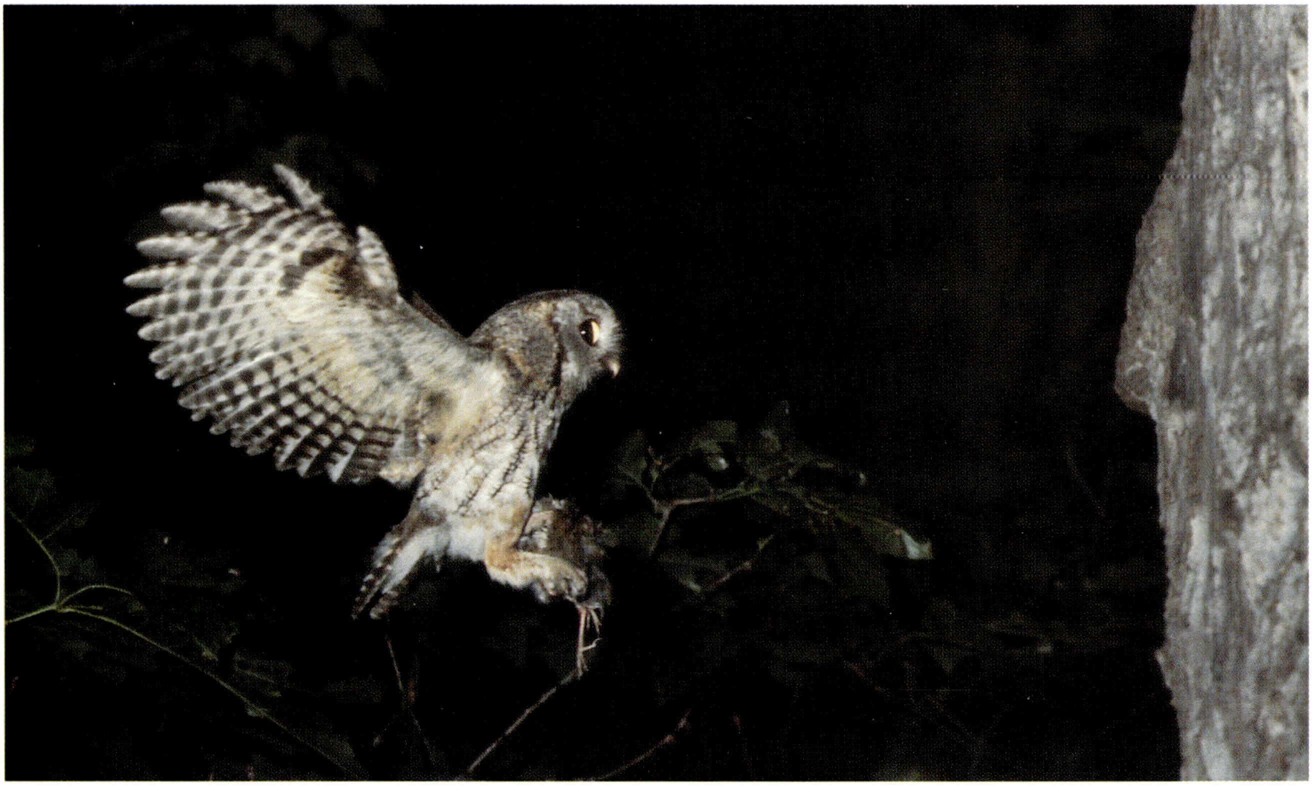

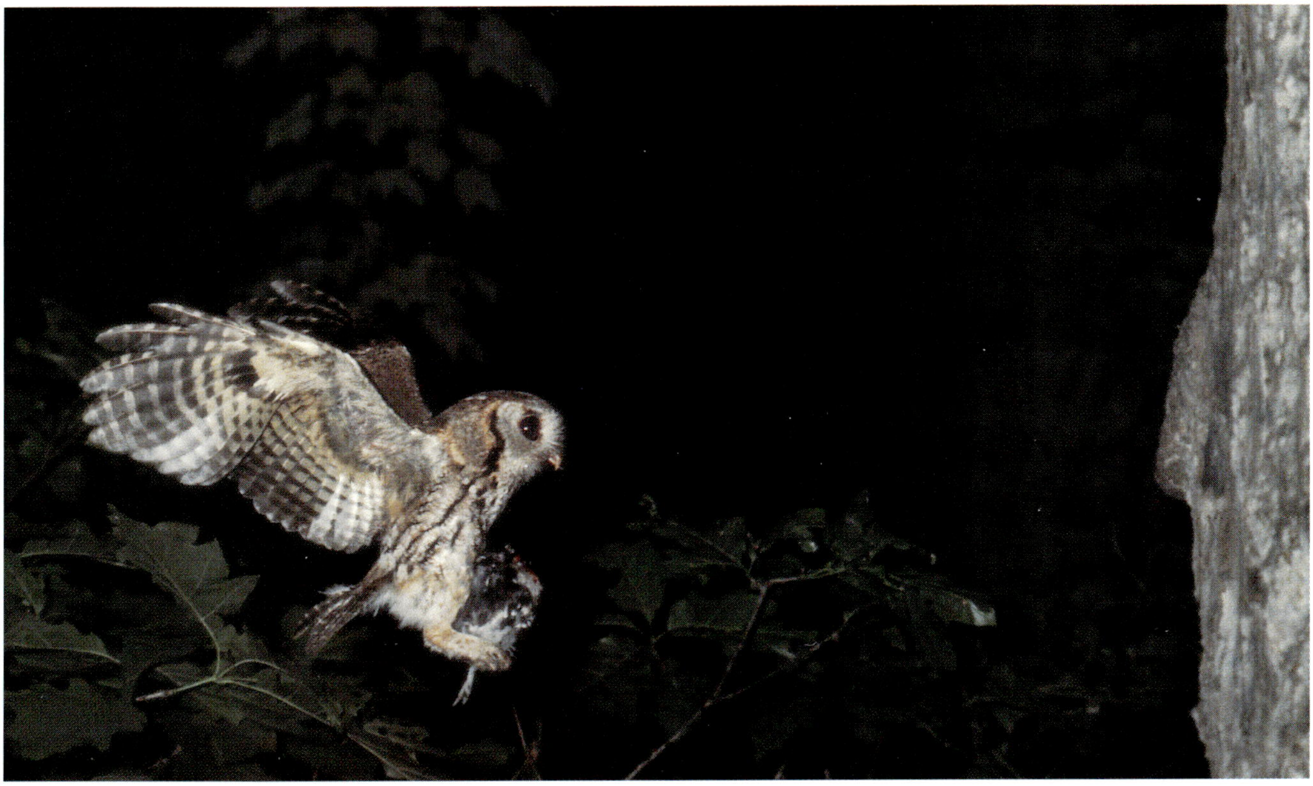

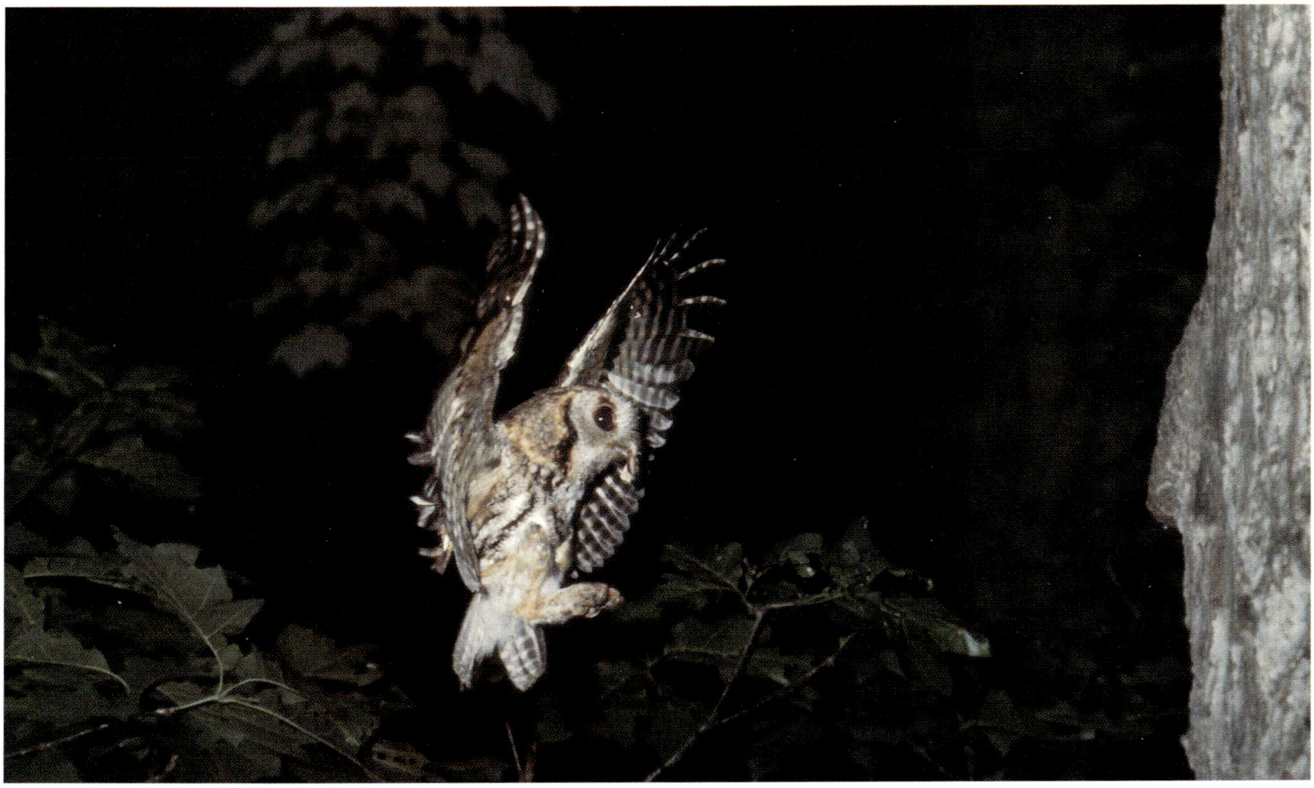

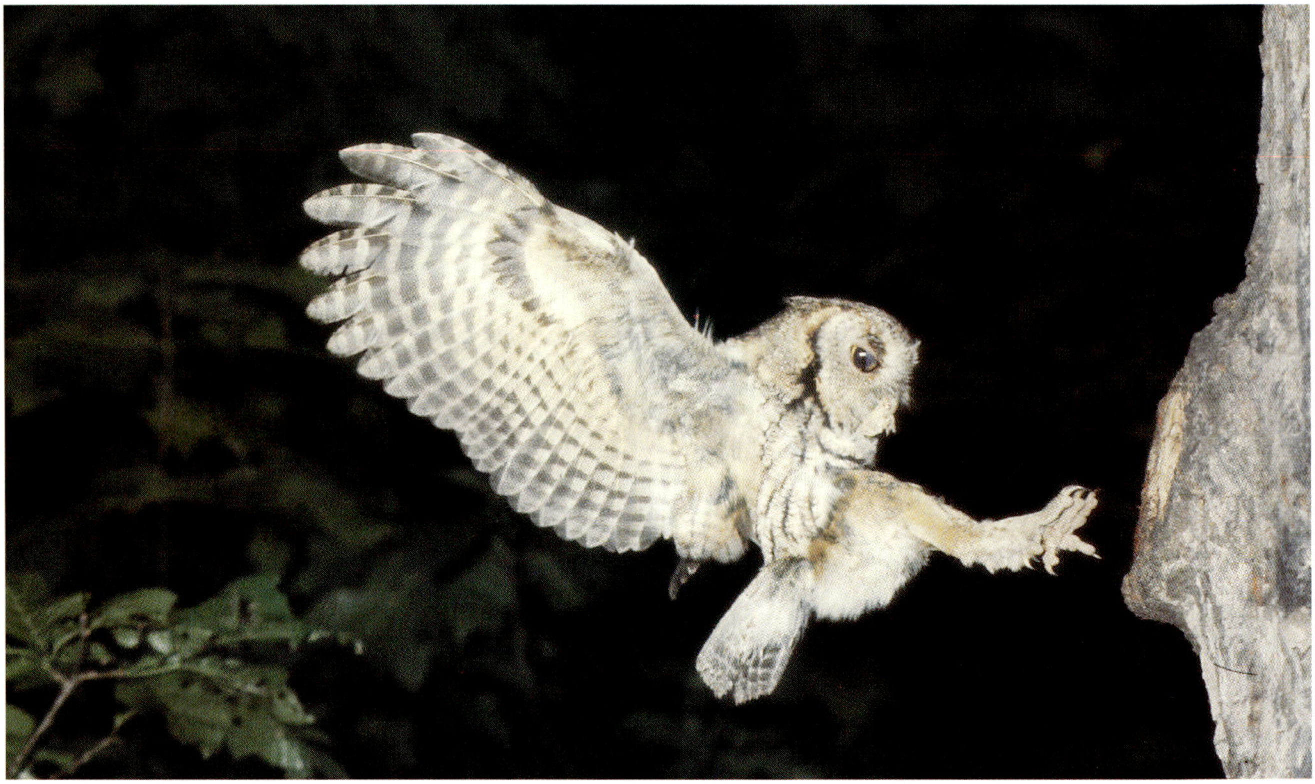

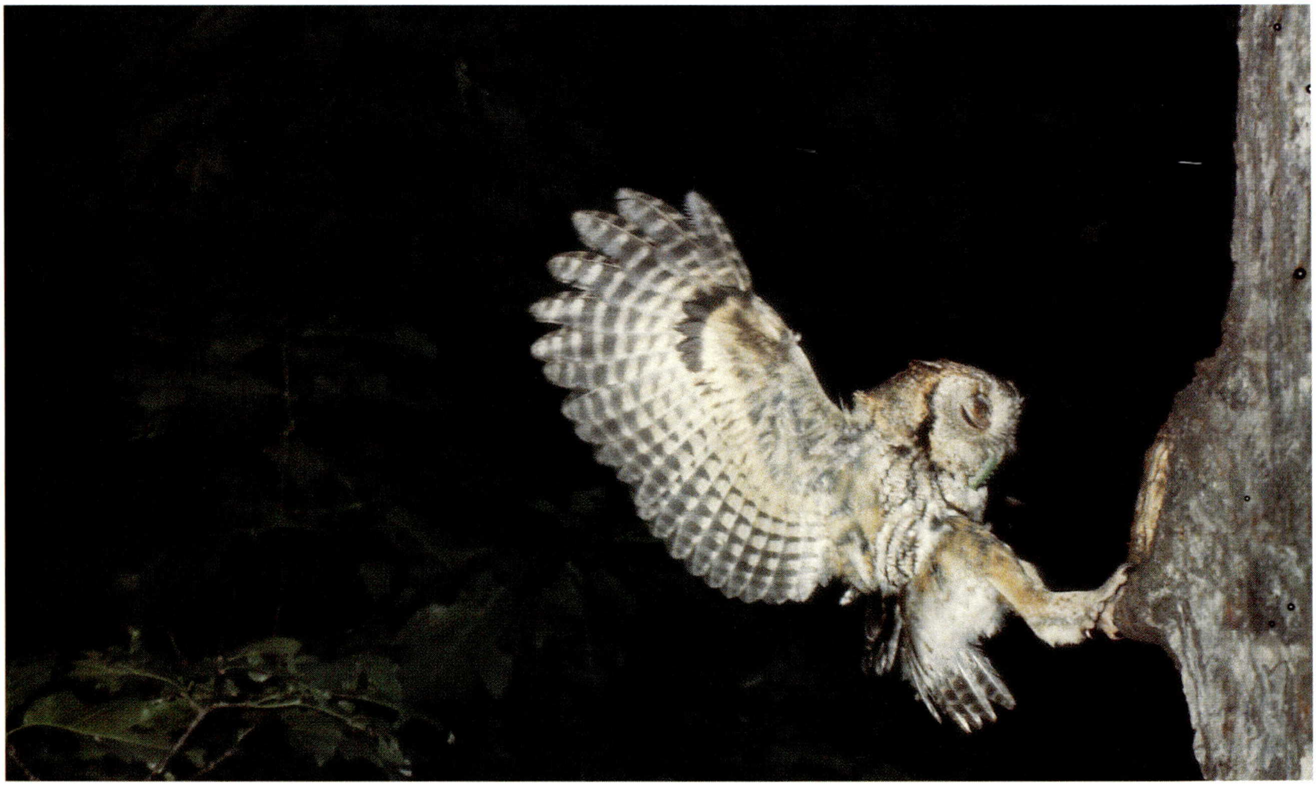

On the Road

Whenever we take a vacation trip on which there might be an opportunity for some hunting with my camera, I bring it along. Although Mary Pat doesn't have the passion for birds that I do, we both enjoy traveling and sight-seeing in remote and scenic areas. We have made a number of trips to the southwestern part of the United States. The sixteen photographs in this section, which I have gleaned from hundreds in my collection, were taken in southern Texas, southeastern Arizona and along the California coast.

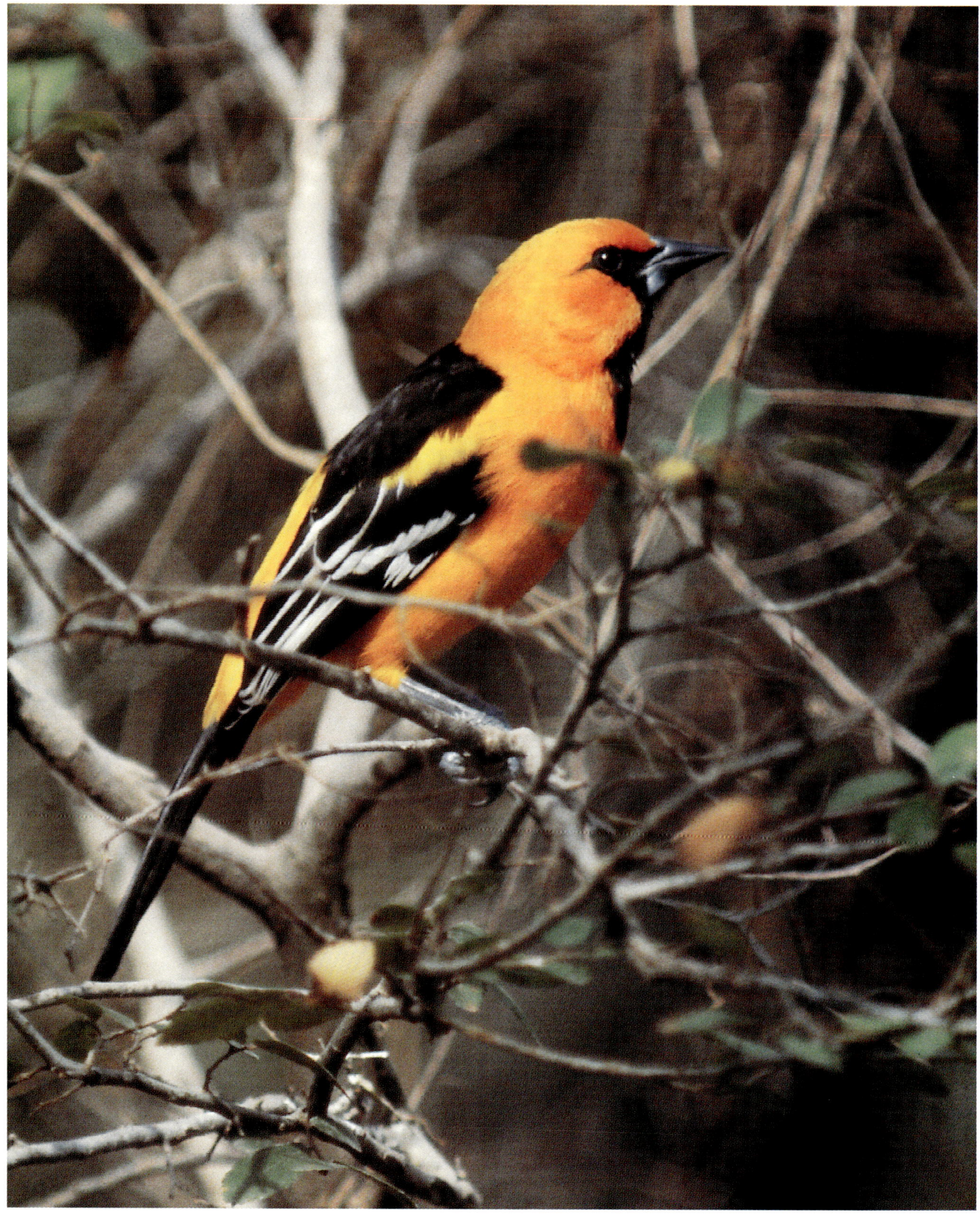

Altamira Oriole

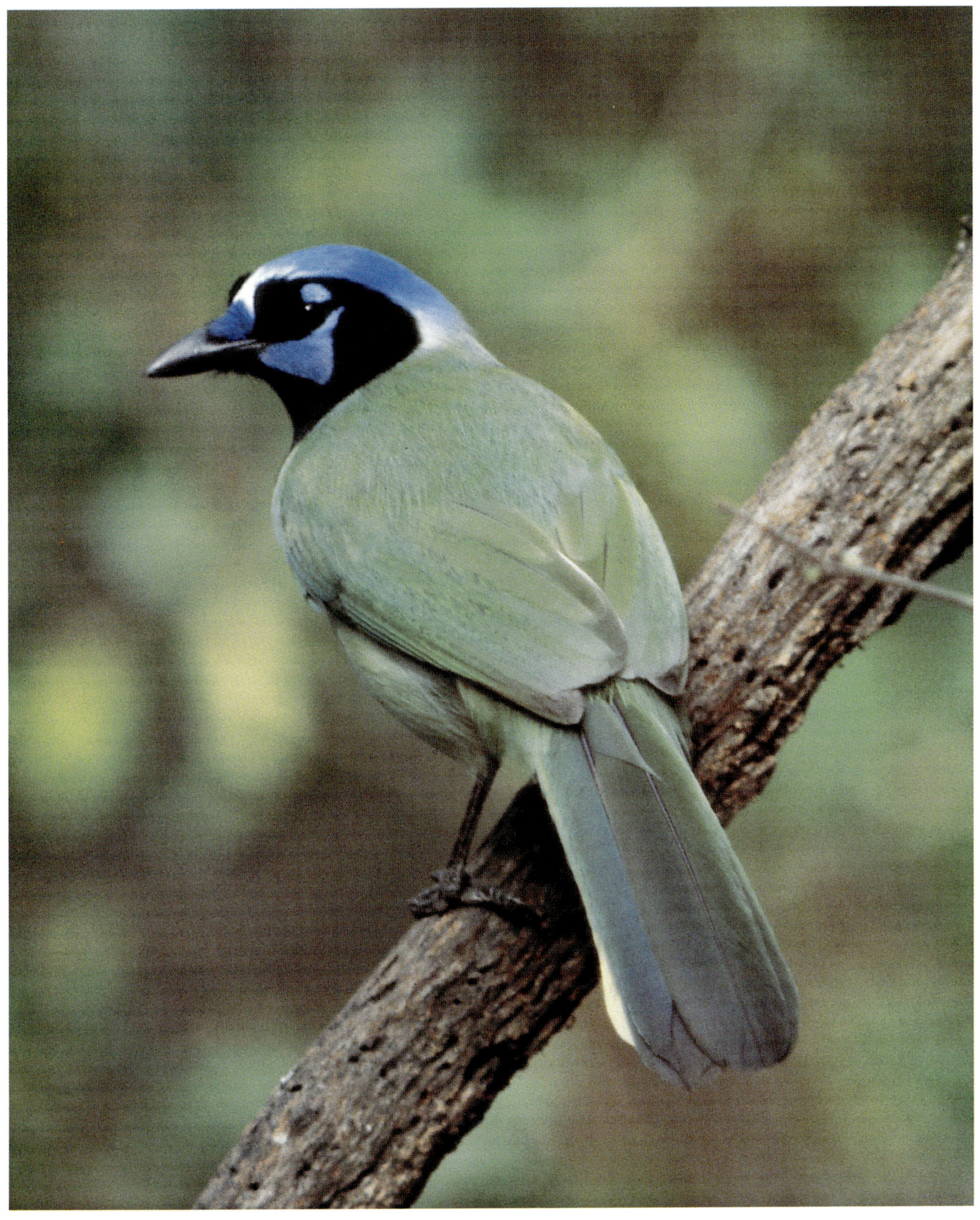

Green Jay

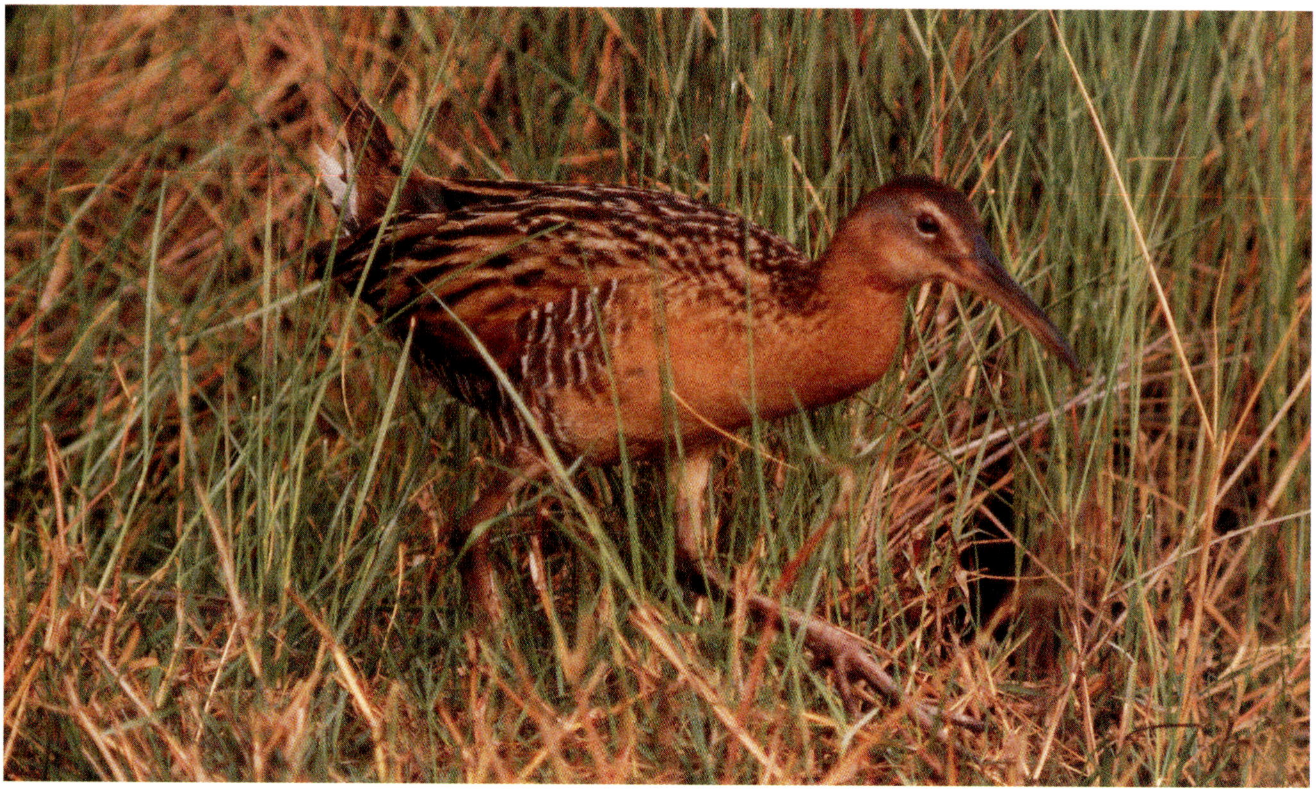

King Rail

Golden-fronted Woodpecker

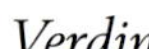

Verdin

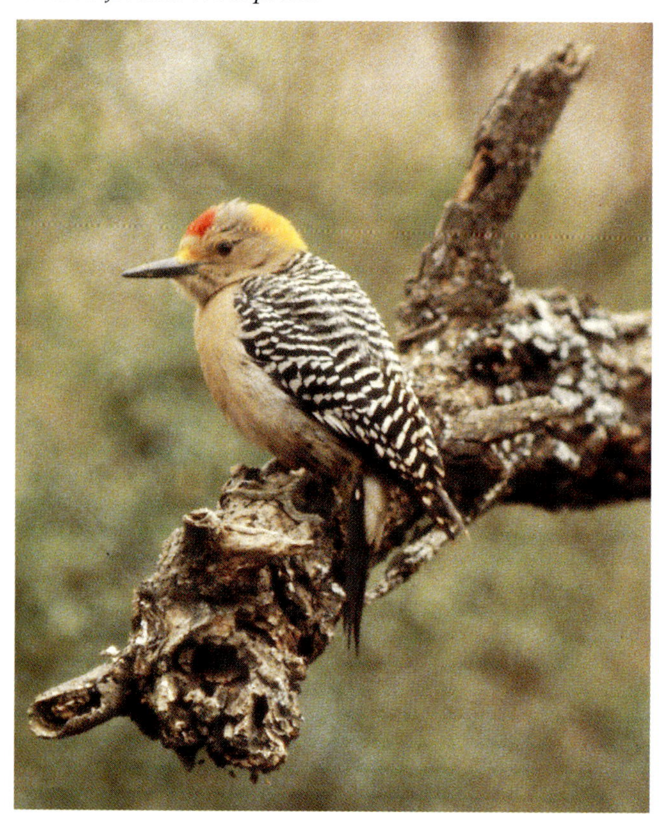

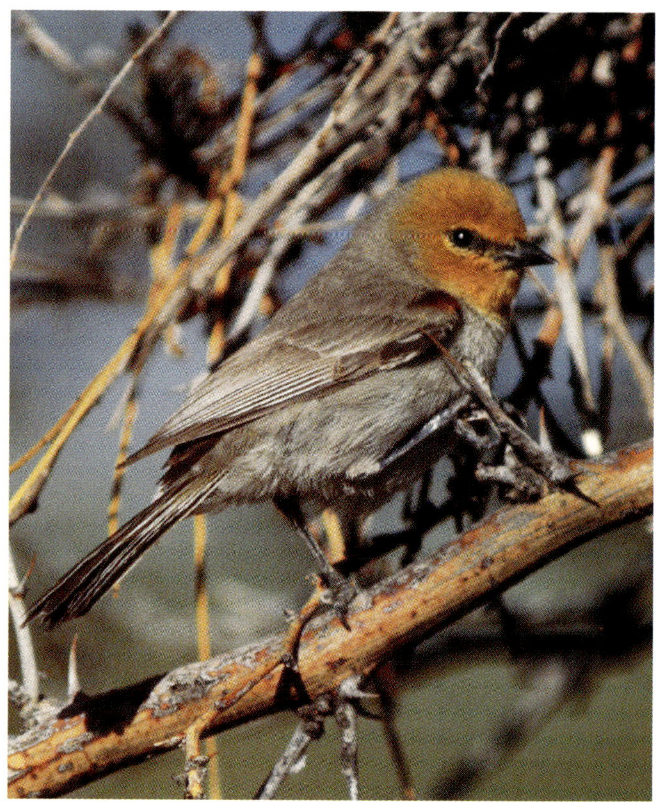

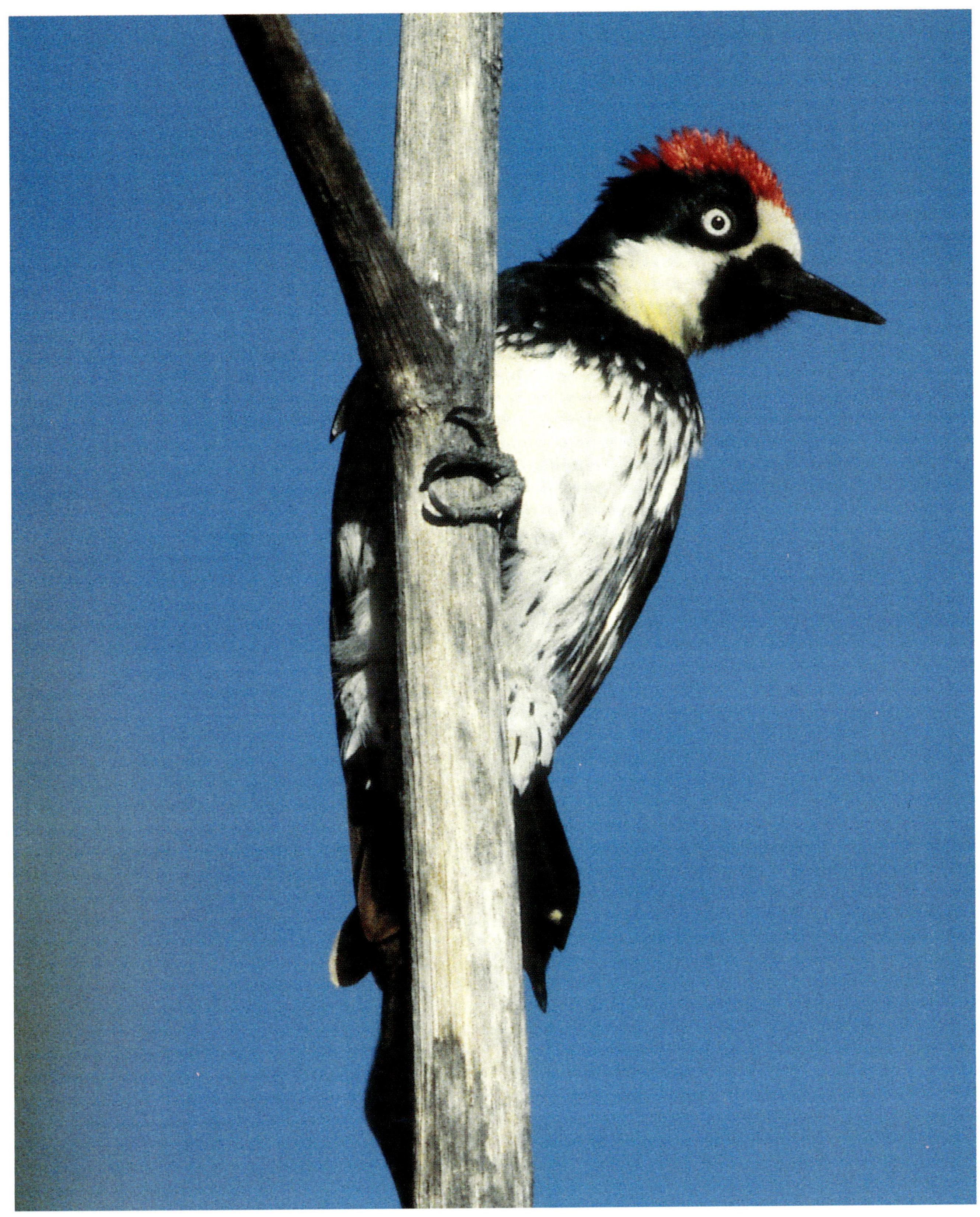

Acorn Woodpecker

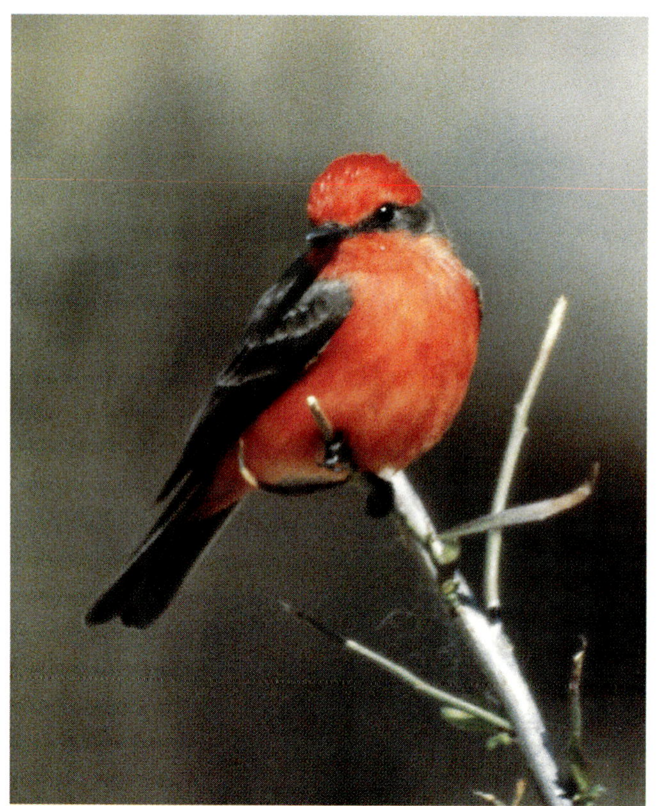

Vermillion Flycatcher

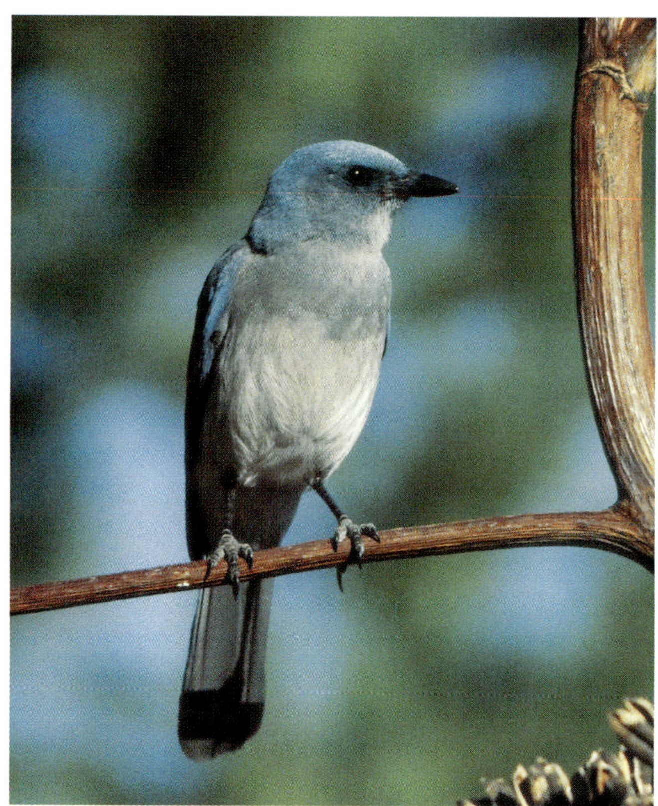

Mexican Jay

Phainopepla

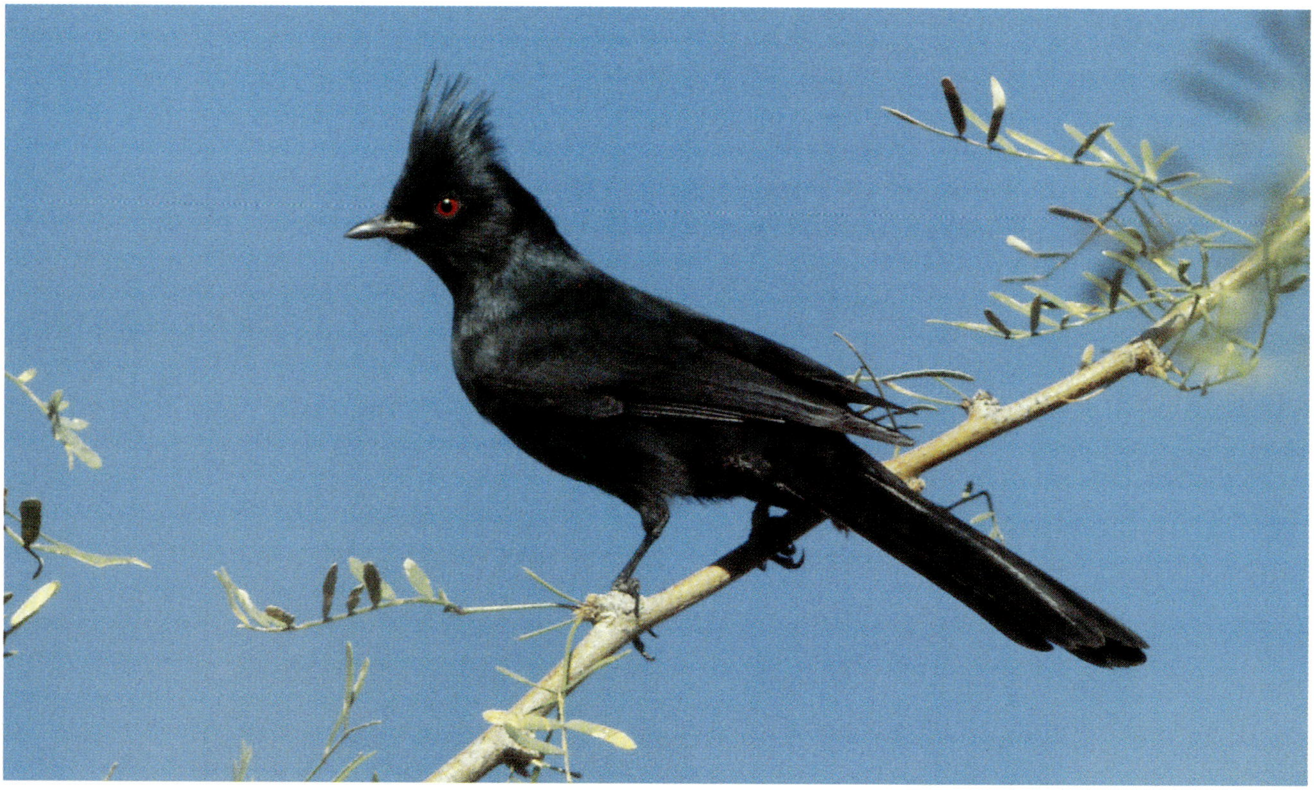

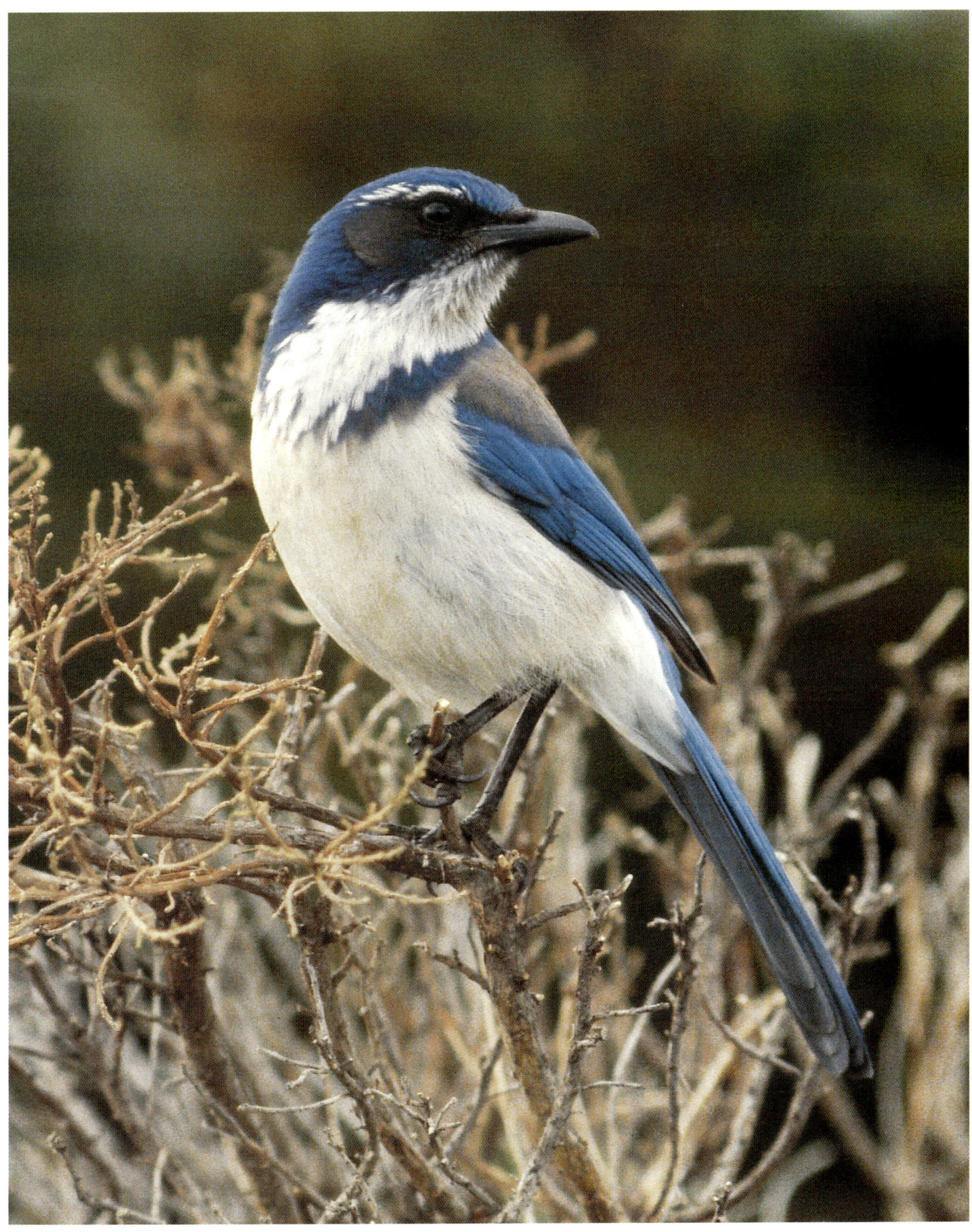

Western Scrub Jay

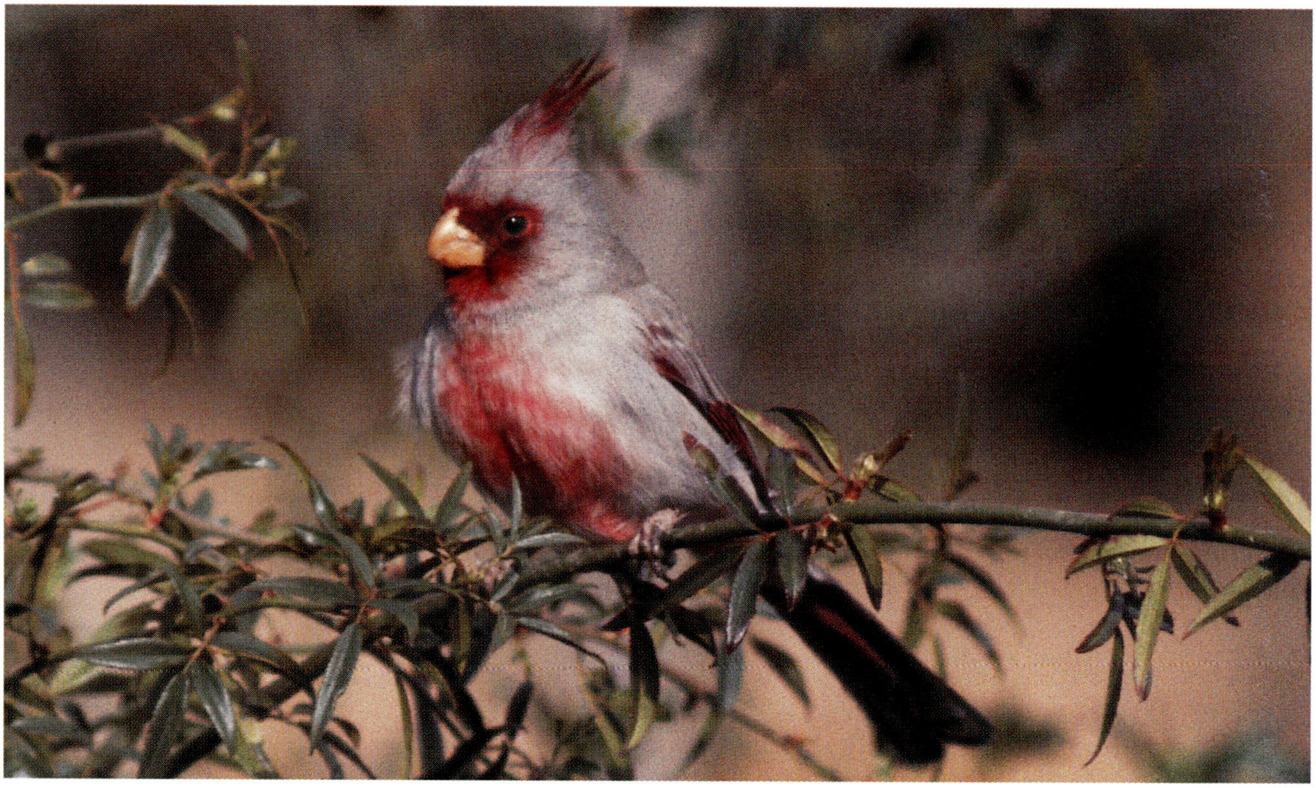

Pyrrhuloxia

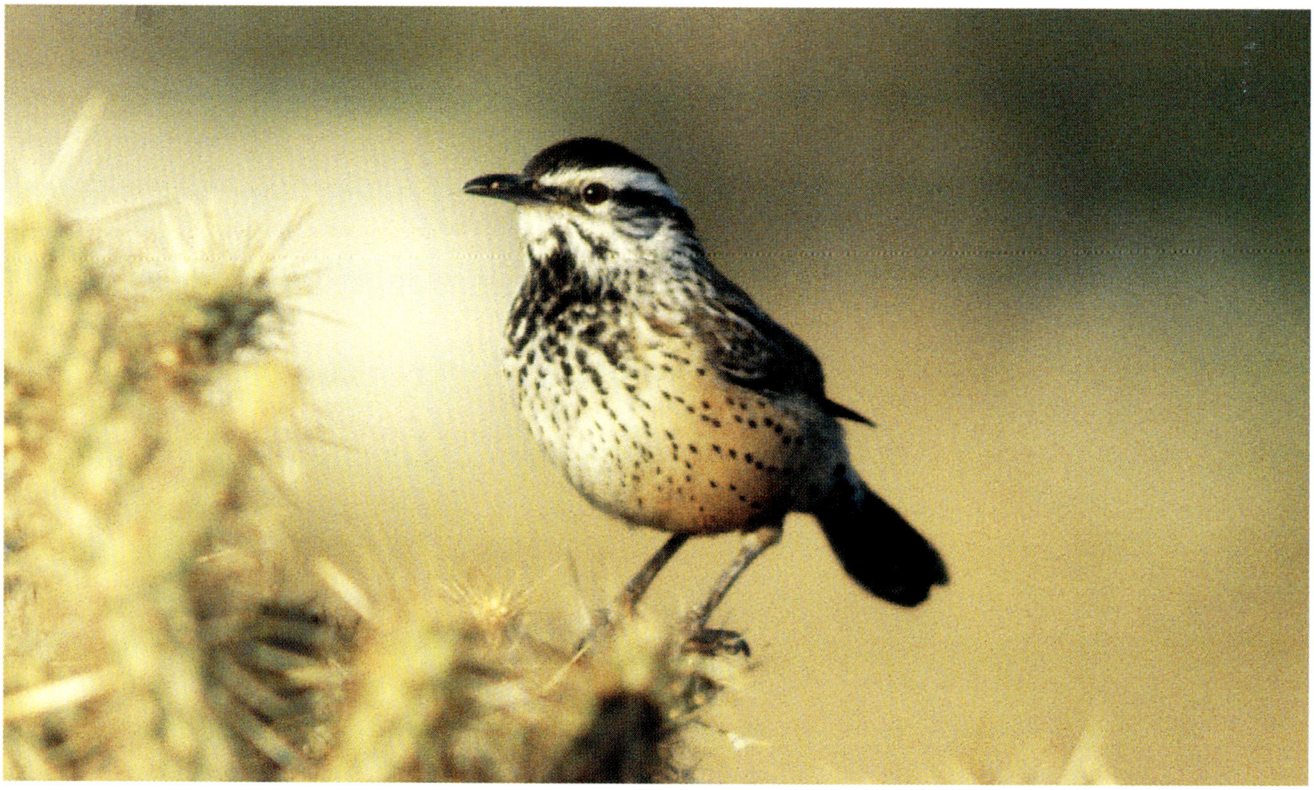

Cactus Wren

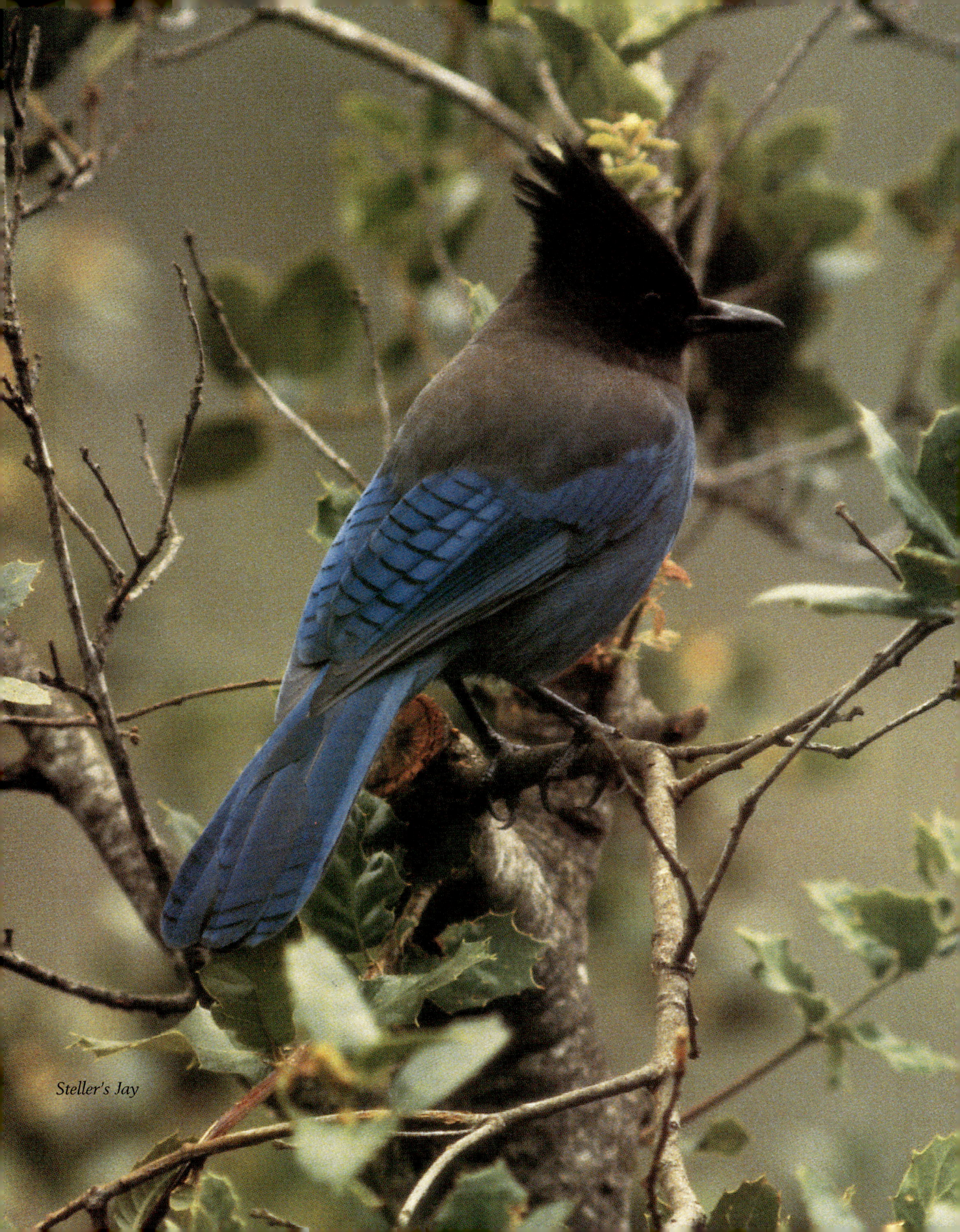

Steller's Jay

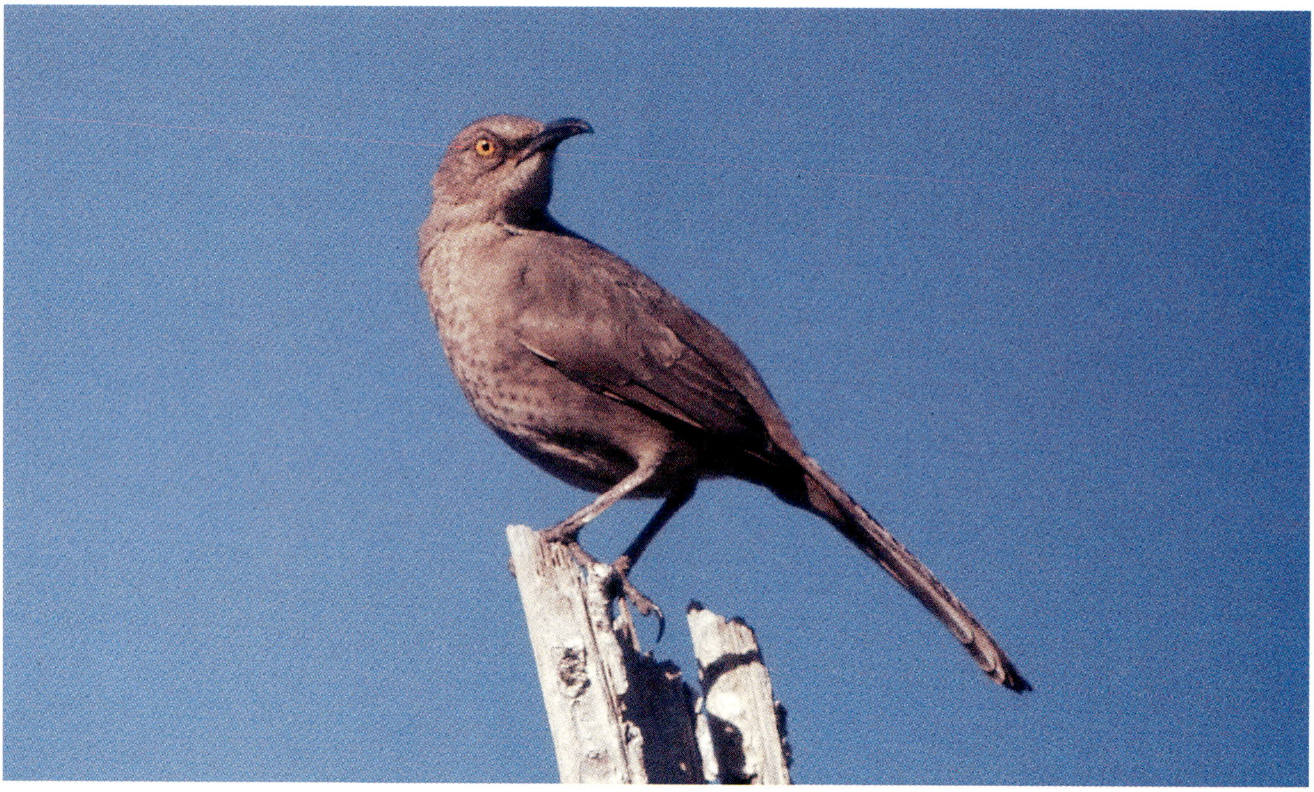

Curve-billed Thrasher

Gila Woodpecker

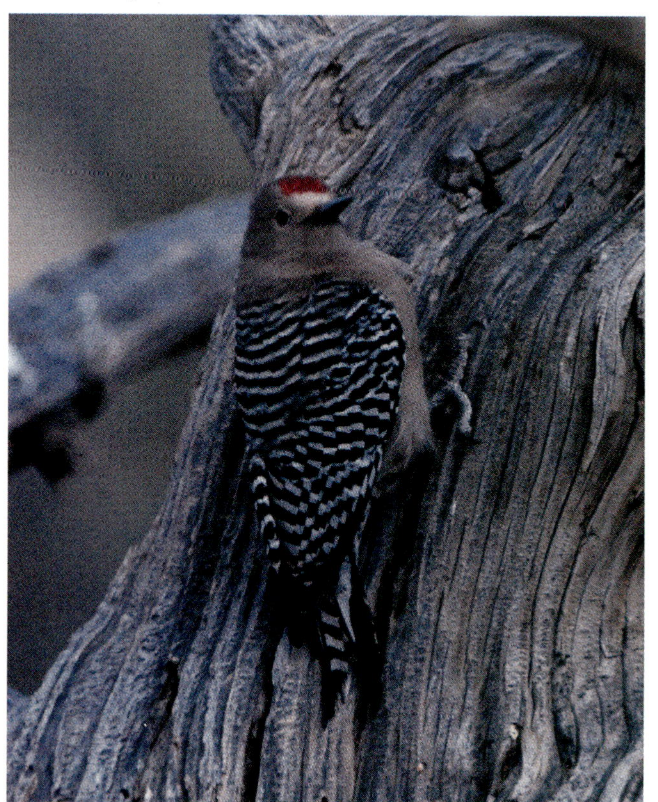

Whimbrel

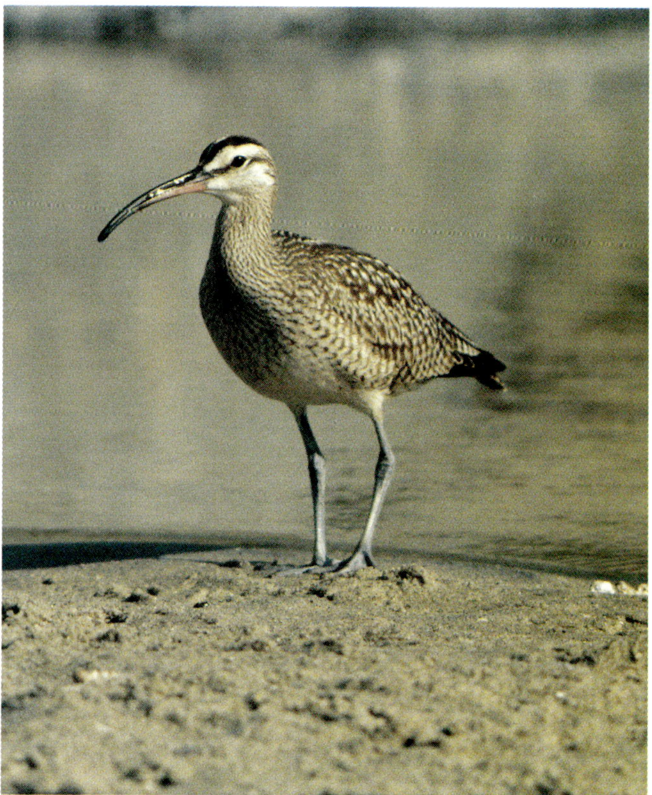

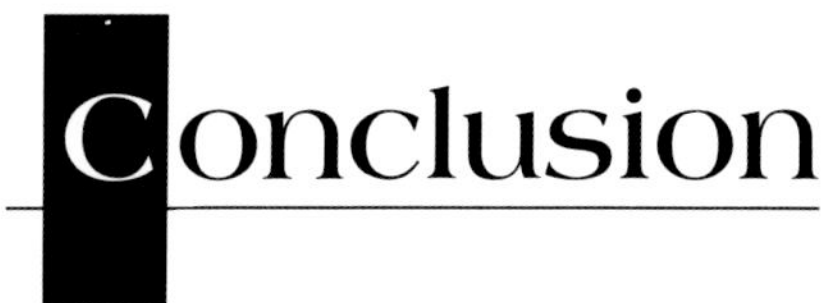

Conclusion

Although a hobby might not be considered one of the "meat and potatoes" issues of life, it certainly can add the spice that makes everything taste better. I find it difficult to describe in words how much enjoyment and stimulation hunting birds with a camera has contributed to my life. I hope the photographs have done a better job.

When I try to imagine a world devoid of the exquisite beauties of nature, one word comes to mind—bleak! I feel regret for those who may have seen but never noticed, and I am concerned that future generations might never have the opportunity to see what we have seen. In my lifetime I have noted many changes, some drastic and some subtle, but too many have been in the wrong direction. If I were to place the blame, I'd quote the renowned comic strip philosopher, Pogo, "We have met the enemy and they are us."

Preservation of our natural treasures in the face of mounting human pressures is a daunting challenge. It's a challenge unlikely to be met until the issue rises to near the top of our collective priority list. If this book contributes in even a small way to the attainment of that objective it will have been a success.

If I could wave a magic wand,
And clearly see what lies beyond,
It would suit me fine if I found
It's one big happy hunting ground.

Index of Photographs